W9-CEU-538

A History of Information Storage and Retrieval

ALSO BY FOSTER STOCKWELL

Encyclopedia of American Communes, 1663–1963
(McFarland, 1998)

A HISTORY OF INFORMATION STORAGE AND RETRIEVAL

by
Foster Stockwell

McFarland & Company, Inc., Publishers
Jefferson, North Carolina, and London

ISBN 0-7864-0840-5 (illustrated case binding : 50# alkaline paper) ∞

Library of Congress cataloguing data are available

British Library cataloguing data are available

©2001 Foster Stockwell. All rights reserved

Copyright ©2000 EyeWire

*No part of this book may be reproduced or transmitted in any form
or by any means, electronic or mechanical, including photocopying
or recording, or by any information storage and retrieval system,
without permission in writing from the publisher.*

Manufactured in the United States of America

*McFarland & Company, Inc., Publishers
Box 611, Jefferson, North Carolina 28640
www.mcfarlandpub.com*

To my wife, Rhoda, without whom this
book could never have been written

Contents

Preface

Knowledge is of two kinds. We know a subject ourselves,
or we know where we can find information upon it.
— Samuel Johnson (1709–1784)

Francis Bacon did not need to tell us that "knowledge is power." Intuitively, human beings have known this from the time someone first discovered something not known before about the surrounding world and communicated that discovery to others. As rapidly as these early segments of knowledge were conceptualized, people began to search for ways to preserve such data through memory clues and repetition, the invention of systems of writing, and the development of many types of storage devices. In modern times, engineers have developed computers and the World Wide Web, both of which have revolutionized storage capacity and eased the process of information retrieval.

Historically, people with special knowledge were viewed as people with unique powers. They often became tribal leaders and medicine men. They often were consulted when decisions needed to be made, and when their knowledge proved false, they were evicted from the community and often killed. For knowledge, though powerful, also can be destructive when misused. It is, of course, human nature to assume that information derived from half-truths and long-lasting myths is "true knowledge."

The early training methods used to impart knowledge on a one-to-one basis eventually evolved into the schools and universities that today train many thousands of individuals simultaneously. At the same time, the repositories of knowledge evolved into libraries and data banks. And it has always been a utopian dream to assemble all knowledge in one place so that any individual can have it ready at hand. It was with this purpose that encyclopedias were first compiled.

This book surveys some of the ways humans have preserved their knowledge. It focuses mainly on the history of encyclopedias, because these single and multivolumed books are still viewed by many persons as the primary

1

storage and retrieval vessels. Yet with the vast data storage capabilities provided by the electronic revolution, printed encyclopedias now are rapidly going the way of the horse and buggy.

A survey of such a vast subject can only touch on the highlights. A full history of knowledge acquisition, storage, and retrieval is almost as vast as knowledge itself. Every book of history, anthropology, and science contains some elements of the story, and no single book could contain them all.

1. The Loss of Knowledge

Almost all the knowledge that humans acquired during their first 500,000 years of wanderings has been lost — more than 99 percent of human history. This tragedy happened because primitive people had no effective method of preserving such information. And when they eventually did develop rudimentary methods of writing, they used these first for recording trivial matters such as imprinting to denote ownership, recording barter transactions, and producing magical incantations — not for the preservation of knowledge at all.

Today we are so accustomed to seeking information in encyclopedias, dictionaries, and on the Internet that it is somewhat difficult to visualize a society in which children grew up learning only those things their parents and other adults passed on to them by word of mouth. The oral techniques that primitive people developed to hold onto their learning — memorized stories and rhymes — helped maintain information, but extensive preservation of knowledge in the midst of such circumstances was at best almost an accident.

As everyone knows, the powers of human retention are so limited it is almost a shame to entrust to the mind the task of keeping exact information. We cannot recall the names of people we met only moments ago. We forget the birth dates of our most important relatives. And we forget to pay our traffic fines and utility bills. Consider the familiar parlor game in which one person whispers the description of a picture or event to another who then passes on this information as correctly as possible to the next, and so on. The description given by the last person is invariably different in many details from the description that began the game.

In addition to the mind's faulty memory is the fact that the human brain, unlike most other parts of the body, is in a state of constant deterioration. Biophysicists tell us that we lose about 100,000 neurons each day of our lives, and we can do nothing to prevent this. We start life with as many as 10 billion neurons, so this rapid loss doesn't mean we will lose all our marbles in a normal lifetime. One would, in fact, have to live about 273 years before they would all be gone. But the technological difficulty of this situation is readily apparent — in every generation, knowledge has to be transmitted by deteriorating old minds to deteriorating young ones.

A cynic might say that the loss of thousands of years of preliterate knowledge is really of no importance since nothing then known can be of much value to us today. But it takes a particularly narrow mind to dismiss out of hand such potentially vast areas of human information. And this certainly is not the conclusion of various botanists and drug researchers who today are combing the lore of contemporary Stone Age peoples to learn about plants and other substances they used as curatives. Some substances, like quinine from the bark of the cinchona tree, already provide quite useful drugs for modern physicians. Native Americans had more than 2,000 kinds of plant foods for their varied diets, yet they left no recipes to tell us how they prepared these delicacies. In fact, we know relatively little about the complex but highly effective economies they developed for the harvesting of products from the seas and land.

Native Americans spoke more than 500 languages in North America alone, some of them as different from each other as English is from Chinese, yet only a few of these were transcribed by later ethno-researchers. Would the forms they used give us any insights into handling international conflict? And every category of religious system known to human beings, including monotheism, evolved somewhere on this continent before there was any way to record the theological insights each contained. According to anthropologist Peter Farb in *Man's Rise to Civilization*, "The Iroquois practiced a dream psychotherapy at the time Europeans arrived in the New World that was remarkably similar to Freud's discoveries 200 years later in Vienna. There are no more marked differences between the two than there are between the Freudian and Jungian schools of psychoanalytic theory." How much other ancient wisdom will we eventually rediscover, and how many skills are lost forever?

Certainly I am not the only one who would like to know how ancient engineers were able to erect the huge stone statues found today on Easter Island. And what was the meaning and purpose of the sophisticated 32,000-year-old cave paintings discovered in 1994 at the Grotte Chauvet cave in France? Such questions seem to flood into consciousness every time we look at the accomplishments of our earliest ancestors.

Difficulties of human memory become most acute when data must be recalled — with precision. An algebraic formula, for example, will yield a different result if the parts are remembered and computed randomly rather than in the prescribed order. Or, if a druggist forgets one detail in a doctor's prescription, he may poison the patient; and a slight change in a radical of a chemical symbol may turn a quiescent substance into a violent explosive.

Preliterate humans, with no means of transcribing vital information, operated at a distinct disadvantage. They had to memorize the habits of every dangerous animal, the poisonous or nutritive value of every plant species, and the location of any fresh water supplies to be able to pass on such knowledge to others within the tribal complex. Those men and women with the best memories naturally became the leaders in each tribe.

A few individuals in every generation undoubtedly made new discoveries that were held briefly as common knowledge before the communal memories gave out. The method used to hold onto these gems of wisdom involved weaving them into stories (we now dub these "myths") that were repeated around the campfire at night. However, we know relatively little about the content of most such stories. After all, archaeologists have been able to learn much more about prehistoric human tools than they have about tribal tales, because clubs and knives remain in the ground to be excavated and myths soon disappear. Still, we can be sure that both tools and tales were manufactured very early, and what first set humans apart from the beasts was just as much the human propensity to dream and fantasize as it was the ability to construct augers and axes.

The stories found among today's primitive peoples probably are similar in purpose to the various myths retold by people over thousands of years. These transmit social codes, relate tribal history, and teach the young. They explain the creation of the world, with the coming of the nature deities and their connection to one another and to humans. They deal with the nature of magic, and they account for rituals and divining practices. Natural phenomena — rain, lightning, fire — often appear as story characters, just as do animals and human actors.

The number of such myths that have been created over the entire span of human development is enormous. Anthropologist Melville Herskovits has estimated that today's African tribes have between 200,000 and 250,000 stories. The number of recorded North American Indian tales also runs into the thousands, and then there are those of the tribes of Polynesia, the tribes of Australia, and many more. The stories are not necessarily simple in structure or short in length. Some take only minutes to repeat, but others are as long as a modern novel, taking many nights around the village fire to complete.

In Australia, the aboriginal tales often tell of totemic animals that wander over the tribal countryside. These animals fight, mate, live, and die, as do the members of the tribe that claims ownership of the myths relating to these animals. Such tales teach the new generation what the old generation knows about the names and characteristics of each place in their territory, together with the routes by which one can travel across it. The stories recall by name each water hole where the animals drank; tell whether the water was sweet, bitter, or salty; and tell where certain animals that provide food for the tribe may be found in abundance.

Most of the stories are rhythmic and repetitive, filled with emotion and visual details that act as an aid to exact transmission from one generation to the next. If the details to be remembered are such things as slight distinctions between several different plant leaves that reveal whether or not a fruit is poisonous, the storyteller might relate a tale that shows how the great god of the tawarra plant ordered the placing of six, rather than four, serrations around the edges of the leaves to remind passersby that this plant had the mystical power of the six great rivers and should be treated with extreme care.

When distinctions in the signs of the weather need to be remembered so that adequate precautions can be taken against natural disasters, the tribes have stories that tell about the wrath of the weather gods. These assure that no mistake will be made in determining whether a vivid sunset points to rain or sunshine the next day. A remnant of this process still exists in the often-repeated rhyme, "Red sky in the morning, sailors take warning; red sky at night, sailors delight."

It is not uncommon to find the same story with significant variations being told by persons of two different tribes within the same tribal grouping. We can assume that the differences are the result of the passage of time and that both groups originally told exactly the same tale. An example of this process appears in the two different versions of creation that are found in the Bible (Genesis 1:1–31 and Genesis 2:4–9), one having God create the animals and man in a particular order over six days while the other has no time period and the trees are planted in a garden for man's enjoyment. Apparently, one branch of early Hebrews remembered the original source in a different way from another.

Some of the more economically developed tribal societies are known to have conducted regular schools for the keepers of tribal knowledge. Such was the case among the peoples of New Zealand and the Society Islands. At these primitive universities, tribal priests instructed groups of select youth in ancestral lore, genealogies, agriculture, religion, magic, tradition, navigation, arts and crafts, and storytelling. The school building was ritually constructed and dedicated by human sacrifice. Students listened to and memorized the stories from dawn to midnight, sometimes for as long as five months at a time. Accuracy of repetition was emphasized, for repetition without error was believed to have magical value. And, indeed, pulling an exact duplicate out of the mind can be as astounding as pulling a rabbit out of a hat. The mark of any well-trained Society Islands chief was his ability to give orations that contained a large number of historical and religious allusions as well as proverbs, similes, and metaphors.

An important element of rhythmic repetition in all tribal stories involves repetition of story line in some and repetition of form in others. Such repetition stimulates memory, as does the device of inserting songs in the middle of many of the tales. But overriding the rhythmic style is the dramatic quality of the storytelling sessions. In the telling, the acting is superb. The teller accompanies each story with hand and body movements as well as changes in voice, and the audience acts as the chorus. Throughout, the teller may question the audience, calling for yes or no answers when characters in the story must justify their behavior.

Both the rhythmic repetition and the use of rhyme have a mnemonic effect that helps to cement the bits of story knowledge into faulty human memories. Whether we are conscious of it or not, we all have put some data into our memories through such a process. Who can forget, for example, "Thirty days hath September, April, June, and November. All the rest have thirty-one, excepting February alone."

Another important element of most of these stories is magic, and this is another reason why exact repetition is crucial. Magic, it is believed, works only if no single element is omitted. Archaeologist V. Gordon Childe, in a discussion of Neanderthal man, once suggested a likely formula for what might have been used in one of their myths. As Childe put it in *Man Makes Himself*, "To make a D-scraper, collect a flint nodule (1) at full moon, (2) after fasting all day, (3) address him politely with 'words of power,' (4)... strike him thus with a hammer stone, (5) smeared with the blood of a sacrificed mouse." This formula was guaranteed to always work, just as the ancient Chinese custom of beating gongs scared away the big dog that was swallowing the sun or the moon whenever there was an eclipse. Chinese peasants performed that rite for thousands of years because it worked every time.

Although rhythmic repetition was the method used to commit knowledge to memory among tribal people, other memory systems were later developed. The Greeks, who gave Western people so many arts, invented a system for memorizing, which is now called "mnemotechnics." They passed it on to the Romans and thence to medieval Europe. The technique is based on the association of things to be remembered with places and images.

It was invented by the poet Simonides, according to Cicero, who describes the technique in *De oratore*, a treatise on the five parts of rhetoric, of which memory is one. Cicero says that to train oneself in this memory faculty, one must choose mental images of places and store other mental images of the things one wishes to remember in those places. In other words, the user of this device needs to associate each memory in a specific order in pictured locations so that the places and images will recall the items to be remembered, respectively, "as a wax writing tablet and the letters written on it."

According to Frances Yates, author of *The Art of Memory*, the usual method used by the Greeks and Romans, although it was not the only one, involved architectural images. To commit a series of things to memory, the subject was advised to associate each item with a particular room in a building or with an object in that room. Thus the first point in a speech to be remembered would be associated with the living room in a house, the second with the kitchen, the third with a stairway, the fourth with a bedroom, and so forth. Illustrations for each point might be related to the various pieces of furniture or other objects in the particular room. The method ensured that the points of the speech would be remembered in their correct order, since the order was fixed by the sequence of rooms and objects in the building. The vividness of architectural images aided the memory, and the Greeks recommended that the images should be as striking and unusual as possible — beautiful or hideous, comic or obscene — since the emotional effect also was an aid to the process of remembering.

Yet whether a person used a specific memory system or not, the one who possessed the most knowledge was usually the one who led and controlled each primitive society. As Francis Bacon said in *Novum Organum*, "knowledge and human power are synonymous."

Throughout history those with special knowledge, or who employed others who had special knowledge, have always managed social affairs, whether it was the primitive hunter who knew where game could be found or the modern businessman who has inside information about what the stock market is next going to do. Thus the tribal leader was not necessarily the one with the greatest strength or skill with a bow. He also did not need to be the one with the greatest mental skill, i.e., the highest IQ, but he was always the one with the greatest store of knowledge. He was the one with the secrets that permitted the tribe to continue to live when all sources of food and water seemed to disappear. It was him that they would follow into ever-drier regions of the desert, without doubting his ability to know where he was taking them. The titles of reference given to leaders of the hunting and gathering bands speaks eloquently of their powers: The Eskimo leader is "he who thinks," and his Shoshoni counterpart is "the talker."

A group consciously or unconsciously chooses its leader because it wants the fullest benefits of that person's knowledge. There are, of course, individuals who struggle to assert themselves by strength alone, but unless they can command the respect of the group — a respect accorded to what they know — they will not hold power for long. In many a tribe it is the feeble old man with an alert mind who commands, rather than the sturdy but inexperienced youth.

Anthropologists have described their amazement at how the leader of a Bushman tribe in Africa can find water in the midst of a parched desert where no plant can live. The leader knows exactly where to dig with his hands to find pockets of liquid nearly a dozen inches beneath the surface, while other members of the tribe digging nearby find nothing. The leader also is the one who can tell the difference between the spoor of a sick animal and that of a healthy one, and see animal tracks where no one else does. He seems to know even the thoughts of the animals, for he can tell the trackers which direction to go when there are no visible signs.

The person with the greatest knowledge in more technically advanced tribal societies is the shaman, or medicine man, who, through his trances, can cure his fellow tribesmen. He is the one who also accompanies their dead to the Realm of Shades, where he serves as a mediator between them and the gods. As Mircea Eliade puts it in *Shamanism: Archaic Techniques of Ecstasy,* "The shaman is the great specialist in the human soul; he alone 'sees' it, for he knows its 'form' and its destiny."

The shaman achieves his place of power because he commands the techniques of ecstasy; because he knows which herbal medicines, incantations, and dance rhythms will cure the sick; and because he can prophesy the future. He is the community doctor, the community's religious innovator, and the guardian of its "soul." He knows how to cure the sick, because he is a man once sick (often his vocation is revealed to the tribe through an illness or an epileptic fit) who has cured himself. He is a man who displays tireless energy, a man who can drum, dance, or jump all night, if that is what is needed, to minister to the ill members of the tribe.

The tribe never confuses the shaman with just any possessed person, and neither should we. For example, the Indonesian and Eskimo shaman owes his prestige to the fact that he can control his epilepsy, not to the fact that he is subject to epileptic fits. He can achieve a degree of concentration that is beyond the possessed. He can sustain exhausting efforts and control his ecstatic movements. His soul can safely abandon his body during states of ecstasy to roam vast distances. It can penetrate the underworld and rise to the sky, challenging the dangers of such mystical experiences, and bring back cosmic knowledge to the tribal group.

The once-necessary role of shaman fell into decline after various methods of writing developed. Now anyone who could read could have access to some special knowledge, and memories did not need to be acute. The first of these writing methods was cuneiform incised on clay tablets, a method invented by the Sumerians in the Middle East about 3000 B.C. The Akkadian-Sumerian system of writing had about 600 cuneiform characters. The Hittites, also living in the Middle East, used about 300, the Elamites about 200, and the Persians only 39. Several thousand cuneiform tablets have been recovered and placed in museums since the first ones were unearthed in 1802. The information gained from these clay tablets has shed much light on the early history of the area.

The Chinese, who independently developed their system of writing about 1500 B.C., had a much more extensive list of characters that they carved on tortoise shells and embossed on bronze vessels. We don't know how extensive the vocabulary of the Shang dynasty (c. 1520 to 1030 B.C.) scholars was, but the total number of words on the excavated shell inscriptions may be well more than one million. A large portion of these, however, consist of formulas repeating the same words again and again. Thus the whole vocabulary represented is estimated at more than 2,500 individual words. Among them, about one-half are legible today and the rest, including many personal and geographical names, have yet to be deciphered.

The Chinese system of writing used today can be traced directly back to these shell and bronze inscriptions. Many consider it the most highly developed word-writing system in the world. As many as 50,000 Chinese characters eventually were developed over the centuries, all based on those first used during the Shang dynasty.

Although a great amount of human knowledge was lost because of the lack of any form of writing, many written documents that could have been preserved were wantonly destroyed through war, prejudice, and common neglect. For example, the scrolls of the famed library of the Ptolemys at Alexandria, according to legend, were burned to heat the public bath water, and the library was destroyed during times of military siege.

The library once stood as one of the finest centers for learning in the ancient world. Ensconced in its halls was the cream of Greek scholarship and encyclopedic learning. King Ptolemy I (367/366 or 364–283 B.C.), and later his son, Ptolemy II (308–246 B.C.), planned nothing less than the collection of all Greek writings. They poured large quantities of gold into the project, and even resorted to piracy in the interest of amassing knowledge. More than once each of the Ptolemys confiscated the book cargoes of ships that anchored in Alexandria's harbor. They borrowed the works of three great playwrights from Athens, copied them, and then returned the copies rather than the originals to the Greeks.

The number of papyrus scrolls that finally filled the Alexandria library storage bins has been estimated at several hundred thousand. But after Ptolemy II died, the scrolls began to molder. Few needed or wanted to read them. In time, no one could understand the works anymore, and they collected a thick layer of dust. Finally, they became the fuel to heat the public baths.

In the mid–1500s, Bishop Diego de Landa ordered the Spanish conquistadors to burn all the Mayan bark-cloth books they could find, because these "contained nothing but superstitions and falsehoods of the Devil." The great collection of Mayan astronomical knowledge was thus destroyed, and so apparently was everyone who knew anything about it. Descendants of the Mayans live today in the forests of Guatemala, tapping sapodilla trees to collect chicle, the chief ingredient of chewing gum, which they sell for food and clothing, but all the knowledge their ancestors accumulated over the centuries is lost.

We don't have many clues as to what the Mayan texts contained besides astronomical lore — only three of the books survived — so there is no way to calculate the loss to humankind. But the incident graphically shows that where the system to hold knowledge is disrupted, or where the knowledge-transmission process is blocked, the information itself disappears.

Fortunately, discoveries made and then lost can sometimes be made again. One of my favorite examples of this is the perpetual reinvention of the double-bottomed boat, which ship enthusiasts now call a catamaran. As a boy, I was excited to read of the "invention" of such a twin-hulled boat when it was described in *Popular Mechanics* magazine. The author of the article said it was a unique way to travel on water, and the pictures were quite thrilling. The double hulls enabled the boat to travel at a greater speed than other boats of the same size and with less rocking from the motion of the waves. The author also said this was the first time such an obvious advantage in ship craft had been employed. A year later I had a chance to see such a boat, owned by a California ice-cream manufacturer, who neighbors said developed his craft at least a year before the one described in the magazine article. The owner, too, claimed originality for his design.

But the twin-hulled boat has a far longer history. It probably was first used in ancient China, and was the basis for the outrigger boats that the Polynesians and Malays have sailed for thousands of years. In 1663, Sir William Petty, the pioneer statistician, member of the Royal Society, and friend of Oliver Cromwell, Christopher Wren, and Samuel Pepys, made quite a stir in London by his invention of a double-bottomed boat that sailed the English Channel. I have looked at Petty's diagrams in the rare-book collection at Chicago's Newberry Library, and they are not much different from those published nearly 300 years later in *Popular Mechanics*. I now suspect that if a historian studied the matter in detail, it would be found that the twin-hulled boat has been rediscovered periodically ever since people first began to cross large bodies of water.

Such independent discoveries are made frequently, and when they happen at much the same time they give rise to all sorts of arguments and lawsuits. An example of this is the independent discovery of an inexpensive way to extract aluminum from its ore. This was accomplished by Charles Martin

Hall of Thompson, Ohio, and Paul L. T. Héroult of Paris, both in 1886. Other examples of such independent discoveries include the invention of the tele-scope in 1608 by three different persons, each unknown to the others, Jansen, Lippershey, and Netius. Then there is the airplane, developed by the Wright Brothers in America in 1903 and by Dumont in France that same year; the independent observation of sunspots by Galileo, Fabricius, Schemer, and Har-riott, about 1610; and the discovery of nitrogen by Rutherford in 1772 and Scheele in 1773. The list goes on and on, but we now need to turn our atten-tion to other methods of knowledge preservation.

2. The Greeks Had a Word for It

It may be a surprise to most readers, but Socrates never wanted his thoughts put down in writing. He complained that written words forced one to follow an argument rather than to participate in one. And he disliked both the alienation that writing imposed and its persistence. He found it most unsettling that a manuscript could travel without its author, with whom no argument was possible. Still worse, the author might die and never be argued out of the position taken in his writing.

We know the philosophy of Socrates today only because his student and friend, Plato, put the man's words down on parchment scrolls for later generations to read. All of Plato's writings, in fact, are in the form of dialogues in which Socrates interrogates others about various ideas. These dialogues include, among others, *Republic*, *Laws*, *Symposium* (on ideal love, which has given rise to the expression "Platonic love"), and *Phaedrus*. Plato founded an institution of philosophy and science in 387 B.C. that became known as the Academy, and some modern scholars consider this to have been the first university in the world. It operated for nine centuries in Athens, and was claimed to provide the fullest education that any intelligent man should ever need.

One reason for the Academy's success was that all its potential students believed it was possible to have every bit of human knowledge available in one place and that most of such knowledge was to be found there. In this belief they were following the ancient Greek concept of the world as an unchanging entity. To the Greeks, knowledge was something static and not dynamic. They held that, once understood, the world could be controlled — that it never changed even as new things were discovered about it.

The Greeks tried to gather all known facts as they searched for rationality in their unchanging universe. In this, they reflected the passionate desire of humankind to acquire all knowledge, and they rigidly held to the illusion that sufficient knowledge would somehow sustain life and make it worth living.

There also was a sense in which the Greek belief was an attempt to circumvent, or wall out, the untidy ambiguities of life.

The Greeks had a name for their outlook. They spoke of *enkyklios*, meaning circular and complete, and they combined this with *paideia*, meaning education. Together, the two words are often translated as the "whole circle of knowledge." Pliny the Elder used the words this way in his preface to *Natural History*, where he says that he treats all the subjects of the circle of learning of the Greeks. And Quintilian, Plutarch, Lucian, Strabo, and Galen used the words to describe a general education or a system of arts and sciences.

The two words were not joined into one until 1531 when Sir Thomas Elyot in his *Bok of the Governour* coined the word "encyclopedia" to the delight of scholars. His action was subsequently approved by Samuel Johnson, Noah Webster, and other noted lexicographers. As Elyot defined it, the word meant "that lernynge whiche comprehendeth all lyberall science and studies."

The Greek concept of a finite world was somewhat different from that of other literate peoples of the time. It was also different from that of most of the preliterate people who lived before the Greeks. Tribal men and women didn't formulate complicated philosophical propositions about root causes, significance, and the ultimate relations of things, as did the Greeks. And they didn't try to collect in one place all that they knew, much as squirrels collect nuts.

This distinction between the Greeks and their forebears is not merely a matter of different levels of sophistication. Primitive men and women created myths that presented deeply philosophical concepts in concrete and graphic ways. And the primitive myths, proverbs, and fables of which we know demonstrate that the subtler aspects of life didn't escape them.

The Greek concept was quite different from that of their contemporaries and neighbors, the Hebrews, who rejoiced in ambiguity and diversity, seeing God's action in the change and movement of history. Where Yahweh to the Hebrews was an enigma never to be understood, Greek gods were rational beings to be placated so that they would disclose their knowledge to the people of the world. The Greek myth about Prometheus stealing fire from the gods symbolizes this idea of knowledge as something humans can eventually gain in whole.

In the ancient Greek world, each of the various philosophical schools — the sophists, stoics, epicureans, and pythagoreans — believed they had the major body of knowledge within their particular circle. They constantly ridiculed others for their inability to see this. Plato, too, believed that his Academy alone had all the essential knowledge, and although he argued that it provided the fullest education one might ever need, he never actually wrote anything to describe his total educational system. It was only later that some of his students attempted to do so.

The first was Speusippos, a nephew of Plato, who took over the leadership of the Academy after Plato died in 347 B.C. The philosopher Aristotle, who had been teaching there with Plato, walked out in a huff after Speusippos assumed the post. The scandal shook all of Athens, so much so that the Academy almost closed down. Aristotle justifiably thought of himself as the rightful heir to the position as Academy head, and he wasn't about to work under a man with inferior talents, as Aristotle assumed of Speusippos.

Inferior or not, Speusippos was a prolific writer, and history accords to this man the title "compiler of the first encyclopedia." Only fragments of his work survive and so we don't know much about this encyclopedia, but we do know it was planned as a teaching aid to be used with his lectures at the Academy. It apparently was a summary of all the knowledge that Speusippos could gather.

Speusippos states that Plato was the son of the god Apollo and not the son of any mortal father at all — a somewhat strange comment by a man who, as the child of Plato's sister Potone, would have known every intimate detail about the family's history, including the true facts about his uncle's birth.

Speusippos also maintained against Eudoxus that pleasure is not good but bad, and that pleasure and pain are opposite evils. But his particular interest was biology. Although he was hardly a keen observer, he attempted to classify all the different species of animals and plants by their resemblances to each other.

Plato undoubtedly picked Speusippos as his successor over Aristotle for more reasons than mere nepotism. Although Aristotle was the greatest intellect in ancient Greece, he also was a controversial figure and would have endangered the Academy politically. Speusippos was the safer of the two. Plato never forgot how the Athens power structure had destroyed his own teacher, Socrates, for being a subversive. Although the Academy might fail under the leadership of Speusippos, the power structure would never suppress it as an institution breeding subversive ideas.

Speusippos ruled the Academy for eight years, fell sick, and then died. Aristotle, who was no longer in Athens, stayed away from the city for five years more before he returned to found a school of his own called the Lyceum and to complete his own compendium of knowledge. But Aristotle was never liked by the Athens city establishment. His Lyceum survived only under the protection of Alexander the Great, then ruler of Athens and most of the rest of the known world. Shortly after Alexander died in 323 B.C., Aristotle fled the city. He died a year later at Chalcis.

Aristotle had been the instructor of Alexander at Macedon after leaving Athens following the conflict over the leadership of the Academy, and his influence on the Great Conqueror was enormous. Wherever Alexander went, he followed Aristotle's advice to seek out the philosophers and learned men of the nations he defeated so that he might consult with them and invite them to his table.

The story of Alexander's encounter with the culture and wisdom of India illustrates the deep chasm that separated the ancient civilizations, in this case the Greek from the Indian. Alexander had just smashed the whole Persian empire and had moved on to the Indus valley in 327 B.C. According to the Greek geographer Strabo, the first Indian capital Alexander captured was Taxila, and shortly thereafter, he sent his officers to find the local philosophers. The Indian philosophers reportedly were sitting in session outside the city. The Greek officers discovered 15 naked men sitting motionless atop a sunbaked rock. Strabo wrote that the rock was so hot the Greeks couldn't step on it without shoes. Through a series of interpreters Alexander's soldiers finally learned from these Hindu wise men that they didn't believe anyone clothed as the soldiers were could ever learn philosophy. The officers were advised to become naked and sit motionless on the scorching rock for a while until they were fully prepared to take in the Indian wisdom. Needless to say, this was not the type of knowledge Alexander was seeking. He wanted the kind of knowledge that might fit into the pages of an encyclopedia.

The Greek concept of the circle of knowledge, preserved forever on parchment scrolls, was attractive to the acquisitive Romans, who in their conquests liked to bring back to their capital the best of everything. As might be expected, the first Roman to produce such a work was the well-traveled general, Marcus Porcius Cato (234–149 B.C.). Having risen to a high position during the Punic Wars against Hannibal of Carthage, Cato became prominent in public life, earned a reputation as a great orator, and after 137 B.C. closed every Senate speech with the words, "Carthage must be destroyed."

Cato was a practical man and clearly saw the dangers of too much Greek influence on the Roman world. His encyclopedia, the *Praecepta ad Filum* ("Advice to My Son"), was written as a series of letters to his son, Marcus Porcius Licinianus. In it he covered the subjects of oratory, agriculture, law, war, and medicine. He emphasized a high moral standard against the decadent Greek influence, and the practical methods by which one could become a success. Perhaps it is good that the entire work was eventually lost, if we are to judge by the remains of some of Cato's other writings.

In everything he wrote, he revealed his practical nature. He explained to the farmer how time could be saved in bad weather by giving attention to cleaning and mending the farmhouse rather than by trying to till the fields in the rain. He suggested a practical way to feed slaves — that is, not too much — and he argued that when a slave became sick it was a sign that the slave was overfed, and that old or diseased slaves should be sold as one sells an old ox or cart. Be sure, Cato wrote, to retrieve the tattered garment every time you give a slave a new one. It can be used for patches.

His medical prescriptions were extensive and odd. To treat an ill ox, the doctor should swallow a raw egg whole and next day a chopped leek's head in wine. How this might help the ox no one is today sure, but it takes a doctor with a cast-iron stomach to keep up this treatment. Cato included charms and incantations for every medical problem, even a dislocated elbow, which should be bound in reed splints and sung over with unintelligible words.

Cato didn't write in Greek — according to him, a "decadent language" — though most literate Romans could read it. Yet his writings so met the needs of the gentleman farmer of his day that he was widely read and quoted. In fact, today he has the singular honor of being listed as the father of Latin prose.

The voluminous Roman writer Marcus Terentius Varro (116–27 B.C.), who was born a generation after Cato died, is perhaps the best representative of Roman encyclopedic learning. Though only a few of his writings remain, it has been estimated that he completed 74 different works consisting of 620 single volumes, or scrolls. Quintilian called him "the most learned of the Romans." And St. Augustine, in a later age, said that Varro appeals to the lover of facts as Cicero appeals to the lover of words. Undoubtedly this is an exaggeration, because the words of Varro tend to exasperate scholars by his interest in minute details. Varro loses himself in curiosities, giving insignificant events as prominent a place as major ones. The reference to Cicero, however, is not unfounded, and Varro dedicated most of his works to that great orator.

Unlike Cato, Varro was not put off by Greek learning, and he made a conscious effort to bring the best of it to the average Roman reader. But at the same time he delighted in poking fun at the most ridiculous aspects of Greek philosophizing. He held one belief that he tried to drive home: that "the good old Roman days" were far better than the times in which he lived — times of ever greater luxury. He presented this theme in essays on covetousness, dinner parties, drunkenness (*A Pot Has Its Limits*), extravagance in marriage, pleasure (*The Battle of the Gods*), flirtation with pretty women, medical prescriptions, the emptiness of certain funeral orations, and the blindness of the soul (*Gladiators with Closed Visors*).

Varro so enjoyed dividing subjects into categories that he was carried away by the process itself. For example, his work *De re Rustica* ("About Agriculture"), which he began at age 80, is a subdivided and re-subdivided work about agricultural plants, sheep, oxen, poultry, zoo animals, dormice, snails, bees, and the management of fish ponds. In the first chapter, Varro lists 50 Greek writers on the subject of agriculture. He then begins to divide his material into many sections and subsections and stops at almost every proper name to discuss its significance and to assume its etymology. It has been suggested by some scholars that had Varro written less and spent a greater amount of his energy on style, more of his works might have been preserved.

His nine books titled *Disciplinarum Libri IX* ("Nine Books of Disciplines") encompass a complete encyclopedia of the liberal arts and cover grammar, logic, rhetoric, geometry, arithmetic, astronomy, music, medicine, and architecture. The texts were often plagiarized in later encyclopedias, particularly those written during the Middle Ages. Varro's *Imagines* covered biography, and was the first encyclopedic work in which pictures were used to supplement the text. It included 700 portraits of noted Greek and Roman personalities, but these have all been lost.

The Romans, unlike the Greeks, never set up competing schools of philosophy. Though they thought that the concept of the circle of knowledge made sense, they made no pretense of knowing all of the available facts. Instead, they drew their knowledge from as many sources as possible, some of which contradicted one another. Thus their encyclopedias were sometimes redundant and included unaccredited materials taken from those of the Greeks.

Because the only surviving section of another encyclopedia written sometime between A.D. 14 and A.D. 37 by the Roman aristocrat, Aulus Cornelius Celsus, deals with medicine, it is often assumed that Celsus must have been a physician. But he was no doctor and the section on medicine wasn't even written by him. It was a translation into Latin of a Greek work by a Sicilian called Titus Aufidius. Celsus translated this work and claimed it as his own, giving no acknowledgment to the author. Only painstaking scholarship in modern times has eventually revealed the source. However, Celsus probably would have a place of honor in the world of translation even if he had admitted it was another's work, for his style is superb. The fact that he didn't admit to plagiarism may account for the opinion of some of his contemporaries that Celsus was a man of only moderate talent.

In any case, it should be remembered that the volume on medicine was but one part of a 26-volume encyclopedia, the *Artes* ("The Arts"), written during the reign of Tiberius (A.D. 14–37). This encyclopedia was designed to cover the whole of a person's life. The first two parts — agriculture and medicine — dealt with the physical life of a man. The last two — rhetoric and the art of war — his life as a citizen. To follow the logic further, agriculture creates the means of life, and medicine protects that which is created. At the same time, rhetoric (which in Roman times covered the complete training in the arts of civil life) might be said to create civil life, which was protected by the art of war.

The part on medicine that has come down to us is the most comprehensive single work on the subject that we have from Greek and Roman antiquity. Its most interesting section concerns surgery and has a fascinating, almost modern account of the removal of tonsils. The section on dentistry includes the wiring of loose teeth and the use of a dental mirror.

Of all the Greek and Roman encyclopedists, undoubtedly the most influential was Pliny the Elder (A.D. 23–79), who lived shortly after Celsus and who completed *Historia Naturalis,* or *Natural History,* consisting of 37 parchment scrolls and 2,493 articles. The work is still studied today, and handwritten copies were the prize volumes of every medieval library. Pliny was a self-taught man who gathered material for his encyclopedia from 473 authors, mostly Greeks. He completed the work in Rome after early military service in Germany, Gaul, and Spain. He later was appointed to be the prefect of the Roman fleet. When Mt. Vesuvius erupted to overwhelm the cities of Pompeii and Herculaneum with lava in A. D. 79, Pliny went to study the phenomenon at close range and, getting too close, died in the ashes.

The main thought that runs through Pliny's *Natural History* is that nature serves humankind. Natural objects are invariably described in their relation to humans and not by themselves. Unfortunately, Pliny tended to accept many old wives' tales as fact so that for a thousand years afterward his fictions appeared, whether with the source credited or not, in many books and other encyclopedias. For example, he says that the herb dittany has the power to extract arrows, as proved by stags that feed on this plant. The arrows that strike these animals fall out as soon as the dittany is digested. Had Pliny checked this "proved fact" with as much scientific interest as he displayed in investigating the volcano, he undoubtedly would have omitted it. On another occasion he tells of the remora, a Mediterranean fish with a suctorial disk on its head. Pliny says that this tiny fish can restrain all the forces of the ocean. Winds might rage and storms might roar, yet the fish withstands their force and holds ships still by simply adhering to them! Pliny further lists the unicorn, the phoenix, the griffin, mermaids, and tritons among the known animals, sketching them with the same care and respect he accords to the lion, crocodile, and elephant.

Finally, the Greeks and Romans produced four other encyclopedias, none of which is worth much discussion. The one compiled by Marcus Verrius Flaccus about 20 B.C. (now lost), however, did become the source material for a dictionary prepared by Sextus Pompeius Festus, an encyclopedic dictionary of the type made famous in 1806 by the American Noah Webster. Julius Pollux wrote *Onomasticon* ("Dictionary of Names") in the second century A.D., of interest only because of its definitions of technical terms and included quotations, while the work of Gaius Julius Solinus of the third century draws so heavily (about 90 percent) on Pliny's *Natural History*, without acknowledgment, and on other works of the time that one hesitates to list him at all except for the fact that several medieval writers copied parts of it into their own encyclopedias. And then there was the Greek Martianus Minneus Felix Capella who, between A.D. 410 and 429, wrote an encyclopedia in a strange mixture of prose and verse that focuses on the wedding of Philology to Mercury, with the first two books devoted to a description of the wedding nuptials. The following seven books are devoted to the seven bridesmaids of liberal arts: grammar, metaphysics and logic, rhetoric, geography and geometry, arithmetic, astronomy, and music and poetry. The pedantic approach of the author and his free borrowing (usually unacknowledged) from Pliny, Varro, Solinus, and other writers did not prevent his work from being treasured for a long period of time, all the way into the sixteenth century.

The encyclopedic gathering together of the early Roman and Greek writers came to an end with the invasion of Italy by the Goths in A.D. 410 and the Ostrogoths in 489. Thereafter, the preservation and development of encyclopedias and other books shifted to the Christian Church, which became the center of all learning.

For one thousand years the fabric of the church gathered the diverse elements of Europe together through religious symbolism and Pauline morality. The church ordered the daily time schedules, reset the yearly calendar to divide before and after the year attributed to the birth of Jesus, turned pagan rituals and mythology into Christian practices and history, and established rules of conduct that were deemed good or bad in the eyes of the religious hierarchy. But we now need to turn from Europe to see what was happening elsewhere — in Asia.

3. Gifts from Asia

Western pundits often talk as if the whole world was discovered by Europeans, but this is a narrow and rather parochial vision. It certainly was not the situation before the Renaissance. On the contrary, the Chinese in 138 B.C. (in the person of the navigator Zhang Qian) were the first to discover the Greeks in Bactria (now part of Afghanistan). And no ancient Greek or Roman, including Alexander the Great, ever got as far east as the Chinese got west through the arrival of Gao Ying and other Chinese in the Persian Gulf in A.D. 97. By the eighteenth century China had become the greatest empire on earth. Its domain extended from the Siberian forests of the Amur region 3,000 miles westward, deep into the plains of Central Asia and 1,500 miles southward into the tropical mountains of Southeast Asia. The countries that surrounded China — Japan, Korea, Annam, Burma, Nepal, and the sheikhdoms of Central Asia — all acknowledged China's suzerainty by sending tribute to the Chinese emperor.

The Chinese had already designed the world's first civil service system; introduced the first paper money; made significant discoveries in the fields of geology, meteorology, astronomy, and engineering; and made many inventions, including gunpowder, porcelain, the magnetic compass, paper, and movable type for printing. And they had written the most extensive encyclopedia ever — the *Yong Lo Da Tian* ("Great Standard of Yong Lo"), which encompasses 11,095 volumes on more than 500,000 pages. It was produced by some 2,000 scholars working under five chief directors and 20 subdirectors, and was designed to include everything that had ever been written on Confucian religion, history, philosophy, arts, and sciences. The scholars who composed this encyclopedia began their work on the volumes in 1403 and completed the massive project four years later. Some 370 surviving volumes are now scattered in libraries all over the world.

We know this about China's history of knowledge because there are more original sources for the facts and events of that country than exist for any other Eastern and indeed most Western countries. Unlike, for example, India, where scholars are still quite uncertain about the chronology of its history, the Chinese have one of the best historiographical traditions in the world. Their ancient records reveal in many cases not only the year and month that a certain event took place, but even the exact day and sometimes the exact hour. There were official historians in every dynasty, starting with that of the Qin (221–207 B.C.), who recorded the contemporary happenings. These eventually became complete dynastic histories, and several Western observers have expressed surprise over the objectivity and lack of bias that these Chinese historians brought to their work.

Why Chinese knowledge and influence declined after the eighteenth century is still a matter of conjecture, and it is not our purpose to examine that here. This has been done exhaustively elsewhere by scholars such as Joseph Needham in his monumental seven-volume *Science and Civilization in China*. Instead, we will look briefly at the way the Chinese educated themselves and collected their information into books that could be read by future generations.

Like the Greeks, the early Chinese established academies of scholars to gather together all their knowledge and pass that learning on to others. The most famous of these was the Academy of the Gate of Chi in Shandong province. Here many of the most brilliant philosophers, some of whom came from great distances, were welcomed and provided with quarters and maintenance by the county authorities, and the most important among these scholars held the rank of Great Prefect. Some of those who worked at this academy were the noted Taoist philosophers Tian Pian, Shen Dao, and Peng Meng; the founder of the Yin-Yang school of philosophy Zou Yan; the Mohist philosopher Song Xing; and the well-known Confucian philosopher Mencius. It is, of course, interesting to note the similarity in dates between the Academy of the Gate of Chi, founded about 318 B.C., and Plato's Academy in Athens that was founded in 387 B.C. as well as the Stoic Academy founded by the Greek philosopher Zeno sometime after 314 B.C. It is just one of several such coincidences in the history of human development.

In no great civilization did education hold so central a place as it did in China. And nowhere else did learned men enjoy such political authority. In fact, scholars almost always have been held in high esteem by the Chinese. One reason for this was China's civil service system, designed by Confucian scholars and maintained by almost every emperor for more than 2,000 years. Under this system, any man who could excel in the government's arduous written examinations, which took many days to complete, would be appointed shortly thereafter to a government post and honored as an intellectual. The system allowed men, and only men, to rise from the lowest ranks to positions of great power on the basis of their intellectual prowess alone, no matter who their fathers might be. Essentially, it made brains predominant over class background, and a few peasants — only a very few — rose to become county and provincial governors.

On paper this civil service system looks like the most egalitarian system ever set up anywhere in the world. In reality, however, those who were educated enough to take the civil service exams were almost always the sons of rich landlords, i.e., boys whose fathers could afford to hire tutors for their education and who were not needed to work elsewhere on the farm or in trade.

Young men studied for years to gain the right to take first the county exam, then the provincial one, and finally the examination at the national level. At each stage of passage they were honored with banquets and celebrations, much as are winning candidates in an American political election. And they were expected to provide gifts for their supporters. The decision to take such exams thus was an expensive one, a fact that also tended to eliminate impoverished contestants. But the system worked well and kept the intellectual level of the ruling elite relatively high.

Most of the early Chinese writings were produced by those who had passed the civil service examinations and they, as government officials, established the first libraries in China — used for their own pleasure and that of their relatives. Yet the production of books and documents in China was remarkable in terms of quantity, quality, and varied subject matter. In spite of the cumbersomeness of the Chinese written language, the number of handwritten and printed books turned out by the Chinese before 1750 was greater than that for all other languages in the world combined.

The imperial court even established an elaborate system of book classification to keep track of all these writings. The system was introduced as early as the first century B.C. It arranged the books into seven divisions. A later, modified, fourfold scheme for book classification was introduced in the third century A.D., and this has now been used by Chinese bibliographers for more than 1,500 years. It is even possible that this four-division system — classics, philosophy, history, and belles-lettres — may have influenced the triad scheme designed by Francis Bacon (1561–1626) in England, which is the basis of modern book classification in the West.

Besides books, Chinese written materials included numerous inscriptions carved into stone, the most gigantic of which is the engraving of the complete texts for more than 105 Buddhist cannons using some 4,200,000 words on 7,137 stone steles that are found in a large cave and other nearby subterranean chambers on the eastern peak of Mt. Fengshan in Hubei province. The single cave library includes 145 tablets representing 14 different sutras that are engraved on its walls. There are also four pillars covered with Buddhist images in this cave. The tablets containing the other carved sutras are in the surrounding chambers.

The invention of printing and movable type — a Chinese invention from around the eighth century despite claims for Gutenberg's discovery in the fifteenth century — were closely related to the influx of Buddhism from India. With its spread in the third and fourth centuries A.D., much religious literature was imported from India, and for the first time foreign books were extensively translated into Chinese and integrated into Chinese life. Taoist works also flourished with the increasing output of Buddhist writings.

For some reason, the Buddhists had always felt the need for unending repetitions of sacred names, sutras, pictures of Bodhisattvas, holy ejaculations, and other religious incantations. By the eighth century these were being block printed on rice- and bamboo-based paper for wide distribution. Not long after that, the Chinese were carving reverse characters out of wood and using ceramic molds to turn words into movable type to be able to print larger documents in more variety. Such printing included many textbooks that were required by thousands of young men in their preparations for the civil examination system. Just as Gutenberg's process in Europe (using metal type) allowed for the mass production of the indulgence grants needed by the Catholic Church, the use of movable wood and ceramic type in China allowed for the mass production of Buddhist scriptures.

The Chinese reverence for education and good literature does not mean that their knowledge base was always secure. Books, in fact, were destroyed and intellectuals persecuted from time to time just as they were in Europe and other parts of the world. Perhaps the best-known incident of this sort was the burning of all the books except those in the imperial archives by Emperor Qin Shi Huang, the first emperor to unify all of China in 221 B.C. This is the same emperor who started the building of the Great Wall and whose tomb has long been guarded by the thousands of life-size ceramic soldiers in battle array, which have been only recently excavated — a must for any tourist visit to Xian.

According to the account universally accepted for centuries in China, the emperor ordered the burning of all the books — except for works on medicine, divination, and agriculture — because he believed the literature of the day was too impregnated with outdated Confucian ideas. During this process, the emperor also put to death many of the literati and their relatives, as well as some of the book owners. Needham says that he doubts the exaggerated nature of this account, because the same kind of stories are told of similar hero-kings in other parts of the world. The official records say little about the event, although it is formally recorded that the emperor worked indefatigably in handling "one hundred and twenty pounds of reports" every day and that he traveled a great deal.

The Qin emperor's palace was described as one of the wonders of the world, and it is expected that when his tomb is eventually excavated (only the ceramic battle army has so far been uncovered) it may also be an extraordinary edifice. Perhaps even some of the documents from his palace archives that were elsewhere destroyed in the "great burning" will be found there. The Chinese archaeologists have said they will not begin excavation of the tomb until they have the techniques to do the job properly. And this may be the case. But so many ancient sites of perhaps more archaeological significance are now being studied in China that it is likely the excavation of the Qin emperor's tomb has been placed at low priority.

Volumes have been written that describe all the Chinese literary achievements, but we will confine our discussion here to encyclopedias, because such works are designed with the intention of covering all existing knowledge. Most Chinese books of this sort are truly remarkable, constructed as they were for the needs of the civil service system and good government rather than recording absolute truths for the general reader. They were carefully composed, revised, amplified, and recomposed from time to time.

The first was *Huang Yan* ("Emperor's Mirror") prepared by order of one of the emperors about A.D. 220 No part of this work, or that of several of its successors, has survived. But other Chinese encyclopedias suggest that the *Huang Yan* was a carefully structured work written in fine literary style. The arrangement of its content was copied by many later encyclopedists. Another encyclopedia put out shortly afterward by Zhang Hua (232–300) under the name *Bo Wu Ji* ("Plentiful Things") was revised by Dong Si-zhuang about 1607 under the title *Guang Bo Wu Ji* ("Extensive and Plentiful Things") and then reprinted in 1761.

About the year 600 the Chinese encyclopedia *Pian Zhu* ("Stringed Pearls of Literature") was completed, a part of which still survives. Shortly thereafter the *Yi Wen Lei Ju* ("Anthology of Art and Literature") of Xun Ou-yang (557-641) was written in 100 chapters divided into 47 sections. This was followed by Yu Shi-nan's encyclopedia called the *Bei Tang Shu Zhao* ("From a North Tang Writing Desk") that he finished about the year 630. It has 160 chapters in 19 sections and emphasizes public administration. An annotated edition, edited by Gong Guang-tao, was published in 1880.

Another encyclopedic work by Du Yu (735–812) that comprised nine sections including economics, law, music, political geography, examinations and degrees, rites and ceremonies, government, the army, and national defense was later combined with eight other works — some of which were historical encyclopedias — and printed in 1747 under the title *Jiu Dong* ("Investigation of the Known"). There also have been several modern reprints of this collection.

Any more extensive list of the many Chinese encyclopedias is likely to be tedious to the Western reader unfamiliar with the Chinese language, and so I will touch on just three more, because they are considered to be so important by modern scholars. However, one should be aware of the fact that there are numerous Chinese encyclopedias of every type — historical, scientific, biographical, and literary. Many are now incomplete because some of the volumes or pages have been lost over the years.

The *Shi Lei Fu* ("Accumulated Knowledge") of Wu Shu (947–1002) was divided into 14 sections containing 100 chapters on celestial and terrestrial matters, mineralogy, botany, and natural history. Later writers added to this work so that by 1699 it contained 27 sections and 191 articles. Wu Shu also compiled a literary encyclopedia of 30 sections that was later incorporated into another, larger encyclopedia.

Around the same time the statesman Li Fang (925–996) and his collaborators compiled the massive and still-popular encyclopedia *Tai Ping Yu Lan* ("An Understanding of Peace and Tranquility"). This contains 1,000 books arranged in 55 sections. It has quotations and extracts from some 1,600 other works, of which a list is given at the beginning of the encyclopedia.

Chinese encyclopedias are difficult to consult, because in traditional Chinese scholarship no indexes existed. Scholars were supposed to know their texts sufficiently well to be able to refer to them for any specific inquiry. Only in recent years have any indexes to some of these volumes been prepared. The one published recently for the *Tai Ping Yu Lan* under the joint sponsorship of Harvard University in the U.S. and Yanjing University in China is an indispensable aid to modern Chinese readers who might wish to consult this encyclopedia.

Finally there is the encyclopedia of natural science written by Shen Kuo about 1086. Titled *Meng Xi Bi Tan* ("Dream System Essays"), it contains a history of China's ancient science and technology. In this book is found the first description of the magnetic compass. It also contains a great deal on astronomy, mathematics, notices of fossils, the making of relief maps, descriptions of metallurgical processes, and biological observations. The author, a scholar in government service, was at various times an ambassador to several countries, a military commander, the director of hydraulic works, and chancellor of the Han-Lin (Forest of Writing Tools) Academy in Xian. Wherever he went he never failed to write down all that was of scientific and technical interest. A shorter work by the same author describes the best way to make an official inspection carriage comfortable so that the rider can get a good view of the scenery or other objects of interest.

No cultures in the Far East other than the Chinese produced encyclopedic works until modern times. Hindu literature, which was already extensive when the Greeks and Romans were writing their encyclopedias, contains no such volumes. Instead, the scholars of India produced elaborate commentaries on Sanskrit texts, much as the Hebrews compiled commentaries on the Talmud.

In the Near East, however, the followers of Muhammad created encyclopedias among the many Arabic books they completed. And while much of early Christianity tended to discourage investigations and learning outside of the sphere of religion, Islam flowered in scholarship and preserved many of the Greek and Roman texts that had been forgotten or destroyed in the Christian world. It was not until the later Middle Ages that Christian scholars began to rediscover this wisdom, some as a result of their contacts with Arabic knowledge.

It is interesting to note that at the time when Columbus sailed to the New World, Islam was the largest world religion. Beginning in the year 622 when the Prophet Muhammad moved from Mecca to Medina, a date known to Muslims as the Hegira, the religion expanded rapidly into areas as far apart and as different from each other as Senegal, Bosnia, Java, and the Philippines. After the death of Muhammad in 632, Muslim generals and their armies accomplished in Asia all that Alexander the Great had done, and half of what the Romans had done around the Mediterranean.

In the year A.D. 800 when Charlemagne was crowned by the pope in Rome, Western Christianity had hardly begun to reach beyond its Mediterranean core into the mostly preliterate world of northern Europe. But 800 years after the Hegira, centers of Islamic civilization were already scattered throughout Asia, Africa, and southern Europe. Arabic is the universal language of the Muslims just as Latin is the universal language of the Catholic Church, and so Arabic inscriptions and literature can today be found wherever Muhammad's followers are located.

The first Arabic encyclopedia was the work of Ibn Qutaiba (b. 828), a teacher and philologist. He was the author of a number of important works, and his encyclopedia, titled *Kitab Uyun al-Akhbar* ("The Best Traditions"), was divided into ten books. These covered power, war, nobility, character, learning and eloquence, asceticism, friendship, prayers, food, and women. Using traditional aphorisms, historical examples, and old Arabic poems, the author intended this encyclopedia to make the knowledge of his time accessible to all educated persons, particularly to those in the administrative class.

Before Ibn Qutaiba's encyclopedia had been rediscovered and published in 1903, it was thought that the oldest Arabic encyclopedia was *Mafatih al-Ulum* ("Key to the Sciences") by al-Farabi (870–950). This author was greatly influenced by Greek concepts and drew on the works of such Greek authors as Philo, Nicomachus, and Euclid for some of his material in an attempt to reconcile Greek philosophy with Islam. The encyclopedia was divided into two parts: Arab knowledge and Foreign knowledge. Some of its subject matter covered philosophy, grammar, logic, medicine, mathematics, astronomy, music, mechanics, and alchemy. *Key to the Sciences* was eventually translated into Latin under the title *On the Origin of the Sciences*, and was widely read in the Roman world.

An Arab encyclopedia put out in pamphlet form and written as a collaborative effort by five authors was the product of a religious or political party calling themselves the Brethren of Purity. The group was founded in Basra and was particularly active from 980 to 999. Their aim was to harmonize reason with authority and to develop a universal system of religious philosophy. Altogether they published 52 pamphlets on such subjects as the origin of life, the stars, love, resurrection, cause and effect, arithmetic, astronomy, the four elements, zoology, magic, government, divination, and astrology. In 1887–89 the pamphlets were gathered together and printed in Bombay, India, under the title *Rasa'ulu Ikhwan al Safa* ("Book of the Sincere Brethren").

Other important Muslim encyclopedias include the *Al Shifa* ("The Healing") by Avicenna (980–1037), a noted medical encyclopedia by Averroes (1126–1198), and the *Prolegoma* ("Treatise") of the Arab historian and sociologist Ibn Khaldun (1332–1406). The latter includes discussions on political establishments and a classification of the sciences.

The influence of Greek thought on many of the Arab encyclopedists is an example of how the Greek concept of a circle of knowledge spread throughout the civilized world. It was pushed by the victorious Greek and Roman armies, and eventually even by Catholic missionaries and medieval diplomats schooled in the wisdom of Aristotle and Pliny. In style and content, the earliest German, Russian, and Japanese encyclopedias were far more Greek in design than they were native to their own cultural heritage. It was indeed a triumph of Greek and Roman cultural imperialism, but an imperial accomplishment that never quite reached into China.

4. The Early Accumulation of Books

The founding of libraries predated any encyclopedia writing, even though the earliest library unearthed seems to have been little more than a repository for deeds and records of trade. Myths in some traditions contend that libraries predated even the advent of human beings. The gods of Egypt, Greece, India, Persia, and Scandinavia, for example, were said to have had their own collections of written knowledge. And the Hebrew Talmud refers to a manuscript collection (i.e., a library) before the creation of the world. The Sanskrit Vedas profess that collections of books existed before the Creator created himself, while the Moslem Koran maintains that such a collection of writings coexisted from eternity with the yet-uncreated God.

There also are non-biblical accounts in the Hebrew tradition about the library of Adam describing how on the seventh day of the first month of the first year Jehovah composed a work on creation written in the Hebrew language. The purpose was to preserve the record of the event and to teach Adam the alphabet. Adam bequeathed this unique library to his son Seth, and Seth then passed it on to Enoch. Eventually it became part of the library owned by Noah, which Noah had to bury in preparation for the great flood because the collection was too large to bring aboard the ark, which was already crowded with animals. According to this story, Noah later dug up this library and it was subsequently consulted by Moses.

The libraries of Cain, Seth, Enoch, and Ham also were listed by Hebrew chroniclers. Seth's was noted for its record of astronomical and astrological works, but Ham's was apparently filled with heretical works that were destroyed in the flood. Because of their content, he was forbidden to take these tomes onto the ark.

It should be noted that for the Babylonians the only library of importance was that which appeared every night in the sky. The stars in the heavens were themselves imaged as great documents in which could be read the destiny of humankind and all the secrets of heaven and earth. We now recognize this concept as the origin of astrology, with the zodiac forming a kind of Book of Revelation.

As these ancient myths and traditions reveal, libraries have played an important role in every culture. Yet the first libraries of which there is any real proof are the clay-tablet repositories of the Sumerians and the clay-cylinder collections of the Assyrians. The earliest was discovered in the ancient city of Uruk, or Eresh, in the lower valley near the Euphrates River. The tablets in this collection date to before 3000 B.C. and are in pictographic script. They were made by inscribing wet clay with the pressure of a stylus. When the tablets were later baked, the clay became hard and the messages imprinted on them were thus preserved.

The Uruk library contained excessively dull works compared to modern standards. Most of the clay tablets in this and various other Sumerian, Babylonian, and Assyrian libraries — Jemdet Nasr, Tello, Nippur, and Nineveh — are related to deeds for land and other private and public business records. Scholars have not yet learned the meaning of all the markings on such ancient tablets, but many thousands of them have been found, and they are housed today in museums and national libraries throughout the world. Qualified persons can even borrow some for study from the Free Library of Philadelphia.

A find of greater significance was the library at Ebla in northern Syria, which was discovered by Italian archaeologists in 1974. More than 16,000 clay tablets were found in the buried ruins of this city, which dates back to around 2400 B.C. The tablets, some written in Sumerian and others in Semitic script, contain more than just records of trade. A few that have been translated provide independent background material for stories found in the opening chapters of Genesis. For example, one tablet gives an account of the great flood that is similar to that found in both the Old Testament and in Babylonian literature. Another tablet refers to a place called Urusalima, which scholars agree is Ebla's name for Jerusalem. This is the earliest known reference to that holy city.

A more efficient, though less permanent, way of preserving records and other writings was the subsequent use of papyrus scrolls by the Egyptians. Papyrus is a reed that grows in the marshlands of the Nile River. The Egyptians cut the reed stems into strips, pressed these together into sheets, and joined the sheets to each other to form scrolls. Until sometime in the 100s B.C., the Egyptians had a monopoly on the manufacture of papyrus and carefully guarded their right to manufacture this material, which they traded and sold to scribes throughout the Mediterranean.

Papyrus rapidly decays in damp climates. For this reason, almost all existing papyrus manuscripts come from such arid lands as Egypt and surrounding countries, and most of those preserved date from 332 B.C. to A.D. 641. One scroll that has survived — the Harris Papyrus #1— totals 133 feet in length. It is now housed in the British Museum Library in London.

Although the ancient papyrus scroll was elegant to look at, it was difficult to consult. Each roll was about nine or ten inches in width and about 30 feet in length, having about the same amount of text as a single chapter in a modern book. One thousand or so lines of text was all that a scroll could hold, and to shuffle through such a roll looking for some particular passage was undoubtedly a time-consuming and cumbersome process.

Ptolemy's library at Alexandria, said to have numbered in the hundreds of thousands of papyrus scrolls, was undoubtedly the greatest library of the ancient world. However, the library at Pergamum, a Greek city-state in Asia Minor, grew to be almost as large, and like the one in Alexandria, was filled mainly with stolen and copied works by Greek and Roman scholars. Established during the reigns of Attalus I (d. 197 B.C.) and Eumenes II (d. 159 B.C.), the very existence of the Pergamum library was an irritation to the Egyptian pharaohs, who apparently wanted to effect, at Alexandria, the same kind of monopoly over the collection and preservation of knowledge that they held over the material on which it was recorded.

In hopes of preventing further acquisitions by the Pergamum library, the Egyptian rulers forbade the export of any more papyrus to that area of the Middle East. But instead of hindering the library from accumulating more texts, the ban only spurred King Eumenes II of Pergamum to search for other writing materials. He ordered his craftsmen, around 150 B.C., to conduct a series of experiments that resulted in the creation of parchment from the treated skins of sheep, goats, and other animals. This material proved to be as good, if not better, than papyrus for the recording of documents. The Pergamum library thus continued to grow at a time when the library in Alexandria had already begun its decline.

This actually was not the first use of animal skins for writing. Scholars of the ancient world sometimes wrote on leather when papyrus was unavailable. The Dead Sea Scrolls, found in the late 1940s in caves near the northwestern shore of the Dead Sea, are all made of leather. But parchment — the word comes from Pergamum — is a form of leather that has undergone a great deal of refinement. The hair or wool must first be removed from the skin of the animal, which is then placed in lime to rid it of its fat. The skin is next stretched on a frame and scraped with knives or scrapers. Powdered chalk is then rubbed into the skin with a pumice stone to smooth it, and finally the skin is sliced into thin layers. Vellum, the highest quality of parchment, is still used today for important writings such as charters, university diplomas, and wills.

The closing of the Pergamum library provides one of the ironies of history. A little more than 100 years after the discovery of parchment, Mark Antony, in his pursuit of Cleopatra, made a gift to her of all 2,000 works in the Pergamum library. Thus the knowledge that the Pergamum had so carefully accumulated over the years in its attempt to compete with the library at Alexandria ended in the hands of the last ruler in the line of Ptolemys, who had ruled Egypt for almost 300 years.

Because parchment sheets cannot be satisfactorily pieced together into rolls as can sheets of papyrus, the scribes and librarians who worked with this new material began the practice of folding several parchment sheets down the middle and sewing them together through the fold. This process eventually was adopted for the production of books and has remained the primary method used in bookbinding ever since.

Today the great collections of papyrus scrolls and parchment foldings of the Roman Empire have mostly disappeared, as have those of ancient Egypt and Greece. But at one time most of the larger Greek temples contained their own scroll libraries, and all the homes of the richest Romans had repositories for such works. In fact, having a library in one's home became such a status symbol that the Latin poet Lucian (c. A.D. 120–200) began to poke fun at the "book clowns" who collected books even when they were too untutored to read them, and the Stoic philosopher Seneca (4 B.C.–A.D. 65) raised moral questions about the accumulation of books by those who didn't use them.

One collection, which had belonged to a Roman nobleman named Lucius Calpurnius Piso, was actually uncovered in its original location: the volcanic-ash covered ruins of Herculaneum. Discovered by excavators in the 1750s, the library was subsequently studied with great care by various scholars and archaeologists. It contained more than 350 scrolls stored in wooden boxes that had been placed in bookcases around the walls of a room. Most of them were written in Greek, but a few were in Latin. They were writings on philosophy, medicine, and literary criticism, as well as some general literature. Additional fragments of scrolls burned and charred by the volcanic eruption suggest that the original collection may have included as many as 3,000 scrolls.

The Roman statesman and general Lucullus (110–57 B.C.), perhaps the richest man in the ancient world, maintained an enormous library in Rome of which there are no remnants. Lucullus acquired the contents as part of booty from various wars, and he was generous in allowing others to consult the works. Cicero, who owned a fine private library of his own, tells of visiting Lucullus to borrow one of the scrolls and there finding his friend Cato surrounded by many of the works written by various Stoic philosophers.

Scrolls and parchment sheets bound into books were quite expensive to produce before the advent of printing, because all writing had to be done by hand and the materials were expensive. Eventually, books in libraries were chained to the shelves to prevent their theft. The chains were long enough to reach nearby desks. But, as far back as A.D. 100, the library of Pantainos in the Athenian Agora displayed this inscription: "No writing shall be taken out for we have sworn it."

The first public library in Rome was one planned but never actually built by Julius Caesar. The plans were entrusted to Marcus Terentius Varro, a man remembered for his encyclopedic works. However, the library was finally constructed in 37 B.C. on Rome's Palatine Hill by the literary patron Asinius Pollio. It was named the Octavian Library after Emperor Augustus, or Octavian. Pliny, in his *Natural History*, refers to Caesar's plan for this public library with admiration, saying, "He made men's talents a public possession."

The idea of having a public library took hold and many others were built. A survey of important Roman buildings, conducted in A.D. 337, indicates that there were then 28 public libraries in the city. The best of these was the Ulpian Library, built about A.D. 110 by Emperor Trajan. It had two separate structures for its collections, one for Greek and the other for Latin texts. It also was designated as the Public Records Office of Rome.

Although the number of libraries grew, the Roman Empire itself remained in almost constant turmoil from A.D. 180 to 285. Barbarian tribes from both east and west conducted massive raids into Roman territory, and to meet these threats, the empire doubled the size of its army. The result was that for almost 100 years the army put emperors on the throne and removed them at will. During one 67-year period, there were 29 emperors and claimants to the throne, only four of whom died natural deaths.

In 306 Flavius Valerius Aurelius Constantinus became emperor of Rome. Six years later, as a result of a vision he experienced before going into a great battle, Constantine embraced Christianity. He later moved the capital to Byzantium and changed that city's name to Constantinople. One of the structures he erected there was a library to contain only Christian books, as distinguished from the other libraries of the ancient world that usually held pagan works.

With Constantine's death in 337, came great disorder, and by 378, when the Roman Empire was clearly in decline, the historian Ammianus Marcellinus was found to be complaining, "The libraries are closing forever, like tombs."

The Christian church that Constantine favored so dominated intellectual life in the latter half of the Middle Ages that we need to be reminded that until around the late 900s educational and artistic activity in Europe sank to a particularly low level. During the latter part of the Roman Empire, the Christian church could hardly even be called a cultural institution. On the contrary, it was still busily trying to demonstrate its cultural respectability a century after Constantine's conversion. Whole branches of arts and letters remained exclusively in pagan hands. The universities and public academies were run by the state with the essential purpose of training men for the civil service. They were in pagan hands and, therefore, taught no theology.

Visigoth warriors from Germany burst into Italy in 401 and nine years later swept into Rome itself, capturing and looting the once mighty city and intellectual center of the Latin world. Some years later, the Vandals plundered Rome for two weeks. They were followed by the Ostrogoths, who remained in that city and in Italy until the 550s. Under the impact of these Germanic invasions, libraries, both public and private, went up in flames or were left to decay.

Even as late as the fifth century, when all such Roman institutions were crumbling, no attempt appears to have been made to create any kind of Christian schools. The first such suggestion came in 536 when Cassiodorus (c. 480–575), a prominent Catholic layman, turned to Pope Agapetus with a request that he be permitted to found a Christian academy of learning in Rome. Cassiodorus was one of the few Christian intellectuals to accommodate the German conquerors. At age 20 he worked closely with the Ostrogoth chieftain, Theodoric the Great, acting as his secretary. Under the Ostrogoths, Cassiodorus eventually rose to a post equivalent to that of prime minister.

His plan for the Christian academy was based on the now-extinct examples of pagan academies at Alexandria and Antioch. But the Pope rejected Cassiodorus' proposal. The Pontiff saw little need to preserve intellectual wisdom, and Cassiodorus left Rome to take up residence at Vivarium, in Cambria. Here he eventually founded a monastery for monks who would devote themselves to the study and copying of manuscripts. For this reason Cassiodorus has been called "the father of literary monasticism in the West." Though Cassiodorus never became a monk, he followed the religious services of the monastery as its patron and, as we shall see later, he also completed an encyclopedia of note before he died.

The monastery Cassiodorus founded no longer exits, but his emphasis on copying manuscripts to preserve knowledge for future generations was later taken up by other monastic orders, particularly the Benedictines. In fact, monks produced almost all of the books written during the Middle Ages. Their work, highly specialized, was conducted in special places in the monasteries called scriptoriums. One group of monks prepared the parchment. A second group did the writing. A third group decorated the manuscripts. Finally, a fourth group of monks put the finished manuscripts in the monastery library, sold some of them, and traded others to different monasteries.

We can imagine those who did the writing sitting hour upon hour at tables and copy desks that were lighted by sunshine streaming through the window, or by candles, and dipping their quills into bottles of ink prepared by their fellow monks. Each completed page was given to another monk for proofreading. It was his job to catch the worst mistakes. But, in such tedious work, many copy errors slipped by. The production of such books was so time-consuming that, when they were illustrated and bound, they possessed a value far beyond that of any modern books.

The rules of the Benedictine order included special mention of the library and its use, putting its supervision under a precentor whose duties included making an annual check of all the books and manuscripts. There also were rules regarding the use of the books, and curses to be invoked against any person who might make off with one of them.

Among the most notable monastic libraries were Monte Casino (established in 529) and Bobbio (614) in Italy; Luxeuil (550) in France; Canterbury (597), Wearmouth (679), and Jarrow (681) in England; and Reichenau (724), Fulda (744), and Corvey (822) in Germany. Their contents included copies of the Holy Scriptures, writings of the early church fathers and commentaries on them, various chronicles, and the philosophical writings of such theologians as Thomas Aquinas, all in Latin. After various universities were founded in the thirteenth century, monkish students, on returning to their respective monasteries, usually also deposited their lecture notes in the order's library.

The growth of the universities reflected Europe's emergence from the Middle Ages and entry into the Renaissance. Now Europeans acquired a great desire for art and learning, and they began to look to ancient Greece and Rome for inspiration. This renewed interest in learning led many aristocrats to establish their own private libraries, while scholars found and translated ancient writings, and writers created literature of their own.

The Sorbonne Library at the University of Paris in A.D. 1250 had 1,017 books, many of them chained. All but four were written in Latin. These exceptions were in French. Rules established for this library in the early 1300s are enlightening. They allowed students and their teachers to use the books only in the building where the books were housed. If any books were taken from one room of the library to another, they had to be returned to the original bookshelf before the end of the day. Permission to take a book out of the building required a deposit equal to the value of the book.

In later years this library was divided into two parts. One division contained the most valuable books, all of which were chained to the shelves or desks. The other section held works of less value and could be circulated. This part was called the common library, while the first was called the reference library.

The famous Vatican Library was not established until around 1450. It was set up chiefly as a manuscript repository. Today it has approximately 350,000 printed books in its collection. The library's manuscripts number more than 50,000, many of which are highly valuable Latin works. And there are also nearly 4,000 Greek and Oriental manuscripts stored there as well.

5. Medieval Scholarship

The period following the collapse of the Roman Empire is called feudalism by economic historians. Yet religious historians sometimes speak of it as a period of spiritual growth because of the widespread interest in religious matters, while others refer to it as the Dark Ages because of the presumed lack of learning that characterized the culture of those times. The most commonly used designations, however, are the Medieval Period or Middle Ages.

After Rome fell to Germanic tribes, civilization sank low in western Europe. Knowledge from the ancient Romans survived only in a few monastery, cathedral, and palace schools. Knowledge from ancient Greece almost disappeared. Few persons received any schooling, and many of the art skills and much of the craftsmanship of the ancient world were lost.

The prevailing attitude toward writing and libraries at the beginning of these times is reflected in the answer St. Anthony (d. 356?) gave to an inquiring sage about how Anthony could endure his desert solitude without the consolation of books. The saint replied, "My book, philosopher, is the nature of created things, and as often as I have a mind to read the words of God, it is at my hand." While this statement has a certain beauty and depth, it also displays a hearty contempt for recorded knowledge.

The Roman system of government and most of their other structures of society were destroyed by the Germanic invaders — persons loyal only to their tribal chiefs or to their own families. By the 800s most of western Europe was divided into large estates ruled by a few wealthy landowners. Where broader social structures were established, this was done only by the Christian church.

Popes, bishops, and other church officials took over the many functions of government. They collected taxes and maintained courts to punish criminals. Their church buildings served as hospitals for the sick, inns for travelers, and, of course, as the only centers for learning. Eventually some of these civil structures were turned over to the kings and nobles, but final authority for all matters still remained primarily with church officialdom.

Because the church had the most literate scholars in its monasteries and nunneries, it supervised the collection, compilation, and transcription of all knowledge. It was here that the medieval encyclopedias were compiled — more than 40 in number. And the great shift from pagan to Christian interests can be seen in the subject matter included in these encyclopedias, as well as the attempt to cover all aspects of any chosen subject with theological thoroughness.

Note, for example, the way Cassiodorus approached the subject of the soul. He says: "Let us first learn why it is named the soul; second, its definition; third, its substantial quality; fourth, whether any form should be attributed to it; fifth, what are its moral virtues; sixth, what are the natural forces by which it holds the body together; seventh, what are its origins; eighth, where is the place of its seat; ninth, what is the body's form; tenth, what distinguishes the souls of sinners; eleventh, what distinguishes the souls of the just; and twelfth, what is the resurrection."

Cassiodorus, as noted earlier, founded the first Christian monastery, and was one of the first churchmen to urge that cultivation of learning be part of a priest's training. He collected the best pagan texts into his library and set monks to making copies of every document. Had Cassiodorus not been so interested in preserving all learning, it is likely that most of the Latin classics would have been lost. Only later did the Benedictine monks also decide to embrace manuscript preservation as a task of their monastic life.

In his 92nd year, when Cassiodorus was still actively at work, he wrote *De Orthographic* ("Art of Writing"), a set of rules for the copying of manuscripts. He urged copyists to study the ancient classics and to make pagan learning the servant of Christian knowledge. Further, he said that the correcting of copied texts should be done with the aid of experts in secular literature. Eventually he added bibliographical notes to the margins of the encyclopedia he composed, partly so that the monks might become aware of the best resources in the library he provided for their use.

Cassiodorus designed his two-volume encyclopedia, *Institutiones Divinarum et Saecularium Litterarum* ("Institutes of Divine and Secular Literature"), not for the learned but for the average monk. Its 36 chapters covered everything from commentaries on the Holy Scriptures to geometry and astronomy. He even explained bookbinding, lighting, and timekeeping. The first volume focused on matters relating to religion and the church. It included sections on the church fathers, readings for unlettered monks, and an admonition for the abbot and the community of monks. This volume was by far the most comprehensive and detailed of the two. Cassiodorus obviously thought the second volume less important, because it was devoted to worldly matters such as grammar, arithmetic, music, and astronomy.

The two-volume encyclopedia became a model for many of the

encyclopedia compilers who followed, even though most seemed to take more interest in the subjects of volume two than those of volume one.

Another significant medieval encyclopedia was that written by St. Isadore of Seville (c. 560–636), a man who grew to adulthood in an environment not unlike that which surrounded Cassiodorus. But this was Spain, not Italy, where the Germanic Visigoths were in control. Isadore had a background in classical education, and spent much of his early life fleeing from the barbarians by moving from one Spanish province to another until he finally settled in Seville. Here he was instructed by his brother, Leander, the archbishop of Seville and the man Isadore would eventually succeed.

After he became archbishop, Isadore presided over many councils of the church, the most important being the fourth national council at Toledo in 633. This gathering addressed political action on the part of the clergy and authorized the direct union of church and state. Isadore favored such union, arguing that "secular princes sometimes occupy positions of supreme authority in the church, in order that their might may protect ecclesiastical discipline. Moreover these powers would not be necessary in the church, were it not necessary to impose by terror what the priests are unable to make prevail by works alone." Although this statement sounds rather unenlightened by today's standards, it actually was one of the more rational positions held by the delegates.

Isadore's 20-volume encyclopedia was called *Originum seu Etymologiarum Libri XX* ("Study of the Origin of Words, Book 20"), or *Etymologies* for short. It would be his principal and longest work, although he wrote at least eight other books, including a history of the Catholic Church's campaign against the Jews. What is particularly interesting about *Etymologies* is that Isadore's starting point is not theology but the liberal arts and secular learning, much of it pagan in origin. Most encyclopedias that came from the quills of medieval theologians started the other way around.

Isadore's encyclopedia was duplicated many times by monastic scribes. About 1,000 carefully copied manuscripts of it have been preserved. It also has been translated from Latin into several other languages and printed in a number of editions. But it was not until 1951 that the first complete Spanish translation was made, even though Isadore's influence had been greatest in that country.

Magnentius Hrabanus Maurus (d. 856), who became the abbot of Fulda in Germany, compiled an encyclopedia called *De Universo* ("On the Universe") that was an untidy mass of copied material, taken largely from Isadore's *Etymologies*. As a work intended to convey all the most important knowledge then available, it was a failure. But it had one virtue that endeared it to the medieval scholars. He began his encyclopedia with God and the angels.

Plagiarism seems to have been a natural outgrowth of the medieval copying process. Several of the encyclopedias produced at this time were assorted without acknowledgment from bits and pieces of others people's work. One such gathering, however, was outstanding for its craftsmanship and also for the fact that it was composed by a woman, the Abbess Harrad of Hohenburg, a convent near Strasbourg, in Alsace.

The encyclopedia, completed shortly before 1195, is one of the finest examples of illuminated manuscripts ever produced. It was called the *Hortus Deliciarum* ("Garden of Delights") and was intended for use by the novices at the convent. The sections on the history of the world rely heavily on biblical stories, but from this encyclopedia we get a good idea of the status of education in the cloister schools of the twelfth and thirteenth centuries.

After the French Revolution, the *Hortus Deliciarum* was placed for safekeeping in the municipal library at Strasbourg. The library was destroyed by fire during the late-nineteenth century, but fortunately, parts of the manuscript had been reproduced on a printing press before this happened. The *Hortus Deliciarum* covered some 650 pages and had 636 pictures containing more than 9,000 figures. In one of these, all the nuns of Abbess Harrad's convent were illustrated and named.

Alexander Neckham, a contemporary of Abbess Harrad, was another medieval encyclopedist of note. He was born on the same night in 1157 as the future King Richard the Lion-Hearted of England, and Alexander's mother was chosen to be Richard's wet nurse. The two boys grew up together. But Neckham decided to become a scholar instead of going with Richard on the Third Crusade.

At a relatively young age Neckham was put in charge of the school of Dunstable, governed by St. Albans Abbey. Later he went to the University of Paris, where he gained fame as a teacher. He eventually returned to England to become the abbot of Cirencester.

His connections with King Richard proved valuable and he spent a great deal of time at court. He also devoted much of his time to writing both prose and verse. He composed noted essays on grammar (his favorite subject), science, Aristotle, and Ovid's "Metamorphosis," and even translated some of Aesop's Fables and turned them into poetry.

Neckham's two-volume encyclopedia was titled *De naturis rerum* ("On the Nature of Things"). Much of it was drawn, without acknowledgment, from Isadore's work. But the fact that he plagiarized so liberally had nothing to do with his nickname "Nequam," which means "wicked" in French, a nickname given to him by his students in Paris. There are indications that he enjoyed this pun on his name, which appears even on his gravestone. In any case, he began the first volume of his encyclopedia with the creation of the world and ended the second with society and sin, much to the approval of his fellow churchmen.

The thirteenth century also saw the appearance, in about 1240, of *De Proprietatibus Rerum* ("On the Property of Things") by an Englishman named Bartholomew de Glanville. He was a Franciscan monk of great learning who later became a lecturer at Magdeburg in Germany. His encyclopedia was probably the most popular of its time. It was translated from Latin into English, French (by order of King Charles V), Spanish, Dutch, and Italian. In 1491 it was printed for the first time in London, in the English translation, and it was again put out in a revived form during William Shakespeare's lifetime under the title *Batman uppon Bartholme* (1582). Shakespeare is said to have been well acquainted with this edition.

The original manuscript had 1,230 chapters in 19 books. Although the work was arranged in the systematic order of most such medieval writings — beginning with God and the angels and ending with weights and measures, numbers, and sounds — it is interesting to note that de Glanville used an alphabetical order within the volumes whenever possible. Thus his lists of animals and geographical places begin with the letter A. Also to be noted is the fact that this scholar — with an exactness not duplicated by most of his contemporaries — acknowledged his principal sources, Isadore of Seville and Pliny.

But by far the most outstanding encyclopedia of the medieval period was *Speculum Maius* ("Larger Mirror") by the Dominican friar Vincent of Beauvais (c. 1190–1264). It represented a turning point in the history of encyclopedic production, as it was the last to be produced exclusively for the use of a limited religious community. In compiling it, Vincent started the modern practice of using assistants. A whole army of young monks were employed to travel to the monastery libraries throughout France to collect cathedral documents. An indication of the wide influence of this encyclopedia during the Middle Ages is the fact that it is mentioned by Chaucer in *The Canterbury Tales*.

Vincent was a librarian, tutor, and friend to King Louis IX. The king asked him to compile the encyclopedia and financed most of its production. In the end, the set encompassed 80 books of 9,885 chapters. A volume on morality, largely a summary of St. Thomas's writings, was added after Vincent died. Much of the work is a collection of extracts, with at least 450 different authors represented, including Arabic, Greek, Latin, and Hebrew writers. It contains, in brief, says the author, "whatever from unnumbered books, I have been able to gather, worthy of consideration, admiration, or imitation as to things that have been made or done or said in the visible or invisible world from the beginning until the end, and even things to come." To be more specific, the work begins with a discussion of the saints of the

Old and New Testaments and then passes on to such subjects as the six days of creation, elements and properties of matter, the first man and the fall and redemption through the sacraments and virtues, natural history, and the history of mankind.

Sometime between 1263 and 1266 Brunetto Latini (d. 1295), an Italian poet and teacher of Dante, compiled an encyclopedia titled *Li Livres dou Trésor* ("The Treasure Books"). It was based in part on Vincent's *Speculum Maius*, but represented a major breakaway from Latin as the only language fit for holding knowledge. Latini was a lawyer and he wanted to reach the cultured classes in Italy, who had largely abandoned Latin to the monks and priests and were now using French in their discourse. So he wrote the text in French, and the encyclopedia was widely used among intellectuals in both France and Italy. Manuscripts of the three-volume work have been found in almost all the dialects then used in France. The encyclopedia was not translated into Italian until two centuries later.

Latini's main interest was politics, and this subject is by far the best and most original in the work. He had begun his career practicing law in Florence. In 1260 he was sent by the Commune of Florence to seek a leader who might oppose Manfred, the illegitimate son of Frederick II and a man who already had attacked and captured the city of Naples and was soon expected to march on Florence. Latini, however, failed in this quest and had to flee to France where he wrote the encyclopedia. Latini later was able to return to Florence, and he became a prominent member of the government there, a position and status he enjoyed until his death.

Giorgio Valla (c. 1430–1499), a noted encylopedist of the fifteenth century, reflected a combination of the best traditions of the medieval world with the intellectual stirrings that later meshed into what we now call the Renaissance. Valla lived during the time when Johannes Gutenberg began to print his magnificent 42-line Bible, and Valla apparently was quite aware of the portent of this event. Yet he chose to produce his own works in handwritten form in the medieval language of the church — Latin. He died in Venice during one of his lectures on the immortality of the soul, a singularly medieval topic.

Valla was an Italian scholar of wide renown, and he was often called Placentius after his birthplace Piancenza. His 49-book encyclopedia, *De Expetendis, et Fugiendis Rebus Opus* ("On Things to be Sought and Things to be Avoided"), shows the influence of Latini's work. He divided all "things" into three kinds — mental, physical, and eternal. The work was later edited by his son and printed in a two-volume edition.

The medieval period was clearly coming to an end when Juan Louis Vives (1492–1540) completed his handwritten encyclopedia, *De Disciplines*

("On the Disciplines"), in 1531. This work was composed primarily for the use of his pupil Guillaume de Croy, a man who became a cardinal and archbishop of Toledo at the tender age of 19.

Because Vives was a well-known Spanish humanist and friend of Erasmus, he left Spain in 1509 to avoid the Inquisition and went to France, where he studied at the University of Paris. He then settled in Bruges in the Spanish Netherlands. He moved to England for three years at the invitation of Cardinal Wolsey, where he lectured at Oxford and was awarded a Doctor of Law degree. Here he was also tutor to Princess Mary. But he was later arrested and banished from England for protesting against King Henry VIII's divorce from Catherine of Aragon. Vives then settled, once again, in Bruges.

His writings were many, although he is chiefly remembered for his works on St. Augustine and the education of women. He held the medieval view that women had inferior minds, but also the enlightened view that they should be educated and that marriage was the legitimate union of one man and one woman for the mutual supervision of their lives. He also emphasized the importance of Latin and Greek as the proper vehicles for knowledge. Because he based much of his reasoning on nature rather than religious authority, he displeased most contemporary theologians. "Truth," Vives wrote, "is a virgin prairie: it is common property; it is not all in private preserve yet nor colonized. There is much left for future generations to discover."

Other medieval encyclopedias — those by Michael Psellus (1018–1078), Pierre Bercheure (1018–1078), Lambert of St. Omar (compiled in 1120), Gregor Reisch (d. 1525), and Raffaele Maffei (1451–1522) — are now of interest only to medieval historians. A consistent problem with these works is that they demand an understanding of church doctrines on every possible question and assume that the achievement of happiness and a satisfactory life lies only within the social setting established by the church.

Every entry in the medieval encyclopedias had behind it a concern for final meanings that makes such works strange to read today. It was as if each author attempted first to effect a direct line to God before picking up the quill pen to write any sentence. With such a relationship to eternal matters, the author was grounded in the past and future of the church in a way that modern persons, even church officials, find hard to understand.

Because all the medieval encyclopedias were handwritten and limited in number of copies, and because most people of that time couldn't read, some memory system was needed to retain knowledge so that it could be passed to following generations. The Greek system of mnemotechnics, though seemingly forgotten after the barbarians sacked Rome, had actually retreated into the monasteries, although there is no mention of it in the writings of Cassiodorus or in the encyclopedia of Isadore of Seville. But it must have continued as a practice there, for it suddenly appears again in twelfth-century books on learning. Yet its purpose was now related to ethics rather than to speech-making for which the Greeks had primarily used it. The memory system, according to Frances Yates in her book *The Art of Memory*, was preserved throughout earlier centuries as a method to enable often illiterate monks, nuns, and novices to remember the corporate wisdom of their particular orders.

Two of the great scholastics, Thomas Aquinas (1125–1274) and Albertus Magnus (1193–1280), describe the memory system in their writings, but they give no indication that it originated with the Greeks. And by 1577 we find St. Theresa describing her steps to perfection as "The Interior Castle," a title obviously derived from the concept of attaching ideas to images of rooms.

Were it not for the stirrings of the Reformation, the mnemonic system as used in the monasteries would have remained a somewhat mysterious device. But the secularizing movement released the wisdom of the church into the hands of every educated person.

Thus it was that Guillo Camillo (1480–1544), who was an ex-priest and contemporary of Martin Luther, brought the mnemotechnic system out of the monasteries and used it to produce a huge device crowded with images that he called a memory theater. It became the delight of the people of Italy and France, and many hailed Camillo as the greatest genius of the age.

Camillo's memory theater was not a theater in the traditional sense, one in which an audience sits and watches a play on a stage. Instead, the spectator stood in this wooden structure where the stage might be and looked out toward an auditorium filled with emotionally striking images of all sorts. The images were placed in 49 niches, or gates, on seven rising grades. The number seven, in this case, was said to stand for the seven pillars of Solomon's House of Wisdom. In each gate were a variety of tiny statues related to the subject for which the gate was named. The Prometheus gate, for example, included such figures as Geryon killed by Hercules in a construct that described minutes, hours, years, and clock-making; a cock and lion related to the rule of government; Sybil with a tripod related to forms of divination and prophecy; Apollo and the Muses related to poetry; and so on, through many more images.

Camillo's theater was thus a virtual museum of what was known at the time — or, at least, what Camillo thought should be known. He assumed that the theater would educate the viewer, because the images were so striking that they would naturally be remembered.

The Greeks, who used memory as a practical tool for rhetoric, would have been amazed and somewhat confused by the excitement and demonstrable impact of Camillo's theater. But the Greek memory system was finally destined for the curio shelf, because by the fifteenth century people had found a far better way to hold onto knowledge — printed books.

In Victor Hugo's *Notre Dame de Paris* there is a description of a scholar in his study high in the cathedral. He is gazing at the first printed book that has entered his sanctuary, a book that is now disturbing his manuscript-filled world. The scholar goes to the window and gazes out at the vast cathedral, silhouetted against the starry sky. His thoughts are on how printed books will eventually destroy this building.

In a sense, this is exactly what happened when memory systems were superseded by printed books. The huge imaginary castles and cathedrals created by individuals for the purpose of holding concepts in their memories, crowded as they were with neatly arranged images, were no longer necessary. Books now had become the new vaults to hold knowledge.

With books, vast amounts of data could be grasped in the hand rather than in the mind. Concepts and principles now could be preserved without having to find emotional and vivid structures to which to relate them. After all, when a mind is totally absorbed with the task of trying to keep assorted bits of knowledge in its memory bank, it cannot be free to be creative or to wander in new directions of thought. Thus the discovery of scientific principles found in experiments, sociological investigation, and technological inventiveness is closely related to the freeing process arising from printed books.

Books have furthermore provided a form of common memory totally unknown to thousands of generations that lived and died before the invention of printing. Consider the fact that, at best, the accounts of an auto accident or a baseball game vary in proportion to the number of viewers and the time elapsed since viewing. The pages of a book can hold a relatively permanent account. And, though the book record may not be an accurate description of the event, since it is only one individual's account of it, those who experienced the event tend to accept this account — make it part of the collective record — because it has the authority of print and hard covers. When people dispute such a printed record, they usually support their arguments with another printed book, rather than turning to the people who experienced the event in the first place.

Thus printing and books, with the establishment of public libraries and the marketing of family encyclopedias, have provided humankind not only with a quantitative leap in terms of the information that a single person can have at one's fingertips, but also a qualitative change in terms of what this information means in their daily lives.

6. The Printing Revolution

We probably owe as much to William Caxton for the form of English we use today as we do to William Shakespeare or the King James Bible. Caxton (1422–1491) was the first printer in England, and his adoption of the London dialect of that time for everything he printed firmly established it as the language we now call English. Other printers elsewhere in Europe did much the same thing for their various native tongues.

Before Caxton's time, it was difficult to travel from one part of England to another because of the confusing array of speech patterns. A person from Kent could not understand the words uttered by a person from Lancashire, and neither could communicate readily with a person from Northumberland. Though the many regions of the country were ruled by only one king, the parts hardly constituted a nation because of the wide divergence of dialects. Within the church, of course, communication was not such a problem; the language exclusively used there was Latin, which could be understood even from one country to another.

Caxton told a story about a merchant of London and a woman of Kent that illustrates the problem created by the many English dialects. To appreciate this tale, we should be aware of the fact that London was no more than 60 miles from this woman's home. According to Caxton, the merchant from London asked the woman for some "eggys," to which "the good wyfe answerde that she coude speke no frenshe." It was only after a second man asked for "eyren" (cp. German "Eier") that "she said she vnderstod hym wel."

The printed word tended to suppress local and regional differences in all languages, and it overcame much of the previous gulf between the written and spoken word. Printing also led to a diminuation of the importance of accidence and syntax, while greatly expanding vocabularies.

Printing, in fact, has been one of the world's most revolutionary innovations. It has led to advances in all scientific fields from anatomy to zoology, and it enabled religious dissent to flourish. It has spread knowledge far and wide through books and newspapers. It has broken down rigid class distinctions based on the ability to read and write. It has enabled the development of a literate working class, a prerequisite to modern industrial society. And it has made modern democracy possible, for this form of government requires a high percentage of literate voters.

Printing particularly gave humankind a new way to preserve knowledge — in larger quantities than ever before. Data, thoughts, and sayings that would have been rapidly lost in the chasm of faulty memory systems, cumbersome writing methods, and inadequate forms of transportation now could be held onto for decades between the covers of books.

Books have permitted us to interrogate the past with some degree of accuracy, to tap the wisdom of our species, to understand the point of view of others and not just those in power. They have allowed people long dead to speak to us. Books are patient when we are slow to understand, and books are never critical of our lapses.

Of course, printing was a mixed blessing, for while we can be thankful that the printing processes brought most knowledge within each individual's grasp, the expanding amount of preserved information, both useful and not, is now far beyond any one person's comprehension.

Even as early as 1500 more than eight million books had been printed, and by the end of the sixteenth century something like 200 million had come off the busy printing presses of Europe. This number is staggering in comparison to the fewer than five million manuscripts that had been produced by monastic scribes over the more than 1,000 years since Cassiodorus first set his monks to the task.

One of the most important aspects of the use of movable type for printing was that it was now possible to edit and correct a text after it was set without leaving any telltale correction marks. Individual letters and words could be replaced in a completed page, something never before possible with carved wooden-block pages or engraved metal sheets. A text could be edited, subedited, and corrected before it was reproduced in a multitude of copies. Whole sentences and paragraphs could be replaced in a later edition of the same page or book. This was particularly important for the revision of encyclopedia pages, where up-to-date information could be inserted without changing the length or appearance of a volume and without having to change any of the surrounding pages.

Actually, the earliest printed pages are hardly distinguishable from handwritten manuscripts, because the type was carefully crafted to imitate handwriting. Yet just as language was eventually changed and standardized by the printing process, so were typefaces. It was only a matter of time before printing became the preferred art, with skilled calligraphers attempting to duplicate the various printing typefaces that were being developed. It also was only a matter of time and engineering before the number of identical copies that could be produced by a printing press was increased from a few thousand pages a month to the present 20,000 or more an hour.

Caxton, like Gutenberg and all the other early printers, made a living by printing indulgences and other documents for the church. The earliest surviving sample of his printing is an indulgence issued by Abbot Sant to Henry Longley and his wife Katherine on December 13, 1476. Caxton also printed church calendars, worship guides, ecclesiastical handbooks, pamphlets of poems and ballads, and probably some political tracts.

He had been a highly successful cloth merchant before he went to Cologne, Germany, to learn the printing trade. He had also lived in Belgium as an English cloth dealer and was head of the Low Countries Mercers' of London association. But Caxton became interested in Gutenberg's movable type, learned the process, and then returned to England to set up his own printing establishment at Westminster. Here, in the remaining 14 years of his life, he turned out a phenomenal number of books (nearly 80) and other publications, totaling more than 18,000 pages of printed material. He further translated 21 books for his press, mostly from French, including Vincent of Beauvais' *Speculum Maius,* which Caxton titled *The Mirrour of the World, or thymage of the same.* It was printed in 1481 and was so popular that a second edition was printed in 1490.

Caxton's books, unlike those of most other printers, had no title page. In this he was following the old practice of manuscript copiers. After all, title pages were a device introduced by printers before there were any copyright laws so that they might clearly identify their own work. Caxton also failed to use punctuation in his translations of poetry from French and Latin. In his prose translations he used only periods, colons, and occasionally paragraph signs to indicate the beginnings of sentences. His pages were never numbered, and his books were bound in stiff pieces of parchment with the edges turned in.

During his lifetime, Caxton's pioneering work had little impact on the rest of Europe and surprisingly little on England itself. This was because the intellectual leadership of the continent at that time, and all the way into the latter part of the eighteenth century, was clearly held by the French now that church authority was declining. The French composed and printed one dictionary after another to assure perfection in literary style and punctuation, and they printed one encyclopedia after another to assure perfection in intellectual tastes. In England, with the exception of translations from French and Latin works, no English-written encyclopedias were printed until after 1700.

The French encyclopedias were so numerous we will discuss here only three of the most notable. One was written by a Catholic priest named Louis

Moréri, who called his work *Le Grand Dictionaire Historique* ("The Great Historical Dictionary"). Completed in 1674, Moréri's encyclopedia emphasized history, geography, and biographies, with the work arranged alphabetically under proper names. By this time printing was already proving itself the handiest way to arrange an encyclopedia, or at least the one by which it is easiest to make revisions to a printed page.

Moréri's work was revised and republished in two volumes after his death. Subsequent editions with additions were brought out until 1759. This, the 20th, numbered ten volumes. Scholars now say that each edition of Moréri's encyclopedia is valuable in that it provides material for the researcher on seventeenth- and eighteenth-century French history. The encyclopedia was translated into German, Dutch, Spanish, and English (by Jeremy Collier under the title *The Great Historical, Geographical, Genealogical, and Poetical Dictionary*). An Italian translation was also started but not finished, and Peter the Great of Russia reportedly ordered a Slavic translation that was never completed.

Worthy as Moréri's work is to researchers, it is filled with numerous printer's errors, editor's omissions, and author's prejudices. The work's popularity, in spite of its faults, infuriated another French encyclopedist, Pierre Bayle (1647–1706), who decided to compose a work of his own expressly to correct Moréri's mistakes. Bayle's project, however, soon grew to encompass much more than just an addendum to Moréri. It became a massive commentary on most of the other French and Latin encyclopedias available at the time. As Bayle put it, "There is no perversion of the truth, however absurd it be, that is not passed on from book to book, from generation to generation." Bayle's encyclopedia became a brilliant exposition of the ideas of the French Enlightenment.

Bayle was the son of a French Protestant pastor, one who had lost his life in the Protestant persecutions following Louis XIV's cancellation of the Edict of Nantes. The young Bayle attended a Jesuit college, where he converted to Catholicism only to return later to his Calvinistic faith. Because Protestants lived in constant danger under Louis XIV and Bayle's own brothers had died for their religious beliefs as his father had, Bayle had to hide his identity while living in France. He eventually fled to Rotterdam in Holland. There he taught and wrote several controversial works, including his encyclopedia, the *Dictionnaire Historique et Critique* ("Historical and Critical Dictionary"). He also edited the *Nouvelles de la République des Lettres* ("News of the Republic of Letters"), one of the first intellectual journals of modern times.

Bayle did great service for all thinking people in suggesting new philosophical questions for discussion. In fact, many of the philosophical problems that Voltaire, David Hume, George Berkeley, and other philosophers of the 1700s wrestled with were first suggested to them by their reading of Bayle's *Dictionnaire*. The encyclopedia was composed in Talmudic style, with each brief article at the top of the page and all sorts of notes on factual, philosophical, and religious matters below. There were even notes on the notes printed in the margins of the two-volume work. This made it a fascinating but difficult text to read. There was often little relation between the subject of an article and most of its content. For example, Bayle had many articles on relatively unimportant people, such as Jérome Rorario and Pierre Jurieu, in which he used the subject matter merely as a takeoff point for profound discussions on the nature of humankind and beasts, the problems of mind and body, and the theories of Baron von Leibniz.

The whole work was tied together by Bayle's prodigious assault against almost all the religious, scientific, philosophical, historical, and moral assumptions of the time. He stressed the importance of examining the historical evidence for all biblical writings, and in doing this antagonized most of the theological conservatives of his day as well as many of the Protestant liberals. He preached tolerance for Jews, Moslems, Unitarians, Catholics, and even atheists, which no one before had publicly done. One argument that particularly disturbed his readers was his contention that a society of atheists could be moral and a society of Christians immoral. The argument was later used to the discomfort of many of the clergy by both Voltaire and Diderot.

As soon as the first edition of Bayle's work appeared, it was praised, criticized, and condemned. It was banned by the French Catholic Church, and the French Reformed Church demanded that he retract or change portions of it. In response to this criticism, Bayle finally agreed to redo his article on the morality of the biblical King David. But after starting this, he continued the process by revising many of the other articles. He published the second edition of the *Dictionnaire* in 1702, three years after the first. The encyclopedia had by then been expanded to three volumes.

Bayle died before a third edition was completed, in four volumes. The encyclopedia was then periodically revised until a ninth edition appeared in 1742 in ten volumes. The first and second editions were translated into several languages, including English, and the work is still considered to be of great importance and value. Thomas Jefferson recommended it as one of the 100 basic books with which to start the Library of Congress.

Bayle's all-consuming desire to correct the mistakes he found in almost every book he opened was a monumental service to the field of scholarship, and one might hope that the standards he set would have prevented the repetition of such failures afterward. But it didn't. Standards can only circumscribe human failure; they cannot eliminate it. Books are still printed with many of the kinds of mistakes and distortions Bayle so deplored. In fact, mistakes have greatly increased, simply because the amount of printed material has so multiplied.

Mistakes are found by sharp proofreaders in almost every printed book. The number that occur on a single newspaper page is astounding. It is virtually impossible to eliminate them all, though for the most part publishers do an exceptional job.

Printers and publishers of Bibles probably do the most exacting proofreading. Yet mistakes still creep in. A court in London, England, fined the royal printer 300 pounds, in 1631, for printing an edition of the Bible with one missing word in the seventh commandment. The printed text omitted the word "not" and thus read, "Thou shalt commit adultery." The printer was glad to pay this huge fine, since he fully expected to lose his head after the single mistake was discovered.

A Bible printed in Edinburgh in 1637 says, "because she had been religious [for rebellious] against me." And Cotton Mather described one printed in 1702 that made David complain, "Printers [for princes] have persecuted me without cause." An 1802 London Bible stated, "I discharge [for charge] thee before God."

But my favorite is the Cambridge Bible of 1805 that says, "Persecuted him that was born after the Spirit to remain even so it is now." The words "to remain" had been written on the page proof by the proofreader in answer to a question as to whether or not a comma should be deleted. The error was not discovered until two more editions of this Bible were printed, one in 1806 and the other in 1819. At least 20 more examples of such glaring errors in published Bibles could easily be cited.

The lucid editor is resigned to the fact that such errors will probably occur with embarrassing frequency. The editor realizes that the work has been made recognizable as the product of human hands rather than of an irrational machine or a superhuman god. The editor struggles for perfection and finds fulfillment in the constant striving after that goal.

Another controversial French encyclopedia was prepared by Abbé Furetière (1619–1688), a member of the French Academy. He had been appointed to a committee of the Academy assigned to complete the task of compiling a dictionary that would be the final authority among all French dictionaries. The committee met with regularity, but the members had such difficulty agreeing on the nature of their task that the project dragged on for many years with little accomplishment. The project had been initiated in 1639 and was still under discussion in 1650 and even in 1670. Part of the problem was that the dictionary's content had been narrowly circumscribed to include no entries on science or the arts.

Furetière, both because he was irritated by the procrastination of the editorial committee and because he disagreed with the policy of excluding science and art, decided to put out his own dictionary (encyclopedia might be the more appropriate word) to be called the *Dictionnaire Unversel des Arts and Sciences* ("The Universal Dictionary of Arts and Sciences"). His announcement of this project caused a furor in French intellectual circles. His conservative opponents in the Academy charged him with plagiarism and theft of the few already approved pages of their proposed dictionary. His liberal friends defended him, correctly pointing out that the conservatives had no idea of the content of Furetière's encyclopedia and were therefore unjustified in charging theft. The conservatives, however, were strong enough to expel Furetière from the Academy, even though this badly split the body into rival camps.

Furetière died before his encyclopedia was published in 1690, but the controversy didn't ebb until long after that. The work included a preface by Pierre Bayle that helped keep the argument going, and the fact that Furetière was a Jesuit priest and Bayle a Protestant skeptic churned the wheels of the French gossip mill. Under the name *Dictionnaire de Trévoux* ("Dictionary of the Fathers of Trévoux"), and with alterations Furetière probably would never have approved, this encyclopedia was sponsored and published by the Jesuits over a period of 50 years.

As to the Academy editorial committee, it was prodded into life by Furetière's action. The committee quickly adopted rules to prevent any of its members repeating Furetière's indiscretion, and then commissioned Thomas Corneille, brother of the playwright Pierre Corneille, to complete its *Le Dictionnaire des Arts et des Sciences* ("Dictionary of Arts and Sciences"). This was published in 1694, 53 years after the decision was first made to produce such a work. Despite its title, this dictionary still omitted entries on science. Subjects related to the arts, however, now were included at the insistence of Corneille. The Academy work became the model for most other French dictionaries and encyclopedias, all of which gave arts a predominant place and more or less neglected the sciences.

Germany, too, produced its share of significant encyclopedias during the seventeenth and eighteenth centuries. The largest and most comprehensive was compiled, with the help of nine editors, by Johann Heinrich Zedler. It totaled 64 volumes and contained 64,309 pages. Zedler originally intended the encyclopedia to be only 12 volumes in length, but the project continued to grow. Even after it was printed (between 1731 and 1750), Zedler provided four more supplementary volumes. The title of this gigantic work was *Grosse Vollständiges Universal-Lexicon aller Wissenschaften und Künste welche Bishero durch Menschlichen Verstand und Wite Erfunden und Verbessert Worden*, which translates into English as *The Great Complete Universal Lexicon of all Sciences and Arts which Have Yet Been Discovered and Improved by Human Understanding and Ingenuity.*

Among the problems with which Zedler had to contend in producing this work was prejudice among the Leipzig book dealers, who feared that the project was so comprehensive no other books would ever again need to be purchased. They conducted a word-of-mouth campaign against the encyclopedia and tried to dissuade investors from giving Zedler financial backing. The book dealers, of course, needn't have worried. The very aim of an encyclopedia — to contain all one needs to know — is an impossible dream.

However, Zedler's project was well supported financially, and the books were sold one volume at a time by subscription. But such a large project was bound to eat up all the investment resources, and the printing costs finally had to be covered by a lottery. It is an irony of history that Zedler never had enough money to purchase a complete set of his own encyclopedia. He never managed to acquire volumes 13 and 14, reportedly a constant irritation to him during his completion of the later volumes.

The 64 volumes had a high degree of accuracy and were much praised for this fact. Zedler included biographies of living people, an unusual feature for the time. As he wrote in the introduction to one of the volumes, "Why should death alone make a deserving man capable of having his biography printed?"

This period also saw the development of new encyclopedias in other European countries. In Switzerland, Johann Jacob Hoffmann published a two-volume work in 1677 titled *Lexicon Universale, Historiam, Chronologiam, Geographiam, Genealogiam, Mythologiam, omnemque Antiquitatem* ("Universal Dictionary of History, Geography, Biography, Mythology, and Antiquarian Subjects"). This was followed in 1726 by Jacob Christoph Iselin's *Neu Vermehrtes Historish-und Geographisches Allgemeines Lexicon* ("New Universal Enlarged Historical and Geographical Dictionary"). In Italy, Antonio Zara published an encyclopedia in 1614, and Gianfrancisco Pivati published a 12-volume set between 1746 and 1851. The first Hungarian encyclopedia, created by János Apáczai Cseri, appeared in 1653, while the first Russian one by V. N. Tatischev, only half of which was completed, came out in 1793.

We will now return to England, where the first purely English encyclopedia was composed and published in 1704, more than 200 years after Caxton set up his printing press at Westminster. The English language by now had been stabilized and unified. There was a wide reading public, and many printing establishments were turning out many types of books.

The encyclopedia was written by John Harris (c. 1666–1719), a clergyman whose first love was science. The work was modern in nature in that it emphasized the sciences, was alphabetically arranged, and included entries by some of the leading scholars of the day.

Harris was a member of England's Royal Society, the oldest scientific association in the world, where he rubbed elbows with some of the leading scientists, men such as chemist Robert Boyle, mathematician Isaac Newton, and experimentalist Robert Hooke. Harris preached on the Boyle lectures in St. Paul's Cathedral in 1698, gave free public lectures on mathematics at the Marine Coffee House in Birch Lane, and was for a year the secretary of the Royal Society. He was further employed by the London booksellers to compile both a *Collection of Voyages and Travels* and the first English encyclopedia, titled *Lexicon Technicum; or an Universal English Dictionary of Arts and Sciences, Explaining not only the Terms of Art, but the Arts Themselves*. It was published in one volume in 1704, with a second edition coming out in two volumes in 1708 and 1710.

Because of his position in the Royal Society, Harris was able to include the writings of some of the greatest thinkers of the day in his entries in the encyclopedia. The *Lexicon Technicum* includes articles by Newton (on acids), by botanist John Hay, and by a number of other leading scientists. Harris also provided bibliographies for the most important scientific subjects, but ignored inclusion of topics relating to theology, biography, and poetry. The encyclopedia was distinguished for its excellent text, line drawings, and even the quality of its printing. The work was so fine that soon the best encyclopedists were turning to Harris' example for their model, and the encyclopedia of Ephraim Chambers particularly owes much to Harris' plan.

But Harris could not manage on his meager income and probably derived little money from any of his writings or scientific pursuits. When he died, he was an absolute pauper. His friend and benefactor, John Godfrey, provided the funds for his burial.

Ephraim Chambers' *Cyclopaedia, or an Universal Dictionary of Arts and Sciences* was completed in 1728. The two-volume work was widely acclaimed for its scholarship. Samuel Johnson cited it as the reference that "formed his style" when Johnson talked about his own *Dictionary of the English Language* to his biographer, James Boswell. Chambers was even given the honor of membership in the Royal Society in 1729 on the basis of the encyclopedia, and later the right to be buried with other noted authors in the cloisters at Westminster Abbey.

The son of an obscure farmer, Chambers received a grammar-school education, after which he was sent to London for apprenticeship with a well-known cartographer and globe maker. Fortunately, his employer took an interest in the clever lad, and encouraged Chambers' desire to acquire ever greater knowledge. The young man eventually conceived of his plan for an encyclopedia that would be larger and more comprehensive than Harris' *Lexicon Technicum*. Chambers then left the mapmaking business and devoted all his energies to the completion of this project. The work, when published, was highly popular and sold so well that two enterprising men in Edinburgh, Scotland, decided to follow Chambers' lead in developing their *Encyclopaedia Britannica* in 1768 (see chapter 13).

Chambers did not cover history or geography in the *Cyclopaedia*, and he ignored biography, so there were no entries on Aristotle or Bacon. Yet there was a philosophical discussion on Aristotelians and one on the experimental approach advocated by Bacon. An article on gravity gave different opinions on the cause of this phenomenon by 12 different philosophers and scientists, all the way from Aristotle to Newton.

Chambers took great pains to put all the subjects in proper relationship to one another. As he explained in the preface, "Our view was to consider the several matters not only in themselves, but relatively, or as they respect each other; both to treat them as so many wholes, and as so many parts of some greater whole." Chambers used this preface to describe his elaborate scheme of divisions and subdivisions of knowledge. All subjects were divided into 47 sciences and arts according to the senses (natural history, anatomy, chemistry, etc.); imagination (grammar, rhetoric, poetry); and reason (physics, metaphysics, logic, mathematics, agriculture, trade, manufacture, law). This system and the many cross-references at the end of the various subjects provided a fine weaving of articles, which themselves were alphabetically arranged. The work was illustrated with 21 large plates relating to subjects such as heraldry, surveying, sundials, algebra, geometry, trigonometry, and navigation.

When Chambers visited France in later years, he was invited to publish a French edition of his *Cyclopaedia*, dedicated to Louis XV, but he rejected this offer on the grounds of ill health. In England he already had seen his work through three editions. By 1752, seven editions of the *Cyclopaedia* had been published in London, as well as one in Dublin. There was also an Italian translation. And the materials for seven additional volumes, compiled by Chambers before his death in 1740, were reworked and published in 1753 as a supplement. Chambers' work finally claims a special place in history as the basis and inspiration for a number of other noted encyclopedias, particularly the far greater French *Encyclopédie* of Denis Diderot.

In England and elsewhere the success of one encyclopedia led to another, as printers and publishers recognized the potential market for such products. The advent of printing had expanded the access to knowledge far beyond what the ancient Greeks and scholars of the Middle Ages ever could have imagined. By a sort of Parkinson's Law the amount of knowledge now tended to expand to fill the number of available printer's forms. All of this knowledge, of course, was neither new nor useful. And the problem now for the reader, who found the number of available books expanding beyond reach, was to sort out the usable data from the mass of redundant and reprinted words and phrases.

Before we go further with this account of knowledge accumulation, we need to look at the one book that many people, from both the past and present, believe contains sufficient knowledge to render all other sources unnecessary.

7. The Uses and Abuses of the Bible

During the seventeenth and eighteenth centuries, many Christians in Europe and America believed one needed only one book of knowledge — the Bible. After all, it was "the word of God," rendering encyclopedias, libraries, or all other sources of knowledge unnecessary. Other books, they warned, might provide only misinformation. Because the Bible held such an important place in many people's minds, it deserves its own chapter in this book.

A few enclaves still exist in the United States where Christians hold to this one-book belief, just as there are groups of people in Moslem countries who believe that the only book one needs is the Koran. Television evangelist Jerry Falwell says in his *Finding Inner Peace and Strength* that, "The Bible is the inerrant ... word of the living God. It is absolutely infallible, without error in all matters pertaining to faith and practice, as well as in areas such as geography, science, history, etc." Most theologians, however, probably would say to Falwell that although the various writers of the books included in the Bible may have been inspired by God, they were still fallible human beings who recorded numerous errors and now-outdated ideas.

Important as the Bible has been to faith and theological understanding, it is filled with contradictory material, shows all the prejudices of the times in which it was written, and provides relatively little information that may help persons in dealing with the crucial issues of the twentieth and twenty-first centuries.

The careful Bible reader is immediately confronted with two contradictory stories about how God created the world and the human beings in it. One of these, Genesis 1:1–30, tells of how God, in a particular order, made first the day and night, then the land in the midst of the waters, then the trees, then the sea creatures, then the animals on the land, and then man and woman at the same time. The other, Genesis 2:4–22, has God creating heaven and Earth all at one time, then plants, and then a man from whom

God extracted a rib to create woman. Both accounts are of interest as explanatory remnants of tribal tales relating to how the world came into existence, but they come from two different sources that clearly contradict one another.

To base one's store of knowledge exclusively on the Bible results in putting blinders around one's understanding. The Bible should not be viewed as an unimpeachable source of knowledge and history, but as a part of the whole teaching and practice of the Christian faith. It has and still performs great service in confronting our social and moral presuppositions, and for this reason alone will probably remain a significant element in human understanding. Through its ancient stories and accounts of actual happenings, the Bible gives us examples of both wise and unwise practices.

Furthermore, its words, as found in the King James translation, provide us with fine specimens of the best in English literature. The great statesman and historian Thomas Macaulay, in speaking of the language used in the King James version, said it was "a book which, if everything else in our language should perish, would alone suffice to show the whole extent of its beauty and power."

Without any acquaintance with the Bible as literature, how can one really understand the works of the novelists Hardy or Hawthorne? How can one fully appreciate the cadence of Galsworthy or George Elliot? And if one starts to read Herman Mellville's *Moby Dick*, which opens with the sentence "Call me Ishmael," would not one feel bewildered. But, like any book, the biblical text needs to be approached with some element of caution.

The Bible was used by Martin Luther to condemn the Roman Catholic hierarchy and, in turn, by the Roman Catholic church to condemn Luther. When translations from Latin were first made so that any literate person might read it, these very persons began to select particular sections to justify their own prejudices. The contents were cited with approval by both defenders of the status quo and by revolutionaries who were determined to overthrow the status quo. Some say that the Bible is the most widely read book of all time, and that may be so; but it is certainly the most misinterpreted one.

Those who claim that this one book contains all necessary knowledge are often ignorant of the fact that there are translations other than the one they are using, translations that differ in significant respects and give diverse meanings to some of their favorite passages. Among these many English translations are the Coverdale Bible, Cranmer's Bible, the Douai Bible, Matthew's Bible, Taverner's Bible, Tyndale's Bible, the Bishop's Bible, the American Revised Bible, the Oxford Bible, and many more. Some of them have printer's or translator's errors that greatly alter particular texts. For example, both the Coverdale Bible of 1535 and the Matthew's Bible translate one of the words in Psalm 91, verse 5, as "bugs," while most others translate the word as "terrors," which gives the psalm quite a different meaning. And the Bishop's Bible of 1568 has Jeremiah 8:22 reading "Is there no treacle in Gilead?" for the more familiar "Is there no balm in Gilead?"

Beyond problems involved in understanding and translating the ancient languages in which the Bible was written, it puts forth concepts that are quite repugnant to modern consciousness. One can find in any translation of the Bible passages condemning witches and mediums that were used in the eighteenth century to justify the murders of countless women. Passages thought to condemn homosexuality were once used to justify burning at the stake persons thought to be gay or lesbian. Some passages glorify war under the guise of patriotism. These have often been used to justify the actions of political leaders who precipitated wars only to build their own fortunes.

Racism, slavery, and segregation have all been validated on the basis of any number of stories and passages in the Bible. Genesis 9:18–27 gives an account of the debauchery of Noah and the indiscreet discovery of his naked drunkenness by his son Ham. When Ham later told his brothers about their father's condition, they averted their eyes from the scene and thus were spared the curse that Noah placed on Ham and all his descendants. This, and the curse on Canaan, Ham's son, have been used by many racists to give biblical justification to their racial hatreds.

Before the American Civil War ended, it was popular for preachers in the southern states to quote Paul's statement in Ephesians 6:5, "Slaves, be obedient to those who are your earthly masters, with fear and trembling, in singleness of heart, as to Christ." It was also a practice in churches at that time to argue that God had sanctioned slavery through Noah, Abraham, and Joseph, and that the biblical record on this was unambiguous.

Many other passages in the Bible can be interpreted as a justification for slavery, and so one needs to remember the culture of the times in which the various chapters of the Old and New Testaments were written. Slavery was then a commonly accepted practice. Neither Jesus nor the apostle Paul condemn it. Instead, they regard it as one of the givens of society. That fact does not detract from the historical and moral significance of either man. But it needs to be kept in mind when one looks on this book as one of the most significant sources of knowledge.

What can be said about condoning slavery in the Bible also can be said about the anti-Semitic passages found in some translations. Both Catholics and Protestants have sometimes used these passages of the Bible to give credence to their anti-Semitic prejudices. According to them, the Jews were the killers of both the Lord Jesus and the prophets. It says so in I Thessalonians 2:14–16; and Matthew 27:25–26 has it that the Jewish people condemned themselves when Jesus appeared before Pontius Pilate by saying, "His blood be on us and on our children."

Most biblical scholars now point out that to justify anti-Semitism through the use of biblical passages is to engage in a critical misreading of the text. None of the passages relating to the life of Jesus is intrinsically anti-Semitic, yet some of them are, unfortunately, still today used to nurture such prejudicial thinking within the Christian church.

Fortunately, all of the most recent Bible translators have taken care to rephrase the most blatantly anti-Semitic wordings found in this book. Pope John Paul II recently issued a public apology to Jews throughout the world for anti-Semitic beliefs and practices of the past within the Roman Catholic Church.

The Bible is also often used to confirm the inferiority of women, starting with the view of Eve as the embodiment of carnal evil. Some passages in the New Testament Epistles espouse the practice of women's submission to the authority of men, just as there are statements that disparage women taking a position of authority or speaking with authority. Consider, for example, I Corinthians 14:34–35: "As in all the church of the saints, the women should keep silence in the churches. For they are not permitted to speak, but should be subordinate, as even the law says. If there is anything they desire to know, let them ask their husbands at home. For it is shameful for a woman to speak in church." Or again, I Timothy 2:11-12: "Let a woman learn in silence with all submissiveness. I permit no woman to teach or to have authority over men; she is to keep silent." Such passages are frequently quoted by biblical literalists, while Jesus' statements in affirmation of the equality of women and of women's roles in the early church are ignored.

In many parts of the Bible women are consigned to anonymity while the men are listed by name. The long list of genealogies at the start of I Chronicles names only the fathers and their sons, and the first chapter of Acts (1:13) lists by name each of the 11 men who gathered in an upper room after the death of Jesus but none of the perhaps equal number of women, with the sole exception of Mary, the mother of Jesus. Another example appears in Matthew 15:39, where it tells of Jesus parceling out seven loaves and some fish to feed a crowd. The text says that by count there were 4,000 men and then, almost as an afterthought, adds "besides women and children."

Clearly, the biblical morality that originally enforced women's subservience to men was imposed to meet the economic requirements of a rigidly male-dominant social system in which all property was transmitted from father to son and in which the benefits of a woman's or a child's labor accrued to the man. For this reason, any reader of the Bible again needs to pay close attention to the cultural backgrounds of the biblical authors to make a correct evaluation of the content of the text. Current anthropological research and feminist biblical scholarship is leading to a greater understanding of this cultural context.

One example of the high esteem in which males were held by the scribes who wrote sections of the Bible can be found in the original Jewish text for I Samuel, chapter 6. Here two milk cows (obviously female) were separated from their calves to pull the cart that was carrying the ark of the covenant. The author of this section converted these milk cows into the masculine gender to show honor to the fact that they were serving the Holy Ark. Of course, it was only natural that persons brought up in such a culture should show their honor and reverence to God by speaking of Yahweh in the masculine form.

Biblical passages are often cited with great approval by the perpetrators of a hierarchical family structure in which the husband holds all authority and the wife is subservient, needing protection. Traditional Christian marriage vows, based on biblical references, call on the husband to love and the wife to obey. Of course, any such relationship of unbalanced power opens up the potential for violence, where dominance may become brutality. Yet the language used today in many Christian services and Christian hymns still reflects the male dominance that ruled the Christian community for many centuries.

For some it is difficult to believe that human society can be ordered in any way other than that depicted in the biblical passages, since they have always lived in a male-dominated society. But social conditions are changing, and women today are moving into leadership positions in government and industry, as well as in many families. What was true in biblical times and most of the centuries since may soon become obsolete.

One of the most controversial issues in the current culture wars is the subject of homosexuality. Here the Bible proves to be of little help in settling the question, despite many statements to the contrary made by biblical literalists. In fact, no credible case against homosexuals can be made from the biblical text unless one chooses to interpret scripture in a way that simply sustains existing prejudices against homosexuals. The term "homosexuality" does not even appear in the King James version of the Bible, nor do any of its cognates. Its first use in any English-language Bible is that found in the Revised Standard Version completed in 1946.

A passage in the letter to the Romans (1:26–27) is usually cited as Paul's most significant comment on homosexuality. Here Paul writes: "For this reason God gave them up to dishonorable passions. Their women exchanged natural relations for unnatural, and the men likewise gave up natural relations with women and were consumed with passion for one another, men committing shameless acts with men and receiving in their own passions the due penalty for their error."

However, theologians point out that this portion of Paul's letter is taken out of context. Paul was not writing about homosexuality at all. He was writing about the fallen nature of humankind that has caused both the Jews and the Gentiles to suppress the truth by their wickedness. They knew God but did not honor and were not grateful to God. They substituted their own thinking in place of God. In other words, the creatures were ignoring the Creator and worshipping themselves.

The story of Sodom and Gomorrah in Genesis 19:1–9, another favorite reference for Bible literalists, has much more to do with the city of Sodom's wickedness in violating the laws of hospitality and its rape of strangers than it does with homosexual practices. According to this story, two divine messengers (angels) came to the city of Sodom, where Lot lived. It was a common Middle Eastern practice at that time to place any aliens outside the security of their own tribe totally at the mercy or hospitality of the tribe into whose territory the aliens had wandered, in this case the city of Sodom. The most inhospitable way to insult such an alien stranger of the male gender was to force him to act out the woman's role in sexual activity. It was, in fact, the ultimate insult that the male citizens of any tribe could administer. The men of Sodom intended only to humiliate the two guests; they had little sexual interest in them. Lot, according to the story, eventually rescued the two divine messengers and protected them by shutting them within his own house.

The Bible reiterates repeatedly that all persons reflect the holiness of God, for all are made in God's image. This is true for men and for women, for heterosexual persons and for homosexual persons, for all races, nationalities, and people of any ethnic background, and it is true for rich and poor, old and young, religious and nonreligious. To discriminate against any particular segment of society in the name of the Bible is to ignore its most important teachings.

But there is more. The Bible not only provides misinterpreted excuses for all the injustices cited above, it also announces God's judgment against such perverse and inhuman distortions of God's humanizing mercy and righteousness. A careful reading of the Bible clearly shows that every time the ancient Jews began to manipulate God's gifts for their own idolatrous purposes, God moved against them.

For example, in Jeremiah 7:14, God is quoted as saying (through Jeremiah) "I will do to the house which is called by my name (i.e., the temple), and in which you trust, and to the place which I gave to you and to your fathers, as I did to Shiloh." In other words, God is here announcing the destruction of the temple that God gave to the people of Israel as a sign of the covenant, along with the whole ceremonial and sacrificial law. The destruction is to take place because the temple is no longer God's house. Instead, it has become "a den of robbers" (verse 9), with the people ignoring the law of the covenant and dealing unjustly with one another, oppressing the unprotected, stealing, murdering, worshipping false gods, and at the same time taking refuge in the temple, saying, "We are delivered" (verse 10). The whole religious structure has become a shambles and God thus states his intention to shatter it.

Again, in the gospels of the New Testament we find Jesus acting on behalf of God against the human perversion of God's law relating to the Sabbath. Matthew 12:1–14 brings this into focus through two statements attributed to Jesus: "the Son of Man is greater than the Sabbath" (verses 6, 8) and God "desires mercy and not sacrifice" (verse 7). In Mark's version of the same event Jesus propounds the terse theological formulation: "The Sabbath was made for man, not man for the Sabbath" (Mark 2:27). Jesus thus affirms his disciples when the hungry group plucks grain to eat on the Sabbath and when he himself heals a sick man on that day of rest. Jesus is clearly pointing out that the legalistic interpretation of the law, with no regard for human need, had turned God's gift against human beings; it had imprisoned and deactivated the human significance of God's commandment.

The letters of Paul push such logic even further. Paul's central point is that the law is God's gift to the people and is intended to direct them in a life according to God's will, a life of active love. But humankind has transformed the law into "a curse," a means of alienation from both God and God's people. "The works of the law" have become a thing in themselves, a kind of spiritual currency that determines human transactions with God and neighbor. The law has replaced trust in relation to God and has replaced love in relation to other human beings. According to Paul, what is needed is the restoration of right relationships "outside the Law."

Interestingly enough, the letter of James, written later by another follower of Jesus, presents the reader with a direct challenge to Paul's faith-against-works position. The paradox is so striking that theologians have resorted to various tricks to try to explain it away. But James' opposition to Paul's thesis is no more striking than that between Isaiah and Jeremiah on the security of the temple, or between the laws established in Deuteronomy and Jesus' teaching on keeping the Sabbath. And the reason is the same: Faith has by now become an excuse for inhumanity. As the letter of James (2:15–17) puts it, "If a brother or a sister is ill-clad or in lack of daily food, and one of you says to them, 'Go in peace…' without giving them the things needed for the body … what does it profit? So faith by itself, if it has no works, is dead." Thus when faith closes in on itself in a religious universe from which human beings and their needs — and specifically their physical, material needs — are excluded, God will not acknowledge such "faith" anymore: it will "profit nothing."

Turning to the field of science, we find that the Bible has really nothing to say at all. Jesus could never have imagined such concepts as Albert Einstein's theory of relativity or Dmitri Mendeleev's periodic table of chemical elements. What medical understanding there is among the biblical writers is the common wisdom of their times, with nothing remotely resembling our present-day knowledge of medical science. Their biblical understanding of plant life, animal life, and human life were primitive, to say the least. Modern biology has tossed into oblivion most of the ideas about nature that are expounded in the Bible. The concepts of physics, subatomic physics, cosmology, and astrophysics would have brought incredulity to every one of the biblical authors.

It is, of course, true that many of the leading scientists of the past were deeply religious. Isaac Newton considered his commentary on Daniel (a book of the Bible) a far more important contribution to human knowledge than any of his discoveries in the field of motion and gravitation, although others now view the commentary as nothing more than a museum curiosity. And the great chemist Robert Boyle had such confidence in the authority of the Bible that he assumed the post of a governor for Society for the Propagation of the Gospel in 1649. A long list of scientists could be compiled, showing the ways many of them defended religion against "mechanistic atheism." But one would be hard pressed to find any who used passages from the Bible to bolster scientific arguments.

The biblical accounts of creation, the sun standing still at the battle of Jericho, and the fish swallowing Jonah can hardly be considered more than metaphors related to faith. Thus to impose constraints on science through the use of the Bible, as some literalists still try to do, is to force the Bible into a role for which it was never intended and to do violence to its text.

Finally, the 66 books of the Bible are not systematically classified nor are they chronologically arranged. The work, however, is justly looked upon as the foundation for the Christian religion. It is thus an important element of the accumulated knowledge of the world, but only one part of it. And certainly one should not use the Bible as a holy encyclopedia for looking up facts about God.

8. Insight, Paradigms, and Prejudice

Before we go further into the history of information access, we need to consider the way in which the organization of facts changes over time. After all, scientists in the twentieth century have finally put to rest the idea that reality never varies and that we gain knowledge merely by absorbing ideas like a sponge being filled with water.

Many people, of course, long suspected that the learning process is more complex. We experience too many optical and aural illusions to think otherwise. We usually see only the things we are prepared to see. We shut out some sounds to more clearly hear others. Smells cancel each other out. Even our sense of touch — probably the most primitive of our five senses — can be fooled by the temperature of objects with which we have been recently in contact.

We now know that our brains have roughly as many processing units as there are stars in our galaxy, and these cells are so numerous that millions of them can be destroyed by the aging process without any noticeable loss of brain efficiency. They receive and transmit messages in quite different a manner from the way electrons encode such messages in a computer. Indeed, human perception, according to researchers, seems to be a matter of our neurons seeking out and finding information about the behavior of objects that has been previously stored in our memories.

They say that we should think of perception as the selection of the most appropriate stored hypothesis according to current sensory data. For example, the image that meets our eyes when we look at an object impacts the retina, which does little more than choose a pattern from the relevant stored data. This is, in fact, rather like selecting information from an encyclopedia.

The many psychological and biological experiments performed to date demonstrate that all of what we know is finally conditioned by our past experiences and the knowledge we have collected in our brains. Knowing is not a passive but an active process by which our neurons elicit responses to stimuli by comparing these with the known models of reality already in our memories.

It is not our purpose here to describe or list all the experiments that have led to the present-day understanding of how the human mind works. These can be found in many basic psychology texts and in technical books on the workings of the brain. However, we will look at one of the most important breakthroughs that demonstrates how humans gain knowledge. This came, surprisingly, from observations of chimpanzees rather than human beings. It was made by Wolfgang Köhler (1887–1967), a German psychologist confined on Tenerife in the Canary Islands during the First World War.

Köhler's enforced isolation on that island proved fortunate, for, besides escaping from the army and artillery shells, he was able to conduct a careful and detailed study of the behavior of the island's great apes. He later described this work in his book *The Mentality of Apes*, and this research helped to establish some of the basic principles about the way you and I acquire knowledge and store it in our minds.

His initial finding was that chimpanzees solve problems by a sudden mental restructuring of the situation. He called this "insight," and used the German word "gestalt," meaning pattern or form, to describe the process. This discovery spawned a new branch of psychology called Gestalt psychology, which emphasizes the tendency of the mind to organize, integrate, and perceive all situations as total structures. The principles of Gestalt psychology are crucial in understanding how you and I acquire knowledge and hold onto it.

In his book, Köhler raised objections to much of the experimentation then in vogue among animal psychologists, experiments that placed cats in mazes, where they had to manipulate levers to escape. Köhler maintained that in such setups cats cannot possibly behave intelligently because the release mechanism is hidden from their normally perceived environment. When cats want to escape from traps, they don't naturally manipulate levers. Instead, they claw, push, and scratch at obstacles, and when possible jump to freedom, climb over barriers, or squeeze through tiny openings. The mazes, Köhler argued, show only that animals can be trained through a trial-and-error process to manipulate levers, but show little or nothing about their ability to solve problems or to think.

Köhler devised his own experiments differently. In one he placed a banana and a stick near a chained chimpanzee. The stick was put within the ape's reach and the banana was placed just a little too far away. The animal could play with the stick, which is natural behavior for chimps, but could not reach the banana without using the stick as a tool to pull the banana closer.

In a very short time almost every one of the chained chimps perceived (had the insight) that it could use the stick to get at the banana. Clearly, the chimpanzees appeared to both see and use the relationships involved in reaching the goal.

This result may not seem particularly remarkable since trained animals, and especially trained chimpanzees, can do many more amazing tricks. But Köhler was not training the apes. He was observing how their minds work. Other Köhler experiments required the chimpanzees to fit together two short sticks to create one long enough to reach the fruit, and to pile boxes into a crude ladder so as to get to bananas that were placed too high for the animals to reach by jumping.

According to Köhler, productive thinking, whether in chimpanzees or humans, involves perception within a larger context. Thus in learning something new, there is a change not only in relation to the portion of knowledge gained but in relation to the context as well. There is a sudden reorganization through insight of the total perceptual field. Thereafter, in similar problem situations, the solution will be dictated by the reorganized perceptual field. If the animal or person adopts an erroneous insight in a problem-solving situation, they will continue to repeat that mistake in spite of failure and frustration until, or unless, they reach some new insight.

One of Köhler's chimpanzees was blocked in this way. It was fixated on its normal method for getting to the fruit. It failed to realize that it simply could not get the banana without the stick tool and pathetically kept trying to reach it by hand.

Max Wertheimer, another pioneer in Gestalt psychology, presented small children in Germany with a far more difficult problem than that of using a stick to obtain food — one that required insight to find the area of a rectangle. Wertheimer's results verified Köhler's conclusion that human beings tend to perceive organized patterns, not individual parts that are merely added together.

Köhler claimed that insight eliminates the trial-and-error factor in learning. It involves a grasp of relationships not immediately evident within a single perceptual field. He said that although there may be a period of trial and error in problem solving, it is not the kind of blind and random process that other experimentalists once thought it was.

A new insight can be triggered sometimes by the most mundane happenings. Such was the case when bacteriologist Alexander Fleming discovered penicillin through a combination of some of the most commonplace circumstances. He failed to wash his petri dishes before he went on vacation. A bit of mold in the surrounding air began to grow in one of them. When Fleming returned and saw the mold, instead of washing out the petri dishes so that he could use them in new experiments, he decided to study and analyze this growth. It proved to be *Penicillium notatum*, a substance that kills germs of many sorts.

Dozens of other scientists before Fleming had undoubtedly found similar mold growths in dirty petri dishes, but they were unable to see anything there but dirty laboratory equipment. Fleming was open to the possibility of a new way of looking at mold and thus had the insight that eventually led to advanced methods of curing diseases.

The same kind of sudden insight in the field of literature allowed Herman Melville to see the great white sperm whale, Moby Dick, as some colossal alien existence without which humanity itself would be incomplete. It also led Henry Thoreau to visualize and describe human civilizations as toadstools that grow up in the night by a solitary road.

It may seem illogical to say that we don't all see the same thing when we look in the same place. After all, the eyes and other senses of human beings are much alike physically and biochemically. But what we see, hear, and feel is always filtered first through what we expect to see, hear, and feel — our particular mental grid system that is created by the ways we gestalt the world. Thus, when you pick up a piece of furniture, you assume its approximate weight ahead of time and brace yourself accordingly. If it turns out to be much lighter, the shock is unpleasant because it's unexpected.

A new gestalt or flash of insight startles us both because it enters our minds so abruptly and because it so totally changes our assumptions. It emerges out of our unconscious to fill our conscious mind and expel the old rational concepts to which we have long been wedded. In cases where we have diligently struggled over an extended period of time for a solution that was never forthcoming because it was blocked by old fixations, the shock can be one of great relief. "Aha!" we shout, or "Eureka!"

Nothing remains quite the same after such a flash of inspiration. Everything seems to shift a bit, and we perceive ourselves as having a more open, free interrelationship with the external world. The gestalt shift thus becomes an experience of sudden growth in knowledge.

Such a new insight is achieved only when one's old fixation is somehow broken. Although exhilarating, this sometimes can be emotionally painful. It hurts to recognize that I have suddenly changed the particular perspective on which I had long relied for understanding things. More than that, it is an admission that all of what I previously knew may have been little more than a personal whim. The pain intensifies as I begin to recognize that my own rational processes of deduction had little or nothing to do with effecting the new gestalt. Instead, happenings outside myself or happenings in my brain cells over which I had no control brought forth the new insight.

The importance Köhler placed on the whole rather than its parts enabled the Gestalt psychologists to offer the first reasonable explanation for the sudden change in appearance that occurs in reversible perspective pictures. The best known of such optical illusions is the Necker cube, named for the Swiss geologist who first described the fact that a drawing of a transparent rhomboid crystal can be seen in either of two different ways, but never in both ways at the same time. The viewer of such a drawing usually experiences a sudden and involuntary change in the cube's apparent position while staring at it. Other such figures include the reversible goblet, the shifting (Schröder) staircase, and the tunnel. These optical illusions are seen first as either concave or convex figures, and then as their opposites.

The Gestalt psychologists' explanation for the reason we see reversible perspective pictures in opposing forms lies in the fact that we always perceive the "best" figure that is consistent with a given image. In most cases "best" may be taken to mean "simplest." When we look at a Necker cube, our minds automatically assign a three-dimensional orientation to the lines so that the whole appears as a cube, because a cube is the simplest of all possible forms that these few lines may take. The simplicity lies in the fact that a cube's edges are all the same length, and the angles are all right and equal angles. None of the many possible appearances of the drawing, including a two-dimensional one, is as simple and regular. The image reverses because the drawing contains another equally tridimensional construction (another cube) that is symmetrical in depth with the first.

But it is not just in optical illusions that one can recognize the gestalt principle that the whole determines the parts. In a picture of a friendly face, for example, we see a nose, mouth, eyes, hair, lips, chin, and ears. Change the width of the nose, the distance between the eyes, the shape of the lips, the part in the hair, the size of the ears, and we see a different face. Its friendliness is not the result of an indiscriminate aggregation of these features, like putting cookies in a jar. The friendliness results only when all the parts are in proper relationship to each other with regard to past experience of a friendly face.

Take a musical chord of two tones, say d and a. When sounded together, they produce the particular musical quality called a fifth. Everyone familiar with music knows that particular quality exists in neither note alone. It can be reproduced only by playing them together. The mutual influence of one note on the other makes for the quality.

Furthermore, most objects we look at overlay and occlude one another in a way that would be confusing were it not that this perceptual system in our brains segregates and sorts them out with ease and rapidity. We look at a bookcase and see only many parallel cardboard and cloth spines. Our mind fills in the other five sides of each object to identify it as a book. We look at a bottle and see only one side. Yet this side's roundness enables our minds to fill out the rest of the cylindrical shape. If the other side, on closer inspection, turns out to be flat, wedge-shaped, or concave instead of convex, we are rather surprised.

In every aspect of perception — visual, aural, or tactile — the mind mentally fills in the gaps to complete the whole. We do this naturally and unconsciously on the basis of sensory clues given to us by the total environment at the moment. Thus the context in which we are moving is as important to what we perceive as the shape, feel, or sound of the various objects.

If our minds didn't work in this way, we would live in a state of constant confusion. The room I am sitting in right now, for example, is filled with an almost infinite number of different variations in light and color. It's just an ordinary study with desk, chair, books, and filing cabinets. But if I were to use a sensitive light meter among its many shadows and light-reflecting objects, I would find the needle in constant motion as I moved the meter around the room. Fortunately, my mind organizes, or gestalts, the variations of light into objects that hold particular meaning for me as a human being because of information previously stored in my brain.

In a real sense this is a simplifying process. The gestalt brings out the most important elements of the room — desk, chair, computer — and washes out the least important ones — shadow on the curtain, spot on the rug, paper in the wastebasket. What enters my mind is an abstraction of the total environment, one that has no more elements in it than I need to act from day to day.

People collectively share insights either because they have learned them from others or because they have experienced the same event in much the same way. And though we speak of an individual achieving an insight, we seldom find two persons having the same insight at the same time. Thus, when we talk of a group holding the same view of a situation, we usually refer to this collective pattern of thought as a paradigm.

Just as individual gestalts change with new insights, collective patterns of thought, or paradigms, change as new discoveries are made and become accepted as facts. Before the voyage of Columbus, for example, almost everyone perceived the world as a relatively flat surface. Heaven was above and hell beneath. Only a few "misguided" philosophers suggested otherwise. Sailors who by accident sailed to the edge of the flat earth would undoubtedly fall off into unknown horrors of nonexistence.

Columbus had the foresight and courage to sail over what should have been the edge, reached what he thought were the islands of India, and came back to Europe with the report that he had reached the other side of the world.

What had been thought of as flat was now generally recognized as being round. A new paradigm was thus formed in the minds of literate Europeans.

Every field of human thought has gone through a whole series of changes such as this. In the study of astronomy, the early Greek philosophers argued over whether the heavens revolved around Earth or Earth around the heavens until Claudius Ptolemy, about 150 A.D., published a highly regarded work that firmly established the paradigm that Earth was the center of the universe. But in 1543 Nicolaus Copernicus showed this to be wrong. Since then many observations of the heavens have modified and expanded the work of Copernicus. We now see Earth as just one tiny planet that revolves around a medium-sized star in a gigantic and revolving galaxy that is itself only one of an infinity of other galaxies that apparently stretch on forever. Rocket ships and ever-more-sensitive telescopes daily confirm this paradigm for us.

Even human understanding of the fundamental action of gravity has gone through a number of paradigm changes. The Greeks held to the idea that objects fall because it is in their nature to do so. As long as the world was considered flat and the sun moved around it, such an explanation was quite adequate. Then Newton (they say because of a falling apple) experienced an insight that explained many aspects of motion that the Greek concept could not. But Newtonian ideas of gravity are no longer adequate in the curved-space world of Einsteinian matter. This new paradigm, in turn, explains many aspects of motion that Newton's theories never could, and it has given scientists a basis for the whole field of nuclear physics.

Yet not everyone accepts these, or most other, new paradigms. There are still a few proponents of the Ptolemaic universe among us, just as there are a handful of advocates for the flat-earth theory. One firm supporter of the Ptolemaic view is Sheik Abd el Aziz bin Baz who, as late as 1966, asked the king of Saudi Arabia to suppress the Copernican teaching because, according press reports, the sheik believes it is a heresy spreading in his land. He argues that the Holy Koran, the Prophet's teachings, the majority of Islamic scientists, and the actual facts all prove that the sun is running in its orbit and that the Earth is fixed and stable, "spread out by God for his mankind." Anyone who professes otherwise, the sheik said, is propounding a falsehood against God, the Koran, and the Prophet.

Thomas Kuhn, in his monumental book *The Structure of Scientific Revolutions*, uses the term "paradigm switch" to characterize the leap in vision accompanying scientific discoveries and scientific revolutions. He demonstrates that the basic theories of even the most rigid and well-established scientific disciplines rest on phenomena and experimental data that are selected and given status by the acceptance of general assumptions and ways of thinking in the scientific community at large. After scientists experience one of the revolutionary shifts away from a previously accepted paradigm, a change such as the Newtonian revolution or the Darwinian revolution, they don't simply see old facts in a new way, but they see new facts entirely.

Kuhn describes these changes in this way: "During [scientific] revolutions scientists see new and different things when looking with familiar instruments in places they have not looked before. It is rather as if the professional community had been transported to a different planet where familiar objects are seen in a different light."

Charles Darwin's great insight gave a new order, or structure, to the animal world, just as Isaac Newton's earlier achievement had given a new structure to the physical world. To realize how revolutionary this insight was at that time, we need to remember that before Darwin, most concepts about the natural world were related to categories that had nothing to do with evolutionary change. The great eighteenth-century French naturalist Comte de Buffon, for example, explained the absence of elephants in the woods and forests of America by saying that nature in the New World was "less active, less varied, and less vigorous" than in Europe, Asia, or Africa. Thus animals larger than the relatively small tapir, according to de Buffon, could not develop there. (The great plains buffalo was yet to be discovered.) Queen Isabella of Spain drew somewhat similar conclusions about human life in America, making parallel comparisons between men and plants. When she was informed by Columbus that the trees of the Indies did not have deep roots, she is said to have replied, "This land, where trees are not deeply rooted, must produce men of little truthfulness and less constancy."

Darwin never actually observed any of the evolutionary changes that he described as taking place. No one could. The process is far too slow. But he did have the insight that some evolutionary process must be occurring. Otherwise how can one explain the similarities and differences within various species of birds, butterflies, and plants? Today the scientific consensus supports this paradigm, and every year new evidence in fossil arrangements, comparative anatomy, embryology, and so on strengthens it.

Darwin apparently achieved his insight only because of the convergence of a unique set of circumstances, including the reading of a book on economics by Parson Thomas Malthus, a trip to the South Sea Islands that gave him a new context, and the absorption of much of the ever-increasing store of knowledge about animals and plants. The opposition creationists argued then, as they do now, that Darwin had gone against God's "natural order" of placing animals on Earth. In this they missed the wisdom of the Genesis story — that Darwin, in initiating a new paradigm of the animal and plant world, was following God's instructions to Adam to name the animals and thus give structure to the natural world.

Several historians have noted that the opposition to Darwinian evolution expressed at the 1925 Scopes Trial in Tennessee had nothing to do with science, but was the result of parents' fears that their children would, if they became better educated, abandon all parental ideas and the tradition-bound community ways. As the prosecutor, William Jennings Bryan, said during the trial, "If they believe [in evolution], they go back to scoff at the religion of their parents. And the parents have a right to say that no teacher paid by their money shall rob their children of faith in God and send them back to their homes, skeptical, infidels, or agnostics, or atheists."

Science advances a little with each new experiment and new discovery. Science advances radically when a new paradigm totally alters the way scientists view their world. This is true even though most scientific paradigms can no more be proved or disproved than can other paradigms, at least in the way that we can prove or disprove a statement of logic or a mathematical formula. Yet each new paradigm that is generally accepted within the scientific community becomes so because it better fits the observed facts than the older one.

One more example comes from the field of chemistry. Here the English chemist John Dalton published his conclusions, in 1808, about the chemical nature of matter. He proposed that each element is made of specific kinds of atoms — atoms that are different from those of all other elements, especially in weight. This leap to a novel understanding of the nature of matter put chemistry on a new course. Thousands of papers and books about chemical substances and their relations to one another were immediately rendered obsolete. Hundreds of years of work by medieval alchemists became merely idle curiosity. Most of the speculations of the early seventeenth- and eighteenth-century chemists had to be abandoned.

Dalton's laboratory calculations of the weights of atoms for several elements were inaccurate, because the measuring instruments of his time didn't allow the exactness we now can achieve. But Dalton's fantastic leap to a new way of viewing chemical elements revolutionized chemical science.

The roots of most prejudice can be found in a rigid adherence to outmoded paradigms. Whether these attitudes come from childhood, schooling, or the general environment, people try to protect themselves from the social forces that might expose their illusions because of the pain involved in rooting out a mistaken attitude. Few of us have the courage of Charles Darwin, who made it a rule to take immediate note of every fact that seemed to run counter to his own beliefs, for, as he said, "I know by experience that ideas and facts of this kind vanish more easily from the memory than those which are in our favor."

In the history of information storage there are many instances in which the knowledge collected is relatively useless because it is so overgrown with prejudicial and outmoded views of the truth. Knowledge collectors, whether they be writers, encyclopedia compilers, or library purchasers, have to engage in a constant struggle to filter facts from their prejudicial coverings. Yet because such collectors are human beings like you and me, they inevitably reflect some of the prejudices of their times. We can readily recognize this in ancient writings. But such attitudes are more difficult to detect in modern books simply because the opinions of the collectors are in accord with the general paradigms of our time, as we shall see in later chapters.

9. Bacon and the New Outlook

England's "golden age" wasn't — at least it wasn't a golden age for those who lived in it. Few people during this time of Queen Elizabeth (1558–1603) actually saw any gold and the period hardly lasted long enough to qualify as an age. True, historians dubbed it the "golden age" not because of monetary wealth but because of its golden authors — Johnson, Marlowe, Spencer, Shakespeare, and Bacon. Yet the percentage of people who could read their works at that time was quite small and largely confined to the literate upper classes.

Daily life for most people was as hard and fear ridden as it had been for all the past centuries of European history. Beggars still roamed the streets of London in hoards, and plagues continued to spread throughout the land. Elizabethan merchants, gentry, and noblemen paid no regard to the rights of black Africans whom they transported into slavery, nor to the Irish whom they robbed and slaughtered with abandon. Furthermore, deformed women were persecuted by their neighbors as witches, while Jesuit missionaries, Unitarians, and Puritans were hanged or hacked to pieces at the stake. The only thing that can be said in this regard about England's golden age was that the victims were not so numerous as those elsewhere in Europe, particularly those in Spain, where the Inquisition was taking a heavy toll.

The glorious and romantic tales of Elizabeth and Essex, and the riches attributed to the pirate-hero Francis Drake, have made us forget that the queen's own palace floors were still covered with straw rather than rugs, and that the best carriage roads were only unpaved footpaths. Most people, including Shakespeare, believed that ostriches could digest iron, that some toads were venomous as well as ugly and yet had precious jewels in their heads, and that elephants were intellectually equal to human beings.

But the seeds of change had been planted by the Reformation and cultivated by Puritan values — thrift, hard work, pious Sundays, and, particularly, each man as his own authority. Although Anglicanism became the official religion in England and Puritanism was treated as a foreign import in Elizabeth's time, it was the highly religious Puritans who were most in revolt against the medieval attitude that accepted without question the authority of the church. The Puritans constantly struggled with the universal problem of finding some way to separate truth from untruth.

Francis Bacon, though no Puritan himself, shared their interest in finding the truth, and he eventually formulated empirical tools with which to do so. His grandfather had been the overseer of sheep for the Catholic Abbey of Bury St. Edmunds. His father was a Protestant lawyer who became a rich landowner and was appointed Lord Keeper of England after purchasing church property confiscated from the Catholics by King Henry VIII. Francis was born in 1561 at York House in London, two years after Queen Elizabeth came to the throne. He was a bright, precocious boy and the Queen apparently enjoyed talking to him, playfully calling him her "young lord keeper."

This future advocate of experimental and scientific methods for solving all problems attended Trinity College of Cambridge University at the young age of 12, and after two years left to study law. In 1576 he was sent by the Queen to join the staff of England's ambassador to France. While there, his father died and he had to return to England. But the French experience had a lasting impact on the young man, because it was there that Francis Bacon first became acquainted with the importance of scientific investigation, which was to be the subject of many of his writings.

The queen appears to have not really liked or trusted Bacon after he grew to adulthood, and he held no important office under her reign. He was, however, elected to Parliament in 1584 and continued to be returned to that body from various constituencies until its dissolution in 1614. After the accession to the throne of James I in 1603, Bacon's advancement was rapid, for King James greatly admired him. Bacon was knighted in 1603, became the Lord Keeper, then the Lord Chancellor, and finally, in 1620, Viscount St. Albans. As the Lord Chancellor, he presided over many of the most important court trials of the day.

However, it is not for his services to the state that Bacon is remembered, but for his writings, which are marvelous in both language and thought. There is probably no other English author, unless it is Shakespeare, whose words are so easily remembered and frequently quoted. Bacon wrote philosophical books that changed the direction of scientific investigation throughout Europe, literary works that are still studied as examples of the best essay form, and legal briefs that exhibit some of the finest models of judicial reasoning in his time.

There is something about the language that Bacon uses, his power of illustration, and his quaintness of expression that lays hold of the reader and lodges itself in the reader's memory. His maxims sparkle on every page of his writings. For example, in just a few pages of his *Novum Organum* we find,

"Man is the servant and interpreter of nature;" "Truth is rightly called the daughter of time, not of authority;" "It is not fruit-bringing but light-bringing experiments that should be sought;" and "Human knowledge and human power meet in one." And, in his essays, the few close-packed sentences of each work expand and change visibly before our eyes whenever we read them with the kind of attention they demand. For his thoughts always refer to the concrete, never abstractions.

To fully appreciate Bacon's scientific originality and farsightedness, we must see him against the background of the science of his day, which was essentially speculative and otherworldly, marked with the imprint of the medieval church. The fundamental science of dynamics didn't even exist, for it was not founded by Galileo until late in Bacon's lifetime. The Earth was still considered the center of the universe around which the sun, planets, and stars revolved, and chemistry was a mere set of recipes. Bacon's older contemporary, William Gilbert, had discovered some elementary facts about magnetism, but these generally were regarded as magic forces that could not be fully understood by humans. Corresponding to this want of scientific knowledge was a lack of mechanical instrumentation to give men power over nature. There were clockworks, waterwheels, and windmills, but no motors to propel land or ship craft, and no power equipment with which to manufacture goods or to conduct sophisticated experiments.

In the area of natural history, Elizabethans still believed in the four elements, the four humors, the four qualities, and the doctrine of excess and balance. They did not know that blood circulates or that the nerves carry impulses to the brain and from the brain to the rest of the body. They substituted a system of invisible fluids, which they called spirits, for the nerves. The practice of medicine was based on the supposed coordination of blood, phlegm, red bile, and black bile. The sick were probably far safer in their own hands than in those of the most learned physicians, who had amassed great quantities of misinformation.

Bacon accused the learned men of his day of uncritically accepting the myths of the Middle Ages. He advocated the testing of all ideas by observation to determine their validity. Even as a teenager he is said to have attacked the Scholastics and their baggage of commentaries on Aristotle's writings. Bacon called that Greek philosopher a wretched sophist, and said his logic was a manual of madness. He further described Aristotle's metaphysics as a superstructure of cobwebs erected on a small foundation of fact. And his negative comments about Plato were, if anything, stronger. Bacon rightly saw that these ancient teachings were based on little but philosophical speculation. As Bacon put it in his essay *Thoughts and Conclusions*, "For when philosophy is severed from its roots of experience, whence it first sprouted and grew, it becomes a dead thing."

He believed that his own method of inductive reasoning should be substituted for the prevailing uncritical acceptance of medieval myths. He was convinced that the ignorance of nature and the consequent lack of power over nature were by no means inevitable. The problem was not one of the inability of humans to discover natural laws but simply their use of the wrong method. In his book *The Advancement of Learning* he argued, "We are not to imagine or suppose, but to discover, what nature does or may be made to do." He envisioned the universe as a problem to be examined and solved rather than as some eternally fixed state established to test each human's ability to suffer.

Bacon's forceful attacks on the knowledge brokers of his day were bound to make him many enemies. As anthropologist Loren Eiseley put it in his book of appreciation for Bacon's contributions to science, a book titled *The Man Who Saw Through Time*: "The great synthesizer who alters the outlook of a generation, who suddenly produces a kaleidoscopic change in our vision of the world, is apt to be the most envied, feared, and hated man among his contemporaries. Almost by instinct they feel in him the seed of a new order; they sense, even as they anathematize him, the passing away of the same, substantial world they have long inhabited. Such a man is a kind of lens or gathering point through which past thought gathers, is reorganized, and radiates outward again into new forms."

Bacon himself was in such despair over the hostility toward some of his writings and the disinterested reception of others that he translated all of them into Latin so that they might survive to another age. He doubted that those who used English had enough sense to preserve their own culture. He viewed books as boats with precious cargoes launched onto the great sea of time, and firmly believed that his ideas would eventually make their impact.

Bacon's emphasis was on the use of induction — the type of logical thinking by which a person ascends from specific, observed facts to the establishment of general laws and principles. This, of course, was not original with him, and he never claimed such originality. The Greek philosophers had long before made the distinction between deductive and inductive reasoning. What Bacon did for the first time was to analyze and record the principles of such reasoning so that people could use it with a full knowledge of what they were doing.

He pointed out that the inductive method involved four steps: first, listing all the known cases in which a given phenomenon occurs; second, listing all the cases in which the phenomenon does not occur; third, listing those instances in which the phenomenon occurs in differing degrees; and fourth, examining the three lists. These steps, he said, would lead to the discovery of an element present whenever the phenomenon was present, absent whenever the phenomenon was absent, and present in degrees corresponding to the degrees of the phenomenon's presence. That element then could be confirmed as the cause of the phenomenon.

Bacon later abandoned his studies of inductive reasoning, asserting that rules for investigation could not be properly laid down beforehand. They must, instead, be worked out in the process of investigation itself.

Bacon always held that the ultimate secrets of nature would prove to be few in comparison with the vast variety of natural phenomena — a surprisingly modern concept. He illustrated this through analogy with language. According to Bacon, words present a bewildering variety of sounds, but the constituent elements of sounds — vowels and consonants — are quite few. The same, he believed, is true of nature. He stressed the importance of not contenting oneself with mere observation to find these ultimate secrets of nature, but of instituting, wherever possible, artificial experiments for the purpose of obtaining more precise data.

He broke new ground by discussing nature as it is actually found rather than as it might exist in an abstract and ideal state. Bacon recognized that nature had already been violently interfered with by humans, that it is constantly being vexed, imprisoned, and forced into new relationships through the activity of human beings. Aristotle had described life from a distance, as if it existed free and uncontained and as if men weren't even observing it. Bacon, to enable people to better control and alter nature, made a contrast between *natura libera* and the real *natura vexata*. He wanted to study and describe the history of humankind's earlier and less-scientific efforts to subdue nature so that this might be a guide to future action. He was, in fact, the first person to recognize that the essence of science in human history is the story of the interaction between humans and nature.

"It is well to observe," Bacon wrote in *Novum Organum*, "the force and effect and consequences of discoveries. These are to be seen nowhere more conspicuously than in those three which were unknown to the ancients, and of which the origin, though recent, is obscure, namely, printing, gunpowder, and the magnet. For these three have changed the whole face and state of things throughout the world; the first in literature, the second in warfare, the third in navigation; whence have followed innumerable changes; insomuch that no empire, no sect, no star seems to have exerted greater power and influence in human affairs than have these mechanical inventions."

Though Bacon expressed hostility toward speculative views of earlier philosophers, he did not hesitate to make use of whatever practical knowledge came from the past. Thus he made use of the Greek art of memory that had been passed down through the ages, a system that he probably learned when he was living in France. In Aubrey's life of Bacon (published in 1813), there is one of the few examples of the design of a part of a building for use in such a memory system. According to Aubrey, in one of the galleries in Bacon's house, there were painted glass windows "and every pane with severall figures of beast, bird, and flower: perhaps his Lordship might use them as topiques for locall use," that is, as objects to which items for recall might be assigned.

In Bacon's *Advancement of Learning*, the art of memory figures quite prominently as one of the arts and sciences that are in need of reform, both in their methods and in the ends for which they are used. He says the art should be used not for empty ostentation but for useful purposes. And although he did not specify what such useful purposes might be, it is likely that he was thinking of things such as memorizing scientific facts to hold them in the mind for further investigation.

Bacon used the term "emblems" for the more traditional word "images" that was used by practitioners of the memory system, and he expanded on this in his work *De Augmentis Scientiarum*, saying, "Emblems bring down intellectual to sensible things; for what is sensible always strikes the memory stronger, and sooner impresses itself than the intellectual.... And therefore it is easier to retain the image of a sports man hunting the hare, of an apothecary ranging his boxes, an orator making a speech, a boy repeating verses, or a player acting his part, than the corresponding notions of invention, disposition, elocution, memory, action."

Bacon realized that every individual's thinking is influenced and shaped by preconceptions about which each person is generally quite unaware. Such prejudices lead us astray, and he labeled them "idols" so that we might be on guard against them. They are four in number. The first, idols of the tribe, "have their foundation in human nature itself." These are the various mental tendencies common to the whole human race, such as the tendency to recognize facts that support one's belief and ignore or pervert those that don't. The second, the idols of the cave (the name comes from the seventh book of Plato's *Republic*), are one's mistaken ideas derived from heredity and environment. The third, the idols of the marketplace, arise from the tyranny of words as a medium of exchange. This category, Bacon said, is the most troublesome of all, for many words and phrases themselves embody false beliefs and inaccurate observations. They are crystallized errors that we swallow unconsciously. Finally, there are the idols of the theater, which arise either from false systems of philosophy or from perverse laws of demonstration. He called them idols of the theater "because in my judgment all the received systems of philosophy are but so many stage-plays. They are worlds of illusion created each by its own author out of his literary imagination."

Bacon's comprehensive view of knowledge is recorded in one published part, called the *Parasceve*, of an encyclopedia he attempted to complete. There he says, "For the history that I require and design, special care is to be taken that it be of wide range and made to the measure of the universe. For the world is not to be narrowed till it will go into the understanding (which has been done hitherto), but the understanding is to be expanded and opened till it can take in the image of the world."

He made a clear distinction between the new workmanlike encyclopedia he had in view and the semi-literary productions of antiquity. As he put it, "Away with antiquities, citations, disputes, controversies, everything in short which is literary. For all that concerns ornaments of speech, similitudes, treasury of eloquence, and such like emptiness, let it be utterly dismissed. No man who is collecting and storing up materials for ship building or the like thinks of arranging them elegantly as in a shop, and displaying them so as to please the eye; all his care is that they be sound and good, and that they be arranged so as to take up as little room as possible in the warehouse. And this is exactly what should be done here."

Readers are cautioned that the information to be collected had to be of wide range and adapted to the measure of the universe, not of humankind. "For the world is not to be narrowed down till it will go into the understanding, which has been the practice hitherto, but the understanding must be stretched and expanded to take in the image of the world as it is discovered. When this has been done we shall no longer be kept dancing within narrow circles like bewitched persons but shall range at large within the circuit of the whole world."

Yet he said that in the attainment of this end it must be remembered that "the history of the arts is of most use. It exhibits things in motion and leads more directly to practice. It takes off the mask and veil from natural objects. As Proteus did not go through his changes till he was seized and handcuffed, so under the constraint of arts nature puts forth her ultimate efforts and strivings. Natural bodies refuse to be destroyed, to be annihilated; rather than this they will turn themselves into something else. We must then set aside all delicacy and daintiness and concentrate specially on the history of the arts, mechanical and illiberal though it may seem. And here we must prefer the arts which expose, alter, and prepare natural bodies and materials; such as agriculture, cookery, chemistry, dyeing, the manufacture of glass, enamel, sugar, rum, powder, artificial fires, paper, and the like. The arts which consist principally in subtle motions of the hands or instruments are of less help; such as weaving, carpentry, architecture, manufacture of mills, clocks, and the like; although these too are by no means to be neglected, both because many things occur in them which relate to the alterations of natural bodies, and because they give accurate information concerning local motion, which is a thing of great importance in very many respects."

Most of Bacon's life was to pass before he finally published any of the fragments of his encyclopedia, but he spent many hours planning and preparing for it. Over the years, he revised and rewrote some parts at least 12 times. He completed an outline of 130 sections, divided into three main divisions.

The first 40 sections were to be devoted to external nature, including astronomy, meteorology, geography, the greater masses (fire, air, water, earth), and the species (mineral, vegetable, animal). The second part, humankind, was to include 18 sections on human anatomy and physiology, structure and powers, voluntary and involuntary actions, situation awake and asleep, conception and growth, and life and death. The third part, human action on nature, was to include 72 sections about medicine, surgery, chemistry, vision and the arts connected with it (painting, sculpture, and so forth), hearing and sound, music, smell and smells, taste and tastes, touch and the objects of touch (including physical love), pleasure and pain, emotions and intellectual faculties, food and drink, care of the person, clothing, architecture, transport, printing, books, writing, agriculture, navigation, the arts of peace, the arts of war, the history of machines, arithmetic, and geometry.

Of course, it wasn't the arrangement of the sections that inspired later encyclopedists but Bacon's insistence that knowledge could be tested to determine its validity. His observational methods gave a measure for deciding what should be saved of human wisdom and what discarded. When later Denis Diderot and Jean le Rond d'Alembert, working in France, compiled their *Encyclopédie*, they frankly and generously acknowledged their debt to Bacon, calling him "the greatest, the most universal, and most eloquent of the philosophers." And they closely followed his recommendation to examine the history of the mechanical arts and crafts, just as did the early investigators of England's Royal Society.

The closing years for this philosopher and man of science were tragic. He always had been careless with his money and had lived an extravagant mode of life. He also followed the common practice of his day in taking presents from those who appeared before him for legal judgments in his position as Lord Chancellor. Eventually, his enemies, of which there were many, cited such gifts to bring him to trial on a charge of corruption. Bacon pleaded guilty, was condemned, and had to pay a fine of 40,000 pounds (an immense sum in those days). He also lost his office and was banished from the court.

Bacon always asserted that he had never allowed such gifts to influence his legal judgments, but he was now a broken man. He spent his last years in seclusion working on his master plan for an encyclopedia of nature and art, which he called *The Great Instauration*. His interest in science never waned, and he died in April 1626 as a result of his attempts to conduct an experiment to see if cold would do as well as salt in preserving meat.

The experiment was a simple one. Bacon cleaned a chicken, stuffed it full of snow, and then waited to see how long the snow and cold would keep the chicken from spoiling. Some days later he wrote to a friend that he was happy the experiment "succeeded excellently well." The only problem was that Bacon became ill from bronchitis because he stood in the snow too long during the exceedingly cold weather to stuff the chicken. The disease caused his death. His will directed that he be buried beside his mother's grave at St. Michael's Church, St. Albans.

10. Diderot Banned

Chevalier de la Barre, a 19-year-old, rather mischievous youth of Amiens, France, was arrested in 1766 on a charge of scoffing at the doctrine of the Virgin Birth and desecrating a wayside shrine. The severe ruling of the courts befitted the prerevolutionary tenor of the times. The young man was sentenced to be beheaded after he had his tongue cut out and his right hand cut off. His remains were burned in the Amiens public square. It was the unanimous opinion of the judges that he committed the dastardly crime because he was seduced by the influence of those involved with the publication of Diderot's encyclopedia.

This ruling illustrates the harsh social climate of France during the years just preceding the French Revolution. It was a time of brutal measures instituted to control public dissent, and dichotomously a time when censors sometimes looked the other way to permit statements of discontent to come from the nation's printing presses. On the surface, France remained the greatest and most modern of any of the states of continental Europe, despite its disastrous wars and indifferent leadership. Its size and wealth, coupled with a seemingly stable social structure, presaged continuing economic growth. France's cultural dominance seemed fully assured.

But there was an undercurrent of revolt growing in all but the upper strata of society. Among the peasantry, where remnants of feudalism still could be found, there was dissatisfaction over the rents and dues that had to be paid to the nobles. For the artisans, working conditions were poor and hours long. A rigid class structure prevented such artisans from moving into the ranks of the bourgeoisie, just as the bourgeoisie were cut off from any upward movement by the hereditary nobility.

The Catholic Church was undoubtedly the single wealthiest proprietor in France. Part of its wealth supported some 2,000 hospitals and 600 colleges, but another part went to support bishops and abbots in conditions of luxury that were a major scandal, considering the relative poverty of the parish clergy. The hierarchy supported the status quo, because almost any change would mean that their fiscal, political, and social privileges would be curtailed. They joined with the nobles of the Parisian and provincial parliaments in condemning all writings that called for change or in other ways seemed subversive.

Knowledge of almost any kind acted to undermine the church's authority and that of the reactionary establishment. For its part, the establishment responded to threats against its power with increasing repression. To speak the truth was the height of folly, for doing so might well have been a proclamation of one's own death warrant. Safety lay in ignorance. Yet despite this, most literate persons were fascinated by those with the courage to speak out against crown and bishop, and they sought out pamphlets and books written by anyone who proclaimed plans for the reform of society on the basis of reason, decency, tolerance, freedom, and utility.

Among the leaders in the movement for Enlightenment were philosophers such as René Descartes, Jean Jacques Rousseau, Voltaire, and Denis Diderot, whose encyclopedia became a center for such intellectual protest. These authors wrote about the need for social and personal reforms based on human and worldly goals, and directed their wrath toward the various malpractices of the religious and governmental institutions.

Their writings greatly appealed to the talented members of the middle classes, who were blocked from advancement because of their social position. And, although illiterate peasants and artisans couldn't read the works of persons such as Voltaire, they too supported these beliefs. After all, they could clearly feel the pain of tax burdens and other obvious iniquities of the French monarchy and didn't have to be told about them any more than a man has to be told about his toothache.

Diderot spent the greatest part of his life compiling, editing, and writing his *Encyclopédie ou Dictionnaire Raisonné des Sciences, des Arts, et des Métiers* ("Encyclopedia or Systematic Dictionary of the Sciences, the Arts, and the Professions"), although he also wrote major works in philosophy, art and literary criticism, some novels and plays, and even works on mathematics. His last project, which remains only as a mass of notes and partially written fragments, was to be a book on the elements of physiology.

In the long run, his encyclopedia demonstrated the power of the written word in times of great political ferment. As each volume was published, it became another revolutionary tool in conveying the vital information needed to bring about the destruction of the decadent government and supporting church.

Diderot once claimed that he had knowledge of every learned subject. And he probably wasn't exaggerating. He understood mathematics, technology, music, painting, sculpture, medicine, politics, education, and economics equally well. He made a decisive contribution to almost every field he touched. He redirected aesthetics and art criticism, was instrumental in changing the face of the theater, and designed some of the first experimental novels. He also had enough mastery of the newly developing field of biology to inject impressive insights into its tasks and methods.

He was born in the ancient city of Langres, near Chaumont, France, in 1713. His mother was the daughter of a tanner, and his father, Didier Diderot, was a cutler whose reputation for fine work brought many orders for such exacting instruments as surgeons' knives. The parents sent their son to a Jesuit school and for a time the boy planned to enter the priesthood. After graduation, he worked briefly with his father but then left for Paris where, he told his father, he intended to study law. When the father later discovered that his son was not in school at all but was wasting his time in the streets and cafés, he cut off all support to the lad.

Diderot became a Parisian bohemian, dressing in rags and living in a garret. All the money he occasionally earned came from ghostwriting. It was at this time that he learned English and gained some income translating English into French. One of the commissions he earned was for six sermons to be delivered by an inarticulate missionary about to go to the Portuguese colonies.

Diderot particularly wanted to discover all the secrets painstakingly concealed by ignorance, hypocrisy, and falsehood. He wished to bring them to light and expose them to public view. In one of his books, *The Nun*, he attacked the then-common practice of abandoning unwanted daughters to a convent, where they were doomed to lives of inane sterility. In his *Philosophical Thoughts* he argued from a deist position that a religion of humanity and reason is the best for humankind. His youthful and near-pornographic novel, *The Indiscreet Jewels*, popularized the sensationalist psychology of John Locke, concluding that a man will fall prey to boredom if he doesn't constantly renew his sensations through a rapid sequence of pleasures and surprises.

Diderot was at his best in the books he wrote in the form of lively conversations. One of these, *Dream of d'Alembert*, is an imaginary exchange between d'Alembert, his mistress, and Dr. Bordeau, a man of wit, wisdom, and prescience. Through their discourse the three characters sketch a vision of the universe in evolution with its matter pulsing with consciousness. They oppose this to the drab world of Newtonian physics that contains only bodies in constant motion. Another book of conversation, *Rameau's Nephew*, is a satire in which the main character is the half-genius, half-vagabond relative of the French musician Jean-Philippe Rameau. In this work, Diderot raises the question of whether the nephew is now a clown and parasite because of his own faults or because of the faults of a society that has cast him into that role.

Like many of those who supported the Enlightenment, Diderot sensed the need to put all the knowledge from a single enlightened mind, or group of enlightened minds in communion with each other, into one written work — an encyclopedia — that might be small enough to be owned and read by any individual. On the basis of such knowledge, he hoped for an advance in the social sciences and in social planning, one that would parallel the very rapid development in physics that occurred after Newton put forth his theory of gravitation.

Diderot strongly supported experimental methods in philosophy and science, as advocated by Francis Bacon. He was a philosophical materialist in that he believed nature was in a state of constant change and all thought developed from movements and changes in matter. His views on the subject, however, were somewhat vague, as were his religious opinions. At times he took an atheist position; at other times a deist one, believing that God existed independently of the world and took no interest in it. But he later suggested that all of nature was indeed God.

Diderot's entry into the field of compiling an encyclopedia was facilitated by his ability to translate English into French. He was hired, in an advisory capacity, to work with the translators of Ephraim Chambers' *Cyclopaedia, or a Universal Dictionary of Arts and Sciences*, which was announced for publication by the Parisian printer André Le Breton. Le Breton earlier had obtained the rights to a translation of Chambers' work through John Mills, an English bank clerk, but the two quarreled and Mills returned to England assuming that Le Breton would fail in the project. Le Breton, however, hired a well-known mathematician named Jean-le-Rond d'Alembert and Abbé Jean-Paul de Gua de Malves to work on the translation. The latter recommended that Diderot be included among the editors.

The very idea of a French translation of an English encyclopedia was a novelty. A number of French encyclopedias had long before been translated into English, for no one doubted the superiority of French scholarship. But who on the continent of Europe would think an English encyclopedia worth translating, or even reading for that matter. Yet Chambers' *Cyclopaedia* was a masterpiece among reference works of the time. It was well written, included the best of the day's science, was alphabetically arranged, and easy to read because of its extensive cross-references. Its sales also were proving to be a bookseller's delight. It already had been printed in five editions in England, and Le Breton thought it likely that sales would be just as good in France.

Le Breton little realized that it no longer would be a simple matter of translation once he brought d'Alembert and Diderot into the project (Abbé de Malves left at an early stage). The two editors, in 1747, immediately began to design a completely new and better encyclopedia, one of the best examples ever of what is possible in such a multivolumed set of books. What was intended to be no more than an adaptation of the two-volume *Cyclopaedia* became a large reference work of many volumes that leveled criticism at the government, championed the Enlightenment, directed satirical jibes at the Calvinist clergy in Geneva, and supported rational skepticism in religion.

Diderot and d'Alembert used Francis Bacon's classification of knowledge as their model. They followed Bacon's advice in asking each of their contributors to view the specific topic to which they were assigned as a part of the whole field of human knowledge. In fact, they were so tied to Bacon's encyclopedic concepts that critics of the *Encyclopédie* charged them with plagiarism of Bacon. To this Diderot wrote a reply outlining the places where the *Encyclopédie* departed from Bacon's system of organization. Diderot and d'Alembert also acknowledged their indebtedness to Pierre Bayle and his *Dictionnaire Historique et Critique*, which also played a part in blazing the trail for free and open exposition of ideas.

Diderot believed a good encyclopedia ought to have "the character of changing the general way of thinking." And d'Alembert stated that the editors were going to provide a work that could be consulted on all matters of the arts and sciences, a work for both those who teach others and for those who teach themselves.

The contributors they assembled for the task were at first a relatively unknown group of writers, with the exception of Rousseau and Baron d'Holbach. But, as fame of the early volumes of the *Encyclopédie* spread, due in part to attacks by its critics, many noted experts were attracted to contribute articles for its pages. Voltaire, Turgot, Quesnay, Necker, Montesquieu, Buffon, Euler, and Condorcet all wrote for the *Encyclopédie*. Eventually, the name of nearly every person who at that time was making literary history in France found its way onto the list of the 160 contributors.

Diderot and d'Alembert used three methods to maintain the relationship of individual articles to the whole work. In the first volume was a chart of their system of knowledge (basically the one developed by Bacon). Then, after each entry title, the editors inserted some indication of where that particular article fit into the general scheme of knowledge. Finally, there were extensive cross-references at the end of each article and within it to other parts of the *Encyclopédie*. As Diderot explained in his entry on encyclopedias, apart from the more obvious references to other headings, which might be expected, cross-references indicating some not-so-obvious relationships also were included.

Diderot set out to remedy one of the major criticisms leveled against Chambers' *Cyclopaedia*— that the articles on trades and industries came from books rather than from observation and experience. Thus Diderot spent a great deal of time in the workshops, examining each machine with care. Whenever possible, he even had the workers dismantle a machine and put it together again while he watched. He learned to work the machines himself and even to master such complicated tools as stocking and cut-velvet looms.

He used technology as a way to inject his rational outlook into the *Encyclopédie* as a whole. In today's world, dominated by the triumph of science, it may be difficult to understand how pictures and descriptions of machines could have had such a revolutionary impact, but we must remember that this was a time when technology and science were held in mean repute. The artisan was considered a fool of the lower classes, with nothing but sweat to contribute to society. Most workers themselves hardly knew or seemed to care about the purpose of their individual operations in the overall manufacturing process other than to make a living.

The arrangement of the *Encyclopédie* was such that different trades and industries were classified into a recognizable pattern. The manufacture of mirrors, for example, was entered as part of the glassware industry, which in turn was listed as one of the extractive industries. Cloth dyeing was related to the science of chemistry, and metalworking was seen in its geological context. Diderot unraveled the folklore of the trades and translated their special languages so that every literate Frenchman could see how a mason erected a stone wall or how iron was smelted to make cannons.

The illustrations, which eventually numbered 2,900 plates, were not merely drawings of machines and workers in action. They were carefully designed to show all the inner workings of the equipment, with detailed cutaways and exploded sections keyed by alphabet letters to the text. Still today they represent models of how good industrial illustrations can be made. For a single machine there was first an overall drawing of it in action. Then there were two sections of it at right angles, one lengthwise and the other crosswise. Next were cutaways of the essential parts of the machine and, finally, drawings of the individual pieces: the screws, nuts, levers, and so forth.

By taking craftsmanship seriously for the first time, Diderot helped set in motion the downfall of the royal family and the rigid class system. Suddenly, in the pages of the *Encyclopédie*, every person became the equal of every other, because they had access to the technical and social know-how of the technicians as well as the scholars of the educated classes. No longer could the few claim the sole right of ruling the nation when Diderot had given a clear picture of how power was maintained and had exploded the religious and social myths that kept people in a condition of servitude.

The nobility sensed the import of the *Encyclopédie* in this way. They castigated it as chaos, nothingness, a work of disorder and destruction, and the gospel of Satan. Pope Clement XIII condemned the work from Rome, and after the French Revolution and its attendant growth of conservative reaction in England, we find Diderot's encyclopedia denounced there in the supplement to the third edition of the *Encyclopaedia Britannica*. The editor calls it "that pestiferous work" in his dedication to King George III, and goes on to say, "It has been accused, and justly accused, of having disseminated, far and wide, the seeds of Anarchy and Atheism."

Opponents of the *Encyclopédie* tried to block the path of the editors and publisher at every stage of its production. Even before the first volume went to press, Diderot was arrested and imprisoned at Vincennes. He was held in a cell for 28 days, and then was confined within the walls of the castle for yet another three months and ten days. The charges against him related to some of his other writings, but their effect was to delay his work on the great encyclopedia. After the completion of the first few volumes, d'Alembert disassociated himself from the project partly because he was ambitious for social status but mostly because he feared the wrath of the power structure. This left Diderot as the sole editor from 1758 to 1772. It probably was due only to his stubborn courage that this great work, reflecting revolutionary and radical political views and anticlerical sentiment, finally was completed after 25 years of untiring labor.

When volume eight was on the press, in 1759, the government ordered Le Breton to stop publication. Later, the police seized 6,000 volumes of a reprint and walled these up in the Bastille. Diderot was secretly warned to hide his papers before they could be confiscated as well. Le Breton eventually was able to obtain private permission to go on printing, but he was under strict orders not to release any part of the work until the whole was finished. Seven years later Le Breton himself was arrested and put in the Bastille for eight days, and the government ordered all subscribers to turn in their copies of the *Encyclopédie* so that they might be destroyed.

Voltaire tells an interesting story about a dinner party given by King Louis XV that took place during this period of the encyclopedia's suppression. An argument developed among the guests over the composition of gunpowder. Madame de Pompadour, the king's mistress, pointed out that she not only had no idea of how gunpowder was made but she didn't even know how her rouge or silk stockings were produced. The duc de la Vallière then said that he regretted the order by the king banning the *Encyclopédie*, which would undoubtedly contain all this information. The king replied that, although he had not actually seen the *Encyclopédie*, he had been assured it was most dangerous. He agreed, however, to examine it and see for himself. The king sent for a copy, and the servants with difficulty finally found a number of volumes. In these, of course, were descriptions of how to make gunpowder, rouge, and silk stockings. Despite this incident, the king maintained his pigheaded stance and refused to recall his order banning the work.

Irony, innuendo, and indirection proved to be the most effective tools for circumventing censorship of the encyclopedia. Cross-references also were effective in eluding the censor's wrath. For example, the reader of Diderot's article on Belbuch, one of the many gods of the Vandals, was referred by cross-reference to an article on immorality. The reader who turned to this second article would get Diderot's deist viewpoint, while the censor, having only one volume in hand for review, missed the seditious point.

Comments on injustice to the poor were hidden in articles on such things as salt. The word "Fornication" was inserted as a term in theology. The first seven volumes of text had been officially reviewed and passed by the censor. The last ten were not. These had to be secretly printed under a false imprint. The total work encompassed 35 volumes, making it the largest encyclopedia in Europe. Besides the 17 volumes of text, there were four supplementary volumes of text, 11 volumes of illustration plates, one supplementary volume of plates, and a two-volume index.

When the entire work was nearly finished, Diderot accidentally discovered that Le Breton was making changes in the text, undoubtedly to avoid the punishment he knew would visit him if the work was printed as Diderot wished. Le Breton made these changes only on proofs that Diderot had already corrected. He thus was able to hide them from Diderot, who naturally assumed that the corrected proofs were the final versions. Because most of the original manuscripts had been destroyed by the time Diderot made this discovery, there was no way to repair the damage. Diderot was in a state of rage, frenzy, and despair. Only with great difficulty was the *Encyclopédie* finished under his editorship.

In fairness to Le Breton it should be pointed out that his changes were not as great as Diderot supposed. Diderot's blind fury at what he considered an unforgivable act caused him to exaggerate the extent of the damage. We know this because a set of 284 *Encyclopédie* page proofs were found in Russia in the 1930s. They were part of Diderot's library that had been sold to Catherine the Great of Russia at a time when Diderot desperately needed money. The pages indicate the kind of alterations Le Breton made. Even though this is a small part of the total number of pages Le Breton altered, the analysis shows that his changes were quite sensible in that they enabled the work to be printed and sold. Otherwise both Diderot and Le Breton, as well as some of the contributors, probably would have rotted for the rest of their lives in the Bastille.

Diderot's writings in the *Encyclopédie* and elsewhere not only influenced the climate of France, they left their mark on German intellectual giants such as Lessing, Goethe, and Hegel as well. Marxists claim Diderot as a forerunner of Karl Marx. Freudians point to his influence on Sigmund Freud, and evolutionists say he anticipated Charles Darwin.

Diderot died in 1784, just six years after Rousseau and Voltaire, with whose names he is inextricably linked as a leader of the Enlightenment. Ten years later, during the French Revolution, Diderot's son-in-law, Nicholas Corroillon de Vandeul, was arrested and put in the St. Lazare prison because he was an aristocrat. His wife, Marie Angélique, the only child of Diderot, appealed to the members of the Committee for Public Safety for her husband's freedom. Her appeal was leveled on the basis of her father's *Encyclopédie*. She pointed out that this had been one of the precursors of the Revolution. The Republicans recognized the logic of her argument and released her husband, clear proof of the revolutionary impact produced by Diderot's banned work.

11. Organizing Knowledge

The problem of finding an exact item of desired information among a mass of stored data is certainly not new, although today's magnitude of data may be. More than 5,000 years ago the Assyrians tried to deal with this problem by inscribing notations on their clay cylinders in characters so small that a magnifying glass is needed to read them. The Sumerians devised a kind of index for their clay tablets. They covered their cuneiform texts with a thin layer of clay on which they inscribed an identifying code. After doing this, they rebaked the whole clay tablet. Then they merely had to scan the coded notations to find the wanted text. Once a particular item had been located, they broke off the thin shell of clay to uncover the inscriptions underneath.

As collections of books and other materials in libraries have grown in number, the problem of identifying the contents of each volume has expanded proportionally. Various methods for arranging books and creating catalogs for them have been applied to ease the process of locating individual titles. After all, arranging books by size or the color of their bindings accomplishes little. Yet finding needed titles in any library can still be a test of fortitude and perseverance.

The golden age of libraries in Europe is considered to be sometime between the 1600s and 1700s, when most of the great collections of books were begun. The Bodleian Library at Oxford was set up by Sir Thomas Bodley in the late 1500s. Today it ranks as Great Britain's second largest. The library of the British Museum, the country's largest, was established in 1759. The Mazarine Library in Paris was founded by Jules Cardinal Mazarin in 1643, while the National Central Library in Italy, based on the book collection of Antonio Magliabecci, was begun in 1714.

Frederick William, ruler of the province of Brandenburg, set up a library in 1661 that became, in turn, the Royal Library, the Prussian State Library, and the German State Library. One of the chief libraries in Russia is the M. E. Saltykov-Shchedrin State Public Library of St. Petersburg, set up by Empress Catherine the Great in the late 1700s. Added to these are the Royal

Library of Denmark, founded in 1657; the National Library of Spain, founded in 1711; the National Library of Portugal, founded in 1796; and many other such institutions that got their start during this golden age.

None of these, at first, were free libraries, and the books they housed were so expensive that many were attached to chains to protect them from theft. Books could be borrowed and taken from the institution only after the borrower guaranteed their return by depositing money or goods to cover the book's cost. This accounts for the following paragraph from the three-paragraph entry titled "LIBRARY" that is found in first edition of the *Encyclopaedia Britannica*, published in Scotland between 1768 and 1771. It reads: "In Edinburgh there is a good library belonging to the university, well fortified with books; which are kept in good order, and cloistered up with wire-doors, that none but the keeper can open, and are now lent out only upon consignation of the price; a method much more commodious than the multitude of chains used in other libraries."

The first American library, the Harvard Library, goes back to the very formation of European colonies in the New World. It was established in 1638, only 31 years after the first permanent settlement at Jamestown. Its collection of books began with a gift of volumes and money for the newly established school in Newtowne, Massachusetts, from clergyman John Harvard. The library was such an important addition (400 books in all) that the school's name was promptly changed to Harvard and the town's name to Cambridge in honor of the institution in England that trained John Harvard. Such was the power of intellectual achievement in colonial culture.

The Harvard Library was small in comparison to some of the private libraries owned by various individuals in the colonies. As early as 1640, Governor John Winthrop, Jr., of Connecticut had a collection of books that numbered more than 1,000 volumes. Rev. William Brewster, one of the Pilgrim fathers, left a private library of more than 400 volumes when he died in 1643. But the largest library in colonial times was that of Cotton Mather. It reached some 4,000 volumes before his death in 1728. His father, Increase Mather, had owned 675 books, but most of these were destroyed by fire in 1676. Both of the Mather libraries were filled with theological works, although there also were books on history, geography, philosophy, and science. Neither of them owned any works of fiction, poetry, or drama.

Benjamin Franklin, as an experiment, started the Library Company of Philadelphia in 1731, and it became one of the first successful efforts to make books available to everyone. It was a subscription library in which members paid dues that were used to buy books. The members could then borrow the books free of charge. This library today still owns the original set of books purchased by the members and houses them along with volumes donated by Thomas Jefferson, William Penn, and George Washington.

The modern free-circulating library, supported by taxes and individual donations, wasn't known until about 1850. A few such libraries had been set up in various towns in England before that time, but the movement there toward free libraries didn't expand until after Parliament passed the Public Libraries Act of 1850. In America such libraries developed at much the same time, although not primarily because of legislation. The incentive here was the American ideal of having free public schooling available for every child.

The American village that pioneered the establishment of free public library service was Peterborough, New Hampshire. The participants at a town meeting, in 1833, decided to allocate part of their annual State Library Fund for the purchase of books for a free library. Previously this fund had gone entirely to support the local school. Individuals also donated books to the Peterborough library, which was housed in a store and managed by the local postmaster. By 1837 this library had 465 volumes, mostly on religion, history, and biography.

The Peterborough model was subsequently followed elsewhere in New England, and in 1849 the New Hampshire legislature took a lead in passing a law that authorized towns to appropriate money for the establishment and maintenance of public libraries, if they so wished. Massachusetts enacted a similar law in 1851, and Maine passed one in 1854.

The tax money now funneled into libraries was sufficient to maintain them and to allow for the purchase of a few books. But the erection of library buildings and the endowment of large collections must be credited to persons such as Andrew Carnegie, the Scottish immigrant who made millions in the steel industry. In 1881 he bestowed upon the city of Pittsburgh the gift of a library building to be used by the steelworkers who lived there. By 1920 Carnegie had provided financial aid toward the construction of more than 2,500 library buildings in the United States, Canada, and Great Britain.

As the number of books increased in these early libraries, it became more urgent that some rational system be devised for cataloging them. Disorganized knowledge is of almost as little value as no knowledge at all. Thomas Jefferson, for his own library, had adopted a plan devised by Francis Bacon in 1605. This classified knowledge into three large divisions: history, poetry, and philosophy. After Jefferson's books were purchased for the Library of Congress, this classification system remained in use there, with some modifications, until the end of the nineteenth century.

The American librarian, Melvil Dewey, devised the Dewey decimal system in 1876, a system still used in many libraries throughout the world. This system divides books into ten main categories, each represented by a three-digit number ranging from 000 to 999. Each of the ten main groups is further divided into more specialized fields. For example, group 300-399, the

Social Sciences, is subdivided into such units as economics, sociology, civics, law, education, vocations, and customs. When a classification needs further distinction, decimals are used. Thus books on useful insects are grouped under 638, while a book on beekeeping might be designated 638.1.

Dewey's passion for organization was apparent even in his childhood when, as a cousin remembered, "It was his delight to arrange his mother's pantry, systematizing and classifying its contents." He was a practical man and claimed that "everywhere theory and accuracy have yielded to practical usefulness." Certainly this is the case with his decimal system, for although many of his classifications are considered badly arranged by today's standards, they have served "practical usefulness" in many libraries for more than 100 years.

Other important methods of book classification include the Library of Congress classification scheme drawn up by Herbert Putnam in 1897. Although based in some respects on the Dewey decimal system, it classifies books into 21 major divisions with numerous subdivisions rather than Dewey's ten, and it was explicitly designed to meet the particular needs of that library's huge collection of books. This Library of Congress system also has been adopted by many research and university libraries throughout the world. An elaborate expansion of the Dewey method is the Universal decimal classification, which uses various symbols in addition to the numbers employed by Dewey to create long and expressive notations for particular documents. This system was developed by Paul Otlet and Henri la Fontaine in France and has been adopted by the International Organization for Standardization, which has ensured its worldwide use. Finally, there is a system called colon classification designed by S. R. Ranganthan of India. This orders subjects by their uses and relations indicated by numbers divided by a colon. The system primarily is used today in India.

Organizing other materials, particularly magazine and newspaper articles, was a problem of even greater urgency. The subject matter in magazine and newspaper articles is almost never revealed by the publication titles, as subjects are by book titles. One of the first acceptable indexes for periodicals was that designed, in 1847, by student-librarian John Edmands to help his fellow students at Yale University find debating material. The Edmands index was expanded and shortly afterward published by William Frederick Poole. In 1876 Poole produced a revised edition of this index at the suggestion of the American Library Association. Still another revision was printed in 1882, covering periodical literature that had appeared between 1802 and 1881. Supplements carried the index through 1906, and the *Reader's Guide to Periodical Literature*, now published annually, brings the Poole indexing service up to the present day.

Another problem for the library archivist is the mass of duplication that clutters bookshelves and fills library warehouses. On the subject of dogs as pets, for example, there are hundreds of different books. They differ only in style of writing and types of pictures. But the contents of these books so duplicate one another that few dog lovers will read more than a dozen of them without retreating in utter boredom.

The same can be said of most other fields of knowledge. There are dozens and dozens of books on the basic principles of atomic energy. One repeats the information found in another. But, while new facts are added to this field of physics every few weeks, these basic books, once published, include none of these new developments. They merely retread old ground. And the same can be said of books on geometry, the Civil War, the life of Lincoln, on reupholstering furniture, and on and on. One wonders if it is wise to store these hundreds of redundant texts in a single library.

The current information explosion, in fact, is probably not so much a matter of adding new ideas and concepts to the repositories of knowledge as it is a matter of piling up duplicate materials in new packages. More bad books and papers only make it harder to find good ones. As mathematician Norbert Weiner once put it during a moment of disgust over the mass of literature reaching his desk, "Keep the monkeys away from the typewriters!"

The solution to the problem of duplication, however, is not one of purging the library shelves. Within each of the hundreds of books on a single subject there is usually at least one gem of knowledge despite, the fact that much of the rest of the material might be considered waste paper. This one gem is probably enough to justify each volume's right to shelf space. So, despite the problem of the sheer bulk of data, libraries undoubtedly will continue to preserve more knowledge than is necessary, just in case the superfluous books and papers contain a unique nugget of information that someone will someday need.

The dream of having a universal compendium of all the most important knowledge located within easy reach on a single shelf has powered the development of encyclopedias. This dream is, of course, utopian, but it has long intrigued librarians and other craftspersons in the field of knowledge. Here, too, one of the primary problems has been that of organization.

Broadly speaking, three methods have been adopted by encyclopedists for their work: the systematic method, the alphabetical method using broad subjects, and the alphabetical method using specific subjects.

Advocates of the systematic method, which predominated for hundreds of years, were greatly influenced in their various arrangements by the ferment among biologists over plant and animal classifications. Thus, around the same time that Carolus Linnaeus (1707–1778) began to separate animals and plants according to anatomical structure and group them by species, genus, and other ascending categories, encyclopedists began to experiment with ways of arranging their subject matter in similar upside-down pyramid fashions, with overarching general categories and subdivisions, all the way down to specific topics.

It is interesting to imagine how different our understanding of the world might be today had Linnaeus classified all of the animals by function, as some of the early scientists tried to do, rather than by bone structure. Bats, birds, and many insects might be in the same class, while men, ducks, and kangaroos would form another group. Or, he might have classified animals by the space they occupy, putting flying squirrels and butterflies together, pairing sharks and seals, and mountain goats and mountain gorillas. It may seem odd to seriously suggest that these arrangements would have been logical, but such classifications actually were proposed during some of the struggles that took place before the present scheme of biological classification was standardized.

Unlike the advocates of the systematic method, those championing the alphabetical method were influenced by dictionaries. In fact, dictionaries were so closely related to the development of modern encyclopedias that even today some one-volume encyclopedias may be called dictionaries. No dictionary, however, is ever mistaken for an encyclopedia. Over time the alphabetical arrangement has become the preferred method, so much so that it is difficult to market an encyclopedia that is arranged in any other way, although a few still retain the systematic form.

In recent years the *Encyclopaedia Britannica* has attempted to combine both types of arrangement, in the hope of meeting all people's needs. The 15th edition (published in 1974) consists of 30 volumes divided into three parts, each designated for a different purpose. The problem with this encyclopedia's arrangement, of course, is that proper use of the set requires much flipping from one volume to another and the mastery of more instructions than are needed to set up a computer program.

The purpose for which an encyclopedia is designed has a great deal to do with the way its text is arranged. If the encyclopedia is to be a means for quick reference, its arrangement must allow easy access and speed in finding material. If it is seen essentially as a starting point from which the browser can embark on a voyage of discovery, it must provide the basic structures for further education.

Ancient and medieval encyclopedias were invariably arranged in a systematic way because their compilers planned them as educational tools. One of the first alphabetically arranged encyclopedias was the seven-volume *Biblioteca Universale Sacro-Profano* ("Universal Reference to the Sacred and Profane") by Vincenzo Maria Coronelli, a Franciscan friar. He published the first volume in 1701. This was followed in 1704 by John Harris' *Lexicon Technicum* (see chapter 6), which used the same method. After this, more and more encyclopedists adopted the alphabetic method. It was popular because of its ease of use for reference purposes. However, this arrangement in no sense eliminates the need for an index, because at least 100 times as many words as important as the subject-entry words can be found in any encyclopedia. The reader who looks for information only under an entry word forfeits access to the great bulk of other reference data in the entire set.

Alphabetical arrangements are particularly handy for the publisher when it comes to making editorial revisions. If a new archaeological discovery is located in the land that once formed the ancient empire of Chaldea, the new information can be inserted in the C volume entry "Chaldea," and the paragraphs in the surrounding articles — "Chalet" and "Chalcopyrite" (a type of copper ore) — can be shortened or dropped entirely to make space for the new material. Such a revision is much more difficult to make when all references to Chaldea occur in long articles on ancient history or archaeology.

But the mark of an alphabetically arranged encyclopedia is its fragmentation. Looking up information in this way tears human knowledge into little pieces, something that appalled the writer Samuel Taylor Coleridge (chapter 12), who cried out against such "an arrangement determined by the accident of initial letters." Opponents of this system argue that fragmentation leads to much repetition of basic information. For example, each time a specific animal is listed, redundant information will appear under the entries of every other species in that genus.

The use of an elaborate cross-reference system is the only way an alphabetically arranged encyclopedia can maintain continuity of knowledge. Such a cross-reference system directs the reader's attention to related and additional information about particular entries in other parts of the work. Pierre Bayle used cross-references most efficiently in his *Dictionnaire Historique et Critique* (chapter 6). But the practice of including them in earlier encyclopedias goes all the way back to Domenico Bandini's *Fons Memorabilium Universi* ("Fountain of the Memorable Universe") (c. 1400). In modern times the German *Brockhaus* encyclopedia, compiled by Friederich Brockhaus, introduced an ingenious system of arrows for its cross-references rather than the common "see also."

The alphabetically arranged encyclopedia has been attacked from many quarters. The Austrian sociologist Otto Neurath, in 1937, suggested that any new encyclopedia of science should be designed like an onion, with the different layers of knowledge surrounding the "heart," or foundation, of unified science. The British novelist H. G. Wells said much the same thing, also in 1937. As he put it, an encyclopedia should not be "a miscellany, but a concentration, a clarification, and a synthesis."

Both men were insisting on a return to the systematically arranged ency-clopedia, which has always been the one loved by scholars. Such an arrange-ment is somewhat related to the way we learn things. We study history, not individual events of single battles; biology, not koala bears or eucalyptus trees. We need a broad construct if we are to learn. Otherwise, the single events and specific things have no meaning. They are like building blocks that can't be stacked if you have no concept of a building. Even the proverbial "man with a grasshopper mind" relates images in his rapidly changing thought processes to some broader picture. He visualizes sonnets and limericks as part of the field of poetry, and poetry as part of the field of literature. The sys-tematic encyclopedia arrangement attempts to preserve such connections, moving from the broadest categories down to the specific parts.

But the encyclopedia user who is looking for particular information without knowing under which general category it falls is likely to be lost at sea in such an encyclopedia. How do you find out what indium is if you don't know it is a chemical element? Even if you know this, do you look for it under the article on chemistry, metallurgy, or basic elements?

Furthermore, no consensus has been reached on which systematic arrangement is best. So each systematic encyclopedia may be quite different from the others. In one systematically arranged encyclopedia, Francis Bacon may be found in the article on philosophy; in another, the article on English literature; in a third, the article on science; in a fourth, the article on Eliza-bethan England. There always will be a problem in determining what to do with material that needs to be included in an encyclopedia but that doesn't fit neatly into the various categories of the particular system in use. When Joachim Sterck van Ringelbergh designed his encyclopedia, *Lucubrationes* ("By Candlelight") in 1541, he found it necessary to include a "miscellaneous" section to house such items. He and others soon were calling this the "chaos" section.

The systematic arrangement is based on the assumption that the user will read an entire article rather than merely leaf through the volumes. Herein lies the basic error in the design of all systematically arranged encyclopedias. No one anymore has the time or inclination to read an encyclopedia from cover to cover. The set is viewed as a reference source, not a textbook.

One of the few present-day encyclopedias that has retained the system-atic form is *Our Wonderful World*. This is a delightful set of books for grade-school children, filled with excellent and reliably up-to-date material. Yet it never has been popular because of its arrangement, a system designed "to stimulate a child's interest in learning." The arrangement is thematic, with five sections to hold all the data: Man, Man's Environment, Its Control, Man's Relation to Man, and His Cultural Relations. To the purchaser who expects to find specific material without having to use the separate dictionary, *Our Wonderful World* appears to be quite sloppy.

The first acceptable indexes for encyclopedias didn't appear until the 1830s, although the first index placed in an encyclopedia was that by Antonio Zara, the bishop of Petina, who completed his *Anatomia Igeniorum et Scientiarum,* ("Anatomy of Talents and Sciences"), in 1614. An index also was used by Johann Jacob Hoffmann in 1677 for his *Lexicon Universale* (chapter 6).

Ideally, the index will include all the names of all the subjects to which an encyclopedia user might possibly refer. It will have entries on every illustration, map, and diagram, as well as entries on every name, topic, and idea. The articles will be clearly stated so there can be no confusion as to what they designate. For example, the word "seal" can refer to an animal or something applied to a document. The word presents no difficulty within the context of an encyclopedia article. But in the index it needs to be clearly designated as "Seal, animal" or "Seal, emblem." The indexer also has to be sure that each subject is entered under both its formal and common names, where these are different. The authors Mary Ann Evans, Lucile-Aurore Dupin, and Samuel Clemens thus should be listed in the index also by their pseudonyms, George Eliot, George Sand, and Mark Twain.

In the end, the space allotted for the index—whether 15 pages, 45 pages, or 300 pages—will determine how many entries it contains. Such considerations are set by the publisher, who makes the decision on the basis of cost factors, not by the editors or indexers. Too large an index may hurt sales to people who want to purchase the subject matter in the articles and not lists of words. Yet too short an index will be quickly recognized as relatively useless by the same potential customers. So the indexer cuts or expands the size of an index to meet the needs of the set's overall design as established by the publisher, in consultation with book designers. Thus the index includes all the words that fit, not those that are necessarily needed to make the volumes complete.

12. Coleridge, Encyclopedist of the Romantic Movement

Samuel Taylor Coleridge not only tried to encompass all human knowledge, he aimed at the impossible task of designing an encyclopedia that might contain it all. His contemporaries considered him one of the greatest intellects of all time because of his sweep of knowledge, which included most philosophic, poetic, scientific, religious, and political matters. Novelist Thomas de Quincey called him "the largest and most spacious intellect in my judgment that ever yet existed among men." The poet Wordsworth said he was "the most wonderful man I have ever known," and essayist Charles Lamb said, "Never saw I his likeness, nor probably the world can see again."

It might be wise to forgive these enthusiasts for their hyperbole. After all, it was a romantic age, and Coleridge himself was one of the great romantics. The romantics as a group rejected the restricting social conventions and unjust political rules of the times in which they lived. They saw the industrial revolution as a happening that stifled the "free spirit" and put chains on one's creative powers. They argued that creative impulses work best when the imagination is unrestrained. With a broad, all-encompassing approach they pursued the ancient and profound mysteries of Egypt and Babylon as well as the irrational wisdom of the Orient in the hope of preserving all the best of past and present culture.

They saw history not in terms of movements and events, but in terms of individuals, persons such as Leonardo DaVinci, Johann Sebastian Bach, and William Shakespeare, who gave themselves for the advancement of all. The romantics also were humanitarians who revolted against the world they lived in because of its commercialism, mechanical outlook, and standardization of culture. To them, the medieval world was a golden age for the laboring man, an age snuffed out by modern capitalism with its smokestack pollution. Jean Jacques Rousseau, one of the formulators of romantic philosophy, talked of the ideal of the free social man. He believed that people are naturally good, but that they have been corrupted by the institutions of civilization.

Coleridge was one who most thrived in the eighteenth-century environment of romantic ideals and imagery. He had a brilliant mind and a gift for poetic statement. Although his life included much pain and loneliness, he was greatly revered by others and almost single-handedly established the new standards for poetry that are credited to the romantic age as a whole.

Coleridge was born in 1772 at Ottery St. Mary in Devonshire, England, the youngest of 13 children born to the family of a liberal clergyman. Because he was the youngest and had great mental precocity, his brothers subjected him to considerable teasing. This, combined with a certain degree of physical awkwardness, set him apart from his siblings, and he spent most of his time, from the age of three, roaming alone about the fields and, at a very early age, reading. By the time he was six he already had read *The Arabian Nights*, *Robinson Crusoe*, and *Belisarius*. His father died when he was eight, and he was then sent to Christ's Church Charity School in London, which was designed for orphans and the sons of indigent clergymen. Charles Lamb was one of his schoolmates. Coleridge would not see his Devonshire home again for eight years.

On holidays, when most of the other students went home to friends or relatives, Coleridge wandered alone through the streets of London. He usually picked up one or more acquaintances on these journeys, since he possessed a genius for communicating his ideas and enthusiasm and would talk to anyone willing to listen. At 15 his passion was for Plato's philosophy, a little later it was for Virgil, and then for the new English "landscape poetry."

He was a good scholar and won academic success at Christ's Church Charity School and later at Cambridge. While attending the university, he made close friendships with two men who also would soon make their mark in British letters, William Wordsworth and Robert Southy.

Coleridge joined with Southy in a plan to found an ideal community, one that would combine the innocence of primitive society with the experience of European culture. They hoped the experiment might become the model for similar communities throughout the world, and that the world thus would be reformed and revitalized. It was a thoroughly romantic dream, comprehensive in scope, humanitarian in intent, and idealistic in outlook.

The two planners were soon aided in this project by a third poet, Robert Lovell, and by a farmer, Thomas Poole, who became perhaps the most devoted member of the group and one of Coleridge's most consistent friends. Poole has left us some details about the proposed commune. It was to be named Pantisocracy, a word meaning equal government for all, and was to be located on the banks of the Susquehanna River in the United States.

Pantisocracy would have 24 members, 12 gentlemen and 12 ladies, all of whom were to have worked together before they moved to the location so that they might know each other well. The men were to farm the land while the women did the housework and took care of the children. The would-be colonists believed that they would have to work only two or three hours a day, and that they could spend the rest of their time cultivating their minds through study and discussion. Coleridge planned to raise money for the land and ship passage to America for all the members by publishing his poetry and giving lectures. He also intended to eventually write a book on the project.

Among those attracted to the plan for establishing Pantisocracy were three daughters of a family named Fricker whom Southy had known since childhood. Soon Lovell was betrothed to Mary Fricker, Southy to Edith Fricker, and Coleridge to Sara Fricker. Coleridge married Sara in 1795 at a time when the scheme for which he had undertaken the marriage was collapsing. This marriage was never happy. It caused him increasing distress, particularly after Coleridge fell in love with Wordsworth's sister-in-law, Sara Hutchinson.

Disagreements between Coleridge and Southy undermined the designs for Pantisocracy. Coleridge learned that Southy intended to introduce domestic service into the colony and to keep his private resources as his individual property rather than putting them at the disposal of the entire group. Southy furthermore argued that they should temporarily establish the colony in Wales before going on to America, and that they should earn money privately for a period of 14 years before pooling their resources. This, Southy believed, would assure a sound financial basis. "In short," Coleridge later wrote to a friend, "we were to commence partners in a petty farming trade. This was the mouse of which the mountain Pantisocracy was at last safely delivered."

Southy finally killed the scheme when he secretly married Edith Fricker. Southy seized this opportunity to sail with his uncle to Spain in November 1975. Coleridge, however, continued to be haunted by the romantic dream of building Pantisocracy for many years thereafter.

Coleridge next turned to political journalism, publishing a radical paper called *The Watchman*. In it he printed valuable poetry, argued against warfare, and championed the abolition of the slave trade. But there was not wide enough interest to support the paper and it failed. He then considered becoming a Unitarian minister, a plan that never materialized.

His friend Thomas Poole raised money for Coleridge from among a small group of the poet's admirers, and Poole eventually prevailed upon the brothers Thomas and Josiah Wedgewood (England's most famous potter) to give Coleridge an annuity. This enabled him to travel to Germany with the Wordsworths, and there to absorb the ideas of the contemporary German philosophers. On his return to England, Coleridge translated into English two plays by the German author Friedrich Schiller.

Coleridge's role in developing the poetry of the romantic period is too well-known to be detailed here. Suffice it to say that through this poetry, and through his literary criticism, he helped to widen human consciousness and to expand the horizons of working poets. In 1798 he published *Lyrical Ballads* in collaboration with Wordsworth. This volume contained the first version of Coleridge's now-much-quoted "The Rime of the Ancient Mariner."

What is not well-known about Coleridge is that he recorded minute observations about subjective sensations that made him a remarkable forerunner of the modern science of psychology. He wrote an essay about his insights regarding learning that was to be included in the encyclopedia he was hoping to someday produce. The essay is surprisingly modern in its descriptions of how the human mind works, reading at times much like some of the research reports of the twentieth-century Gestalt psychologists.

In his essays on philosophy, he distinguished three different categories of relationships between things: those that are related by nature whether the relationships are perceived by human beings or not, those that exist only because the mind establishes them, and those that combine natural relations with humanly established relations. The first, which he named "things of the law," include all the relationships seen in natural laws, moral standards, and intellectual truths. Mechanics and astronomy are among the subjects that fit this category. The second, which he called the "relations of theory," include only those things that exist when the mind arranges them into a particular pattern to understand and control them. Disciplines included here are medicine, chemistry, and physiology. The third, called by Coleridge the "relations of fine arts," includes matters of taste and principles of the arts. Arithmetic and geometry are among these.

Such relationships, he said, are marked by union and progression. Things are not related by accident. "They are united by *ideas* either definite or instinctive." He claimed at first that all ideas are instinctive. The boy, for example, "knows that his hoop is round, and this, in after years, helps to teach him, that in a circle, all the lines drawn from the center to the circumference, are equal." Successive ideas thus generate from some need, and the process is that of progression.

The three categories of relationships that Coleridge considered to be a major advance in the philosophy of learning may appear to be of little value for most of us today. But we should take to heart his insistence on the need to develop some method or learning system that will enable us to progress from one segment of knowledge to another. According to Coleridge, the thinking person must be trained to gain the benefits of a method. One should not be as "the man who flutters about in blindness, like the bat; or is carried hither and thither, like the turtle sleeping on the wave, and fancying, because he moves, that he is in progress."

Of course, those who are engaged in serious and intentional learning eventually develop shortcuts for their own grasp of such segments of knowledge, shortcuts that suit their particular personalities and inclinations. Yet there are a few overriding principles as outlined by Coleridge that everyone will find valuable. The first is that you can learn best if you start with that which you already know and use this as the basis for moving to those things that you don't. This principle is so obvious that it is surprising how many people "flutter about in blindness" looking for answers to questions for which they have no background by which to grasp the answer, should one emerge. Another basic, yet simple, principle is that it is always best to start from general knowledge and move to the specifics.

Coleridge delivered a series of lectures at the Royal Society in London in 1808 that made him quite famous in his own lifetime. These were on the principles of poetry. In 1813 he delivered a second series of important lectures on literary criticism and successfully produced his play, *Remorse*. He was aided in this latter project by yet another poet friend, Lord Byron.

But starting about 1800 Coleridge's health began to fail. He had been taking opium to relieve the pain of rheumatism, and he now sought relief in more drugs and in travel. He claimed that his poem "Kubla Khan" came to him in the midst of an opium dream. By 1816 Coleridge had moved into the home of his physician, Dr. James Gillman, and was under the doctor's supervision from then on until his death in 1834. He never again was well, and he never could conquer his addiction to opium.

While ill, Coleridge wrote his ideas regarding his plans for an encyclopedia, an essay that eventually appeared in the first volume of the *Encyclopaedia Metropolitana*. Titled "Preliminary Treatise on Method," the essay began by stating that the primary purpose for any such work is for it to be a device that enables human beings to think methodically. He believed that his own design provided such a method for learning and that such methodizing in preparation for an encyclopedia had never been attempted before, or, if it had, was done too poorly to be recognizable.

He went on to say that what he wished to communicate by compiling an encyclopedia was the need to apply a scientific method to the process of learning. He thought his particular arrangement would do this. It would "present the circle of knowledge in its harmony" and give a "unity of design and elucidation." His method involved strict principles to connect one subject to another. All is chaos without a method, Coleridge argued, and the chaos will continue forever unless the human mind intervenes to classify and arrange that chaos. "Mere arrangement, however, is not properly methodical, but rather a preparation toward Method; as the compilation of a dictionary is a preparation for classical study."

The development of a method cannot be a spontaneous thing, he continued, but is an act of the mind, a manifestation of the intellect. The method, to be of value, must exhibit a progressive transition from one step to another, as well as basic relations between the many parts. As soon as the individual becomes trained to see not just things but the relations between things, that person then will begin to see the path that moves from one thing to the others related to it.

Successive ideas, he said, germinate from the first intuitive idea. "Thus, from the idea of a triangle, necessarily follows that of equality between the sum of its three angles, and two right angles." He furthermore pointed out that the relation between things cannot be united by accident; they are united by an idea, which can be either definite or instinctive, and that union is a progressive one.

This progression, which he calls his method, requires "a constant wakefulness of mind; so that if we wander but in a single instance from our path, we cannot reach the goal, but by retracing our steps to the point of divergency, and thence beginning our progress anew."

In terms of the state of mind to be adopted in applying his method, he said, "The habit of Method, should always be present and effective; but in order to render it so, a certain training, or education of the mind, is indispensably necessary. Events and images, the lively and spirit-stirring machinery of the external world, are like light, and air, and moisture, to the seed of the mind, which would else rot and perish. In all processes of mental evolution the objects of the senses must stimulate the mind; and the mind must in turn assimilate and digest the food which it thus receives from without."

He made a distinction between metaphysical and physical ideas, saying that the first relates to the essence of things, such as the purely geometrical idea of a circle, while the second implies their actual existence. "Thus, the laws of memory, the laws of vision, the laws of vegetation, the laws of crystallization, are all physical ideas, dependent for their accuracy, on the more or less careful observation of things actually existing."

He then gave many examples to demonstrate how people have intervened to make order out of chaos. These included mundane things such as putting order in the arrangement of the kitchen and living room, as well as the ordering process used in mathematics and physics. Even poetry, according to Coleridge, exhibits a distinct method in its rendition, a method that he illustrated with examples from Shakespeare's plays and poetry. Shakespeare, he said, "studied mankind in the *idea* of a human race; and he followed out that idea into all its varieties, by a *Method* which never failed to guide his steps aright."

Coleridge gave high praise to Francis Bacon for developing some of the basic principles of "the Scientific Method." He compared Bacon to Cicero — "the first and most eloquent advocate of philosophy"— and spoke of him as the "British Plato." Although Coleridge deplored Bacon's writing style, which he pointed out did not equal Shakespeare's, he said that the only difference between Bacon and Plato was that "the one more especially cultivated natural philosophy, the other metaphysics." Coleridge considered his own method to have made a union of the work of these two philosophers, and thus to be "a complete and genuine philosophy."

Naturally, his method, if used in an encyclopedia, would require that such a work be organized in a systematic (his term was philosophical) rather than an alphabetical arrangement. He said that this systematic arrangement would predominate and whatever alphabetical arrangement might be found, together with all references, would be only auxiliary to the rest of the text.

He envisioned the encyclopedia divided into four great sections. The first would cover the pure sciences (grammar and the forms of languages, logic, mathematics, metaphysics, morals, and theology). This section would take up two volumes. The second section, six volumes, would be devoted to the mixed and applied sciences (mechanics, hydrostatics, pneumatics, optics, astronomy, experimental philosophy including chemistry and physics, the fine arts, the useful arts such as agriculture and commerce, natural history, and applications of natural history such as anatomy and medicine). The third section, eight volumes, would cover history and biography and would include pages of maps and charts. The fourth section, eight volumes, would be used for miscellaneous and lexicographical matters such as the origins of the English language. This would be the only section that might be alphabetically arranged. He also planned to have a one-volume index that would bring the total work to 25 volumes.

Coleridge was invited to develop his ideal encyclopedia by publisher Rest Fenner, who had already printed some of Coleridge's earlier works. Fenner's associates were Thomas and Samuel Curtis. They sought out the poet and critic for this task because he was so well respected and personally knew many of the leading scholars of the age.

Because Fenner and his associates were happy to have a man of Coleridge's stature to head their project and because Coleridge was eager to put his ideas into practice, no contract was signed. Coleridge was happy to proceed even though he could foresee the great deal of drudgery that would be involved and knew he would have to give up some of his plans for other writing.

But the association did not last long. The *Encyclopaedia Metropolitana*, as imaged by Coleridge, was as much a utopian dream as Pantisocracy had been. Coleridge was too ill to leave his doctor's home, yet Fenner insisted that he move to the Camberwell district of London, where the printing presses were located. When Coleridge could not comply, Fenner appointed Thomas Curtis, his associate, as general editor. Coleridge was reassigned to be advisor and contributor.

Then, when Coleridge discovered that the publisher was making changes in his overall design, he withdrew in full from the project, and thereafter constantly described it as a fraud. Thomas Curtis, too, left the project in a short time to move to America. After this it was discovered that Fenner had earlier cheated Coleridge out of some of his book royalties, which increased the bitterness between the poet and the publisher. Thus what might have been one of the greatest encyclopedias of the century, one containing the comprehensive approach of Samuel Taylor Coleridge, was never completed. In its place, the *Encyclopaedia Metropolitana* Fenner eventually published proved to be a miserable failure. It collapsed under financial difficulties after a second edition was printed and put on the market between 1849 and 1858.

The work was issued in 28 volumes, with two for the pure sciences, eight for the applied sciences, five for history and biography, 12 for miscellaneous matters, and one for the alphabetical dictionary. There were 22,426 pages altogether with 565 illustrative plates. The second edition had more volumes but fewer pages.

The *Encyclopaedia Metropolitana* did have a number of distinguished authors represented in it besides Coleridge. It contained excellent entries by astronomer Sir John Herschel; physicist Peter Barlow; mathematicians George Peacock, Augustus de Morgan, and Charles Babbage; and Archbishop Richard Whately. The post of general editor, after Curtis departed, passed from Rev. Edward Smedley to Hugh James Rose and then to Henry John Rose.

The failure of the *Encyclopaedia Metropolitana* can be attributed to several factors. Its lack of alphabetical arrangement was confusing to a public that had by now begun to accept that system in the recently established *Encyclopaedia Britannica* and Abraham Rees's *Encyclopaedia* (1802–1820). The *Metropolitana* also took too long to complete (from 1817 to 1845) and cost much more than Fenner had estimated.

Critics sometimes have mistakenly charged the failure to Coleridge's romanticism rather than to Fenner's business sense. As one writer in the *Quarterly Review* put it, "The plan was the proposal of the poet Coleridge, and it had at least enough of a poetical character to be eminently impractical." However, the classification system developed by Coleridge enables editors today (even those engaged in publishing alphabetically arranged encyclopedias) to plan their work with a view toward a rationally assumed hierarchy of branches of knowledge.

13. The Strange History of the *Britannica*

The *Encyclopaedia Britannica*'s reputation as the best among English-language encyclopedias is probably due more to effective marketing than to content. Many people even think the *Britannica* is a British publication although it has been owned and published by Americans in Chicago since 1920. One reason for this is the continued use of the word "Britannica" in the title and the fact that the publishers have chosen to cultivate British spellings ("encyclopaedia" for encyclopedia, "honour" for honor, and "centre" for center).

In 1768 when a small pamphlet-sized booklet called the *Encyclopaedia Britannica* was first offered for sale in Edinburgh, Scotland, literate residents of that city showed almost no interest. It was thin, covered but a few pages of subject matter alphabetized under A, and was produced by a relatively unknown local printer. Its subtitle seemed to be nothing but overblown puffery — "A dictionary of arts and sciences, compiled upon a new plan, in which the different sciences and arts are digested into distinct treatises or systems."

This first booklet was followed each week by another until the 100th installment appeared. In this last one there was a description of how to bind the parts together so that they would form a complete three-volume set of books. Sales of each section helped finance the printing of subsequent parts.

Since then, the *Britannica*, or "EB," as it is fondly known, has become an institution — the oldest encyclopedia in continuous publication in the English language. It has moved from England to the United States, has been on the verge of bankruptcy four times, and has been transferred to several different ownerships, including twice with the mail-order house of Sears, Roebuck and Company. It also has been accused of English bias, American bias, heresy, and excessive religious propaganda. Two full-length books have been published to denounce it and another to defend it.

Britannica's rise to institutional giant came close on the heels of the "knowledge explosion" created by the industrial revolution. Just as printing brought encyclopedias and other books out of the monasteries so that those with money could purchase them, the new promotional techniques developed during the industrial revolution brought encyclopedias into the homes of almost every family, even those with little or no interest in reading.

The fascinating history of the *Encyclopaedia Britannica* begins when Colin Macfarquhar, a job-printer in Edinburgh, joined with Andrew Bell, an engraver of dog collars, to produce an up-to-date compendium of all knowledge. Bell was a short man, only four and a half feet tall, with a nose so embarrassingly large that he would sometimes wear a papier-mâché addition to mock those who ridiculed him. Marfarquhar was a hardheaded businessman with contempt for authority. He already had been fined for printing a Bible without the Crown's permission and for publishing a pirated edition of Lord Chesterfield's *Letters to His Son.*

The two hired 28-year-old William Smellie as their editor. Smellie, also a printer by trade, was a scholar and friend of the Scottish poet Robert Burns. But Smellie was particularly noted for his addiction to Scotch whiskey. People said Smellie, when drunk, was "a veteran in wit, genius, and bawdry, who liked to quote long poems in their original Latin."

Within two years Smellie had written and pasted together the 2,659-page set from sources such as Francis Bacon, John Locke, Benjamin Franklin, and Voltaire, all without acknowledgment. "Utility," he asserted in his preface to the pamphlet-marketed first edition, "ought to be the principal intention of every publication. Wherever this intention does not plainly appear, neither the books nor their authors have the smallest claim to the approbation of mankind."

The three-volume *Britannica* included a long description of Noah's ark, with an illustration showing how it looked afloat, as well as a terse, denigrating definition of Woman: "The female of man, See Homo." It advised that tobacco could desiccate the brain to "a little black lump consisting of mere membranes." The entry on Edinburgh was given four times as much space as the one on London. California was described as "a large country of the West Indies," and Virginia as a land that "may be extended westwards as far as we think fit." The whole work was salted with 160 excellent engravings by Bell, including a handsome, though inaccurate, map of North America.

The only section that seemed to arouse much interest was a 40-page article on midwifery. This was an explicit text on obstetrics that included several pages of Bell's engravings showing the birth of a baby in great detail. When this section of the encyclopedia appeared, there was a public outcry. King George III issued an order demanding that owners throw these pages away and that the printers destroy the engraving plates. It is somewhat surprising, in retrospect, that the king overlooked the much longer section on anatomy, an article that was just as explicit in its description of sexual organs as the midwifery one was on matters relating to birth.

After the various pamphlet-sized signatures were bound into three equal-sized volumes, the first was found to span only a tiny part of the alphabet, from AA (the name of several rivers) to BZO (a town in Morocco). Volume two covered CAABA (a temple in Mecca) to LYTHRUM (a genus in botany), and volume three went all the way through the rest of the alphabet to ZYGO-PHYLLUM (another botanical genus).

Macfarquhar and Bell conducted a persistent sales campaign, and eventually more than 3,000 people bought the first edition, enough to justify publication of a second. However, other than the slight upset over the article on midwifery, little public attention was paid to this work. The Scottish author James Boswell, who meticulously described all the intellectual doings in Edinburgh at that time, never even bothered to mention the *Britannica*.

Bell and Macfarquhar decided that the second edition should include biographies, a proposal that infuriated Smellie, who resigned the editorship in protest. He was succeeded by James Tytler, a man derisively known as "Balloon Tytler" because he had made the first balloon ascension over England. Tytler agreed to work on the second edition for an incredibly low salary, probably because he already had endured a period of misery in debtor's prison. This edition was completed in September 1784, and the encyclopedia now filled ten volumes. Again it had engravings by Bell. It also had a fascinating article on flying, written by Tytler, that gave complete working instructions for the design, building, firing, and flying of a balloon. In this article, Tytler suggested it soon would be as common for a man to call for his wings as for his boots.

Tytler's handling of American history was as faulty as Smellie's understanding of its geography. Although Tytler's edition discussed the Salem witch trials, it omitted the American Revolution that ended three years before and had been widely covered in the British press. It referred to the city of Boston, but made no mention of Philadelphia or New York. Tytler eventually emigrated to America and died in Boston in 1805.

A constant problem for the Scottish and English publishers was the illegal printing in America of pirated editions of British works. One enterprising American publisher, Thomas Dobson, did more than just copy the *Encyclopaedia Britannica* when he printed it. He rewrote sections that might be offensive to Americans and removed the word "Britannica" from the title as well as the encyclopedia's dedication to King George III. Dobson put his own signature in place of Bell's on the engravings, and sold the completed volumes at a cheaper rate than the Edinburgh publishers. Such pirating continued to plague British publishers until the United States Congress approved the international copyright law in 1891.

The third edition of the *Encyclopaedia Britannica*, which began its release in 1788, was edited by Macfarquhar and George Gleig of Stirling in Scotland, a man who was later consecrated as a bishop of the Episcopal Church of Scotland. This edition now filled 18 volumes. The fourth edition, completed in 1810, was edited by James Millar, a zoologist and chemist, but a man "slow and dilatory and not well qualified," according to the *Britannica*'s new owner and publisher, Archibald Constable. The set had been enlarged to 20 volumes. Fifth, sixth, seventh, and eighth editions followed, with the last one having 21 volumes and being put on the market in 1860.

The prestige of the *Britannica* grew with each succeeding edition, and the editors eventually were able to enlist the efforts of some of the most famous scholars in Europe as authors for their articles. Sir Walter Scott wrote on drama, David Ricardo on economics, James Mill on government and education, and Thomas Malthus on population. Harvard University President Edward Everett, the first American contributor, provided a biography of George Washington. Another contributor, Lord Rayleigh, the physicist who later won a Nobel Prize, was commissioned to write an article on light, but he missed the deadline. His article was then rescheduled under optics, which came later in the alphabetized volumes so had a later deadline, and then rescheduled again under the subject the undulating theory of light. When Rayleigh finally completed the piece, it had to be published under the entry on the wave theory of light.

The most celebrated *Britannica* was, and still is, the 24-volume ninth edition, completed in 1889. This became known as the Scholars' Edition, because of the excellent articles it contained and the fame of the authors who contributed to it. This edition included poets Matthew Arnold and Algernon Charles Swinburne, physicist Lord Kelvin, zoologist Thomas Henry Huxley, and the Russian revolutionary Peter Kropotkin. Huxley's article supported the then-unpopular theories of Charles Darwin, while Kropotkin's supported anarchism. For this and other reasons the editors, Thomas Spencer Baynes and W. Robertson Smith, felt it necessary to warn readers in their introduction that knowledge was increasing so rapidly they should be cautious in dealing with the contents.

Baynes and Smith made no attempt to simplify or popularize the articles, and many were therefore useful only to scholars. But the thorough coverage of the humanities and the brilliant literary essays made this set a unique compendium of knowledge. Many of the articles were reprinted in the later editions (all the way through the 14th), even though the information they contained had by then become hopelessly outdated.

The ninth edition was published and sold volume by volume rather than by signature sections. Each volume was reviewed in leading periodicals as it came out, much as a volume of essays might be reviewed today. The work was popular not only in England but also in America, where it helped to meet the thirst for worthwhile reading matter at a time when books filled leisure hours much as television does today.

In 1897 two hard-selling Americans, Horace E. "Hell Every Hour" Hooper and Walter M. Jackson formed a British company to market the *Encyclopaedia Britannica*. They teamed with the *Times* of London in a campaign to hawk the set at 60-percent discount rates, a campaign that incidentally helped the *Times* out of one of its own financial crises. The two Americans made the same arrangement for the tenth edition, which was basically a reprint of the ninth with 11 volumes added to update it.

There were many objections, however, to the raucous, black-type, banner headlines used in the advertising pages of the *Times*. Readers were told that they could avoid medical, household, and legal expenses by purchasing the set because: "The doctor, the carpenter, the lawyer have all gone to the *Encyclopaedia Britannica* to learn. WHY NOT GO DIRECT and save the expense of an intermediary?" One affronted member of Parliament wrote to Hooper: "You have made a damnable hubbub, sir, and an assault on my privacy with your American tactics."

But the marketing program resulted in the sale of 100,000 sets of the encyclopedia and earned the *Times* a great deal of money. An unusual feature of the campaign was the delivery of the entire set to the purchaser after a down payment of only one guinea had been made. The balance could be paid in easy monthly installments. This was a striking innovation in the publishing field. Never before had anyone been allowed to buy a set of books without paying the full price in advance. Thanks to "The *Times* Easy System of Payment," readers now could enjoy the work while they were still paying for it. Hooper and Jackson concluded their sales efforts by acquiring ownership of the *Encyclopaedia Britannica* in 1901.

Hooper was more than a master promoter. He had a genuine interest in publishing the encyclopedia. As soon as the campaign for the tenth edition was finished, he began to plan for a new and greater work. He appointed Hugh Chisholm, the former editor of the influential *St. James Gazette* and a man who had worked on the tenth edition, as the editor-in-chief of the 11th edition. It took nearly eight years to complete.

The 11th was immediately recognized as an outstanding achievement, "the Monarch of Encyclopedias," according to the American ambassador to Britain; "like the Bible," according to Hooper. Its 1,500 contributors included 166 Fellows of the Royal Society. There also were 56 presidents and secretaries of learned societies represented, 47 members of the staff of the British Museum, and many other leaders of the British intellectual establishment.

Hooper had cleverly worked out an arrangement for Cambridge University sponsorship of the encyclopedia (an arrangement the university was later to regret), after he suffered a breach with the *Times*. This gave the set an intellectual status few encyclopedias have ever achieved. The editors, apprehensive about the limitations imposed by the alphabetical arrangement of the text, provided a table of contents in which all knowledge was broken into 24 major categories, from anthropology and ethnology to sports and pastimes. Supplements to the 11th edition, which became the 12th and 13th editions, were published until 1929.

Meanwhile, philanthropist Julius Rosenwald had taken the encyclopedia to Chicago in 1920. He purchased it through his firm, Sears, Roebuck and Company. This was a near disaster for *Britannica* sales, if not for Rosenwald. The mail-order house was not the proper marketing agent of an encyclopedia, and within three years Sears lost nearly $2 million on it. They sold it back to Hooper's widow and her brother, William Cox, for a mere $265,000. Surprisingly, Sears again bought the encyclopedia in 1928 for cash and a sizable amount of Sears stock.

The 14th edition (24 volumes), which came out in 1929, marked the first attempt to popularize and Americanize the *Britannica*, which for 160 years was primarily British in content and approach. Separate editorial offices for this edition were maintained in London and New York, and the set was dedicated to both the reigning British monarch and to the president of the United States.

Yet the 14th edition suffered the fate of many enterprises launched just before the Great Depression of 1929. Although 20,000 copies were sold during the first year, sales fell precipitously until they reached a low of 4,400 sets in 1933. Economic conditions made it impractical to consider the issuance of any new edition for nearly 30 years thereafter, but each year that passed rendered more parts of the encyclopedia obsolete. Finally, a plan of continuous revision was devised in which selected articles were periodically updated for printing without changing the edition number. Thus editorial expenses could be spread over a number of years, and alterations could be adjusted to the current income from encyclopedia sales.

But because sales continued to drop under Sears' management, the encyclopedia was turned over to the University of Chicago in 1943, with William Benton, who had made a fortune as an advertising executive and a name in politics as a United States senator, putting up $100,000 for working capital. Benton could market almost anything. Within 18 months, the University of Chicago had earned more than $300,000 in royalties.

The 14th edition became increasingly fragmented because of its revisions, consisting of little more than "deferred maintenance," according to Robert M. Hutchins, who had become chairman of *Britannica*'s Board of Editors. The continuous revision process also resulted in overlapping entries and articles that contradicted each other.

Britannica salespersons, however, could still boast about the impressive list of contributors in the "new edition," even though many of them had written their articles more than 30 years earlier and some were now long deceased. New contributors were added only as the budget permitted. The sales department described the encyclopedia as "the greatest treasure of knowledge ever published.... It is truth. It is unquestionable fact." With each revised printing they repeated that "there is no edition of the *Encyclopaedia Britannica* greater than the current one," and "When you buy the *Britannica*, you are getting the best there is ... more useful in more ways to more people."

One member of the sales force in the 1940s was "Yellow Kid" Wyle, an ex-convict on parole who later authored a book in which he boasted of his exploits as "America's greatest confidence man." Only a few weeks after he joined the *Britannica* sales department, he had become the top seller for sets of the encyclopedia. He seemed to be able to persuade customers to sign contracts for the books when no one else could. But he was later fired when unsolicited manuscripts appeared in great number at the encyclopedia's editorial offices. Apparently, his sales technique involved seeking out persons with special interests in particular subjects and then telling them that the *Britannica* editorial department had selected them to write an article on that subject. Wyle implied that their article would be included in the next revision, and, "almost as an afterthought," suggested that they might want to order a set immediately. The flattered "contributor" invariably signed a contract for the encyclopedia and usually convinced friends and associates to do likewise.

Although the sales manager was upset by Yellow Kid's approach, it was not far removed from some of the methods that *Britannica*—and many other encyclopedia sales departments—had long advocated. The *Britannica* sales manager had nothing but praise for another top salesperson, Edward Noonan, who always operated in towns near colleges. Noonan's technique was to talk to the students and their professors about the encyclopedia while serving them sodas and ice cream at the local drugstore. The customers never suspected that he sold encyclopedias until he held the contract for books in front of them, pen in hand. He shared his commissions with the local druggists, who had allowed him to work at their soda fountains. Another *Britannica* salesperson of high repute was a man who sold a set to a passing motorist who had picked him up after an accident in which his car nearly went over a cliff. The book seller is remembered with awe because he kept his mind on the sale, even though he had nearly lost his life just moments before.

By the time the 15th edition appeared in 1974, the condition of the continuously revised 14th had become a scandal. Although the company announced each year that millions of words in the set were altered to bring it up to date, the actual number of word changes was considerably less. For example, in the 1983 printing the word "monastery" was used in place of "abbey," and "butterfly" and "moth" replaced "lepidoptera." Such minor revisions met the demands of the United States Copyright Office, which grants a new copyright to an updated book only when a certain percentage of its pages have been altered by at least one copy change. Yet to justify their claims for massive alterations, the publishers included in their advertised count all the words on any page on which a single word had been changed.

The disgraceful condition of the set was apparent in the fact that scholars were advising that no one use the various "new" printings for any research, librarians were sending people to the dog-eared copies of the 1929 printing rather than the later ones, and sales of subsidiary *Britannica* products — books, films, and educational tools — were surpassing those of the encyclopedia itself.

Critics pointed to the jargon and esoteric details that often cropped up in the 14th edition. They cited the fact that for 15 years an abstruse physics formula had been repeatedly printed upside down. Apparently no one noticed the mistake until the author of the article himself saw it and pointed it out.

Harvey Einbinder in his book *The Myth of the Britannica* gives a whole catalog of the errors he found in the 1963 revision of this 14th edition. That edition still contained these sentences in an article on feathers: "Swan quills are better than those from the goose, and for fine lines crow quills have been much employed. Only the five outer wing feathers of the goose are useful for writing, and of these the second and third are best." It is probable that this part of the article was written a century earlier, or at least sometime before 1884, when Lewis Waterman introduced one of the first practical fountain pens. It is difficult to imagine what type of encyclopedia reader would need such information in 1963.

Einbinder said that in many instances the problem with this edition, however, wasn't one of forgetting to delete outmoded bits of text or one of making inappropriate deletions to allow for the addition of new text, but it is one of attempting to avoid any discussion of controversial issues. He cited as one example the encyclopedia's handling of the decision to drop atomic bombs on the civilian populations of Hiroshima and Nagasaki during World War II. Two brief paragraphs in the 1963 article on atomic energy and two more, with virtually the same data, in the 75-page survey of World War II dispensed with the entire subject of atomic warfare and gave ridiculously low figures for the number of deaths that actually occurred. More accurate figures were available at the time from both United States and Japanese sources. Einbinder suggests that the underplay was motivated by the fear that the subject might be painful to most Americans.

The 15th edition of the *Encyclopaedia Britannica* proved to be an encyclopedia of a completely new design, one divided into three different parts, each with a different purpose. The three-part design was conceived by Mortimer Adler, who had earlier developed the index to the *Great Books of the Western World*, another product marketed by the *Britannica* company and one that reduced all knowledge to precisely 102 Great Ideas. Although much criticism had been leveled at Adler's index, which he called a *Synopticon*, because it so limited the rather vague and misty area of ideas which are never the same for any two people, the *Britannica* Board of Editors was enamored with Adler's design.

The plan, however, was opposed from within the *Britannica* offices by Sir William Haley, a former editor of the London *Times*, who had been hired to oversee the production of the 15th edition. Haley had served during the Second World War as director general of the British Broadcasting Corporation. He stayed at the encyclopedia for only a little over a year since he could not stomach Adler's particular organization of knowledge. He wanted a much larger encyclopedia than the 15th would become, and one containing "great articles," not Adler's "great ideas."

Under Adler's design, the first volume (called *Propaedia*) is a topical index that breaks down the contents of the other 29 alphabetical volumes into ten areas of information. The next part is a ten-volume short entry encyclopedia (*Micropaedia*) containing entries no longer than 750 words each for the reader who wants a quick answer. The 19-volume third part (*Macropaedia*) contains the major articles, some of which are almost book-length in size.

Einbinder approved this edition, but many others did not. They pointed out that the number of units presented in the first section hardly constituted a system in the strict sense of the word. Its subdivisions, such as "European Culture Since 1800" and "Visual Arts, Western," because they are imposed on the record of history to fulfill the needs of Adler's system, tend to distort the historical significance of such events.

During the creation of the 15th edition, *Britannica* pioneered the idea of using computers to edit and set type for encyclopedia pages. Although this is routinely done by most publishers today, including all the American encyclopedia producers, at that time computing was in its infancy. A special room had to be built to house the red-jacketed robots. They required dry, cool air to function properly. They also needed a special crew of technicians to feed articles onto their memory disks.

One of the many advantages of this expensive process was said to be that, at the press of a button, the computer would print out all the material on hematology that had been fed into its memory banks, or all the information it had received about the Rocky Mountains. When it was hooked to an electronic typesetter, it could produce whole books and pamphlets on command.

But the computer engineers encountered many problems in trying to make the machines work properly. In some instances it took months to iron them out. One evening, before the crew went home, the machines were activated to print a series of edited articles during the night while the offices were closed. When the crew returned the next morning, they found hundreds of printed pages, all in illegible and grammatically indecipherable Greek.

Apparently, when the machine had come to a Greek symbol in reproducing material for a physics article, it neglected to return to the normal alphabet, because a human operator had neglected to insert the proper signal into its program. The mass of printed but useless pages was the last straw for the executives at *Britannica*. The computers were moved out of their special room and junked, and the editors returned to traditional methods of editing and printing. It would be some years before the *Britannica* employed computers again — the second time successfully.

In 1986 the *Britannica* experienced one more computer problem when a worker at the encyclopedia altered portions of the set's text because he was angry about being laid off. Before leaving, he created pandemonium by doing a search and replace on the entire encyclopedia with the two words God and Allah.

The earlier ninth edition, though not easy reading for the average person, was certainly a great encyclopedia. So was the 11th, and so were parts of the 14th before it underwent the mish-mash revision process. Portions of the 15th undoubtedly are also excellent. In fact, the "Best of *Britannica*" would make a most interesting book in its own right. After all, much useful information can be gained from almost any reference work, if properly used.

But the idea that the 15th edition is "one of the great intellectual contributions in the life of modern man," as the *Britannica* sales department wants everyone to believe, isn't the case if we are to gauge the encyclopedia's past performance. One is led to wonder whether superlative statements that twist the truth beyond endurance are needed to sell sets of the *Encyclopaedia Britannica*.

14. Modern Encyclopedias Worldwide

Toward the end of Jonathan Swift's classic satire, *Gulliver's Travels* (1726), the hero comes across a professor busily creating an encyclopedia. The man has attached all known words, in their proportion of verbs, nouns, prepositions, and so forth, onto wires and levers of his own design. Whenever he gives a turn to one of the levers, a row of words appears in random order. One of the professor's assistants then transcribes onto a piece of paper each phrase that has been generated. The purpose, the professor explains to Gulliver, is to create "a complete body of all arts and sciences."

This encyclopedia-making process is just one of several "scientific pursuits" that attract Gulliver's attention at the Grand Academy of Lagado. Others include an architect working on a method for building a house from the roof downward, an agriculturalist trying to breed sheep devoid of wool, and various individuals bent on softening marble for pillows and pincushions.

The chapter is great fun, and it takes on added meaning when the reader knows that the satire was directed at the pompous scientists of the Royal Society who in Swift's work behave like inmates of Bedlam. Needless to say, those same scientists took strong exception to this section of the book when it was published.

Today we can look at this chapter with the advantage of hindsight and see its obvious shortcomings as well as its monumental insights. Swift little realized that the Royal Society would someday develop into one of the world's most important centers for scientific advance and that it would become a prototype for the collection and exchange of international scientific data. At the same time, astute readers have noted that Swift, in this chapter, depicts planets circling Mars fully a century and a half before astronomers discovered any of the planets that circled Mars. He also herein predicted the now common practice of ripening fruit in all seasons, even though Swift was poking fun at any such suggestion. He also was amused at the Lagado "scientist's" attempts to extract sunlight from cucumbers, something we now manufacture as vitamin D, although what we get from cucumbers is vitamin C.

As far as the professor's word machine is concerned, it bore a resemblance to the first computer invented by Charles Babbage a century later. The professor's method of compiling sentences foreshadowed some of the recent computer investigations in the field of transformational grammar.

The very idea that anyone might try to compile "a complete body of all arts and sciences" was not what Swift found so amusing, only the manner in which this was being done. He shared with his targets at the Royal Society the common belief that one of the legitimate aims of philosophy is the accumulation in one place of all human knowledge, or, in this case, one encyclopedia.

Over the past 2,000 years more than 2,000 encyclopedias have been designed and compiled, most of them with that purpose in mind. Some of these have been published in many editions. A collection of such books probably would fill more than two miles of shelf space if they could be assembled in one place. In this chapter and the next, we will consider a few of the most notable ones produced over the past two centuries. In this one we will deal only with those published outside of the United States.

We can begin with Germany, where the printer and bookseller David Arnold Friedrich Brockhaus (1772–1823), who preferred to be known as Friedrich Arnold Brockhaus, purchased the rights to print a new encyclopedia when he was attending the Leipzig Book Fair for the first time. Brockhaus was an imaginative and energetic person with an international outlook. He already had commissioned German translations from various Danish and English writings, and he had organized a project for the promotion of a periodical that was edited in Paris, published in Amsterdam, and printed in Leipzig.

The encyclopedia he purchased was the brainchild of Dr. Renatus Gotthelf Löbel (1767–1799) and a lawyer named Christian Wilhelm Franke (d. 1831). The two had been collecting and editing the work for several years, and two volumes of their encyclopedia had even been printed. Their intention was to fill four volumes and to include the most important information on theoretical knowledge and the fine arts then available. But Löbel died shortly after completing the text for the third volume, and though Franke continued to compile the work, he knew he could not market it and so he sold the publication rights to F. A. Leupold, a Leipzig publisher. During the next few years the ownership changed hands three times and the encyclopedia's scope was expanded to six volumes. Enter Brockhaus, who at this point purchased the rights.

Brockhaus immediately made arrangements with Franke to complete the sixth volume and to prepare two supplementary books. These supplements were necessary because the first two volumes, which had been offered for sale in 1796, did not include any information about the significant events in Europe between that date and 1809, the year scheduled for the publication of the rest of the set. There was no mention, for example, of the fact that Napoleon had seized power in France in 1799 and no discussion of the beginnings of unrest in Latin America.

The completed Brockhaus encyclopedia was given a rather cumbersome title — *Conversations-Lexikon oder Kurzgefasstes Handwörterbuch für die in dir Gesellschaftlichen Unterhaltung aus den Wissenschaften und Künsten Vorkommenden Gegenstände, mit Beständiger Rücksicht auf die Ereignisse der älteren und Neueren Zeit*— but the set achieved great popularity in large part because of the owners' determination to make it as accurate and up-to-date as possible. The title was then changed with each new edition, all of which also sold out relatively quickly. By the fourth edition, published from 1817 to 1819, the encyclopedia had grown to ten volumes in size, and it contained an impressive list of well-known German scholars as authors. And by the 13th edition (16 volumes) the name had become the *Brockhaus-Conversations-Lexicon,* though most people referred to it as the Brockhaus.

This encyclopedia became a model for many subsequent works of this sort produced in Europe during the nineteenth and twentieth centuries, and it broke new ground among encyclopedias by issuing a yearbook to its tenth edition (1857–1864), something most other encyclopedias consistently do today. After Friedrich Arnold Brockhaus died, the publication of the encyclopedia and its supplements was continued by his sons and grandsons. Albert Edward Brockhaus (1855–1921), a grandson, was even commissioned by the Russians to produce a 43-volume Russian encyclopedia based on the German work. Although this was completed in Russia in 1906, plans for further editions of the project collapsed after the Soviets seized power in 1917.

At the end of World War II, when the Soviet army occupied Leipzig, the Russian authorities treated the Brockhaus printing house with more leniency than they did most other printing plants. It is said that this was because they had fond memories of the great Russian encyclopedia that the Brockhaus family had provided their country during the days of the czar.

Joseph Meyer (1796–1856) published another major German encyclopedia, the *Neues Conversations-Lexikon,* in the 1840s. This was a work of high standards, and it was particularly noted for its fine handling of scientific and technical subjects. Its sixth edition (1902–1912) comprised 24 volumes. This encyclopedia, however, became identified with Nazi propaganda during World War II, and so it was discontinued after the war.

The Herder *Konversations-Lexikon,* first published in 1853, is now known as *Die Grosse Herder* ("The Great Herder"). Its scholarship, accuracy, and thoroughness earned it a wide audience even though its content tended to provide only a Roman Catholic point of view. A fifth edition was published in ten volumes from 1953 to 1956. Various smaller versions of this encyclopedia also were published over the years.

One other German encyclopedia, the *Allegemeine Encyclopädie der Wissenschaften und Künste,* needs mention. Edited by Johann Samuel Ersch (1766–1826) and Johann Gottfried Gruber (c. 1774–1851), the encyclopedia was planned to be so comprehensive that it could never be completed. The production of this encyclopedia began in 1818 and by 1889 included 167 volumes. The first part, covering information under the letters A to G, filled 99 volumes. Many of its entries were quite large. The one on Britain took up 414 pages; the one on Greece, 3,688!

In France, Pierre Athanase Larousse (1817–1875), a teacher who was the son of a blacksmith, began to publish *Le Grand Dictionnaire Universel du XIXe Siecle* in Paris in 1865. It was anticlerical in tone and combined the features of both a dictionary and an encyclopedia. This French work went into many editions, the latest of which was issued in the 1970s.

Inspired by the success of the Larousse enterprise, the French politician Ferdinand-Camille Drefus decided to put out his own encyclopedia, *La Grande Encyclopédie.* He published it between 1886 and 1902. It comprised 31 volumes and was an outstanding achievement, containing authoritative articles by leading French scholars, excellent biographical material, and relatively complete bibliographies. Although much of the content is now out of date, it is still considered an important source for many subjects.

Not to be forgotten is one other French encyclopedia of note, the *Encyclopédie Française,* which began publication in 1935. This was printed as a loose-leaf set of 21 books arranged in systematic order. The loose-leaf binding permitted supplementary pages to be provided to owners of the encyclopedia whenever information on the earlier pages was updated. The new pages could be inserted in place of the old ones without affecting the design of each volume.

This encyclopedia is still being produced and a number of the volumes already have been completely replaced by revised pages. The design of this encyclopedia was highly praised by the British historian H. G. Wells in his "World Brain" article (see below).

Although the market for encyclopedias in nineteenth- and twentieth-century Britain often seemed inexhaustible, not all publishers made a profit from such books. Many failed because their sets were too poor in quality or because they were not competitively priced. Among the best sellers, however, was *The New Cyclopaedia* designed by Abraham Rees (1743–1825), a well-known

Presbyterian minister. It was a completely original and finely illustrated work, and when completed in 1820, it offered strong competition in England to the *Encyclopaedia Britannica*. Reese, shortly before he designed this encyclopedia, had been an editor and reviser of Chambers' *Cyclopaedia*, originally designed by Ephraim Chambers (chapter 6). He had done such a scholarly job on that project that he was honored by election to the prestigious Royal Society. Reese's own encyclopedia was largely his own work, although it contained articles on music by Dr. Charles Burney and articles on botany by Sir James Edward Smith, a famous botanist and founder of the Linnean Society.

Another successful encyclopedia was *Chambers's Encyclopaedia* (1860–1868), published in ten volumes by Robert and William Chambers, which should not be confused with the earlier Chambers' *Cyclopaedia*. The Chambers brothers set up their printing company in Edinburgh, Scotland, where William Chambers had earlier founded the *Chambers's Edinburgh Journal*. In addition to their encyclopedia, the brothers compiled and published a large number of other reference works.

The *Chambers's Encyclopaedia* was printed in a number of further editions until 1935. In 1944 the encyclopedia was taken over by another company and completely revised under the editorship of Margaret B. Law, who once had been on the staff of the *Encyclopaedia Britannica*. In its revised and modernized form, it is still popular in England today.

Some other well-known nineteenth-century British encyclopedias were the 18-volume *Edinburgh Encyclopaedia* (1809–1831), which was edited by the well-known scientist Sir David Brewster, and the 22 volume *London Encyclopaedia* (1810–1829), edited by Thomas Curtis, the former editor and publisher of the encyclopedia initiated by Coleridge (chapter 12).

There also was the 29-volume *Penny Cyclopaedia* (1833–1846). The editors of this work stated in their introduction that they were not attempting to set up some system of knowledge as many other encyclopedists had, but they wanted only "to give pretty fully, under each separate head, as much information as can be conveyed within reasonable limits. But while it endeavors to present in detail the explanation of those terms of Art and Science, the right understanding of which is independent of any system, it also attempts to give such general views of all great branches of knowledge, as may help to the formation of just ideas on their extent and relative importance, and to point out the best sources of complete information." A full index to the work was promised but never issued.

Although it was the Americans who had the reputation among Britishers for bombastic sales techniques, it was in Great Britain that the first encyclopedia was produced with the sole aim of selling a commercial product other than books, and in which the content was determined by the sales staff rather than the editors. This was the *Pears' Cyclopaedia*, initiated in 1897 by Thomas J. Barratt of the Pears' Soap Company. Barratt was the mastermind of the Pears' advertising program, which had turned a small London cosmetic shop into a huge international soap combine. "Any fool can make soap," Barratt liked to say. "It takes a clever man to sell it."

Barratt claimed, on massive billboards and posters plastered everywhere, that Pears' Soap was pure, healthy, and made one beautiful. He procured testimonials from doctors, chemists, and the famous actress Lilie Langtry to give credence to that statement. In England he erected billboards containing reproductions of John Millais' classic painting "Bubbles" as an advertisement for Pears' Soap. And in the United States he obtained an endorsement for the product from the best-known preacher of that time — Henry Ward Beecher. Full-page newspaper advertisements showed this prominent clergyman saying, "If cleanliness is next to Godliness, soap must be a means of Grace."

In the end *Pears' Cyclopaedia* proved to be an innovative way to combine cleanliness with the human drive for knowledge. Every time a person picked up this one-volume encyclopedia to check a place name or a brief biography, he was confronted with, "Good morning! Have you used Pears' Soap?" Eventually this encyclopedia even became a standard reference work, and it is still popular today. Probably few of its present readers know of its original soap-selling intent, for it is no longer filled with the brazen huckster pages it contained during the first years of publication.

One-volume works such as *Pears'*, although held in disdain by the publishers of encyclopedia sets, have some advantages over larger works. These books are inexpensive to purchase, so people accept the cheap paper and flimsy bindings characteristic of low production costs. Such books also can be replaced as soon as the next year's edition is printed. Thus these books have the kind of built-in obsolescence that manufacturers of automobiles and refrigerators might only dream about. The yearbooks that are published to supplement encyclopedia sets comprised of many volumes achieve a similar obsolescence, but the number of purchasers of these yearbooks is limited to those who already own the sets.

The earliest of these quick-sell, one-volume encyclopedias was the British *Enquire within upon Everything*, founded in 1856. Its publication was suspended 96 years later in 1952. *Whitaker's Almanack*, also started in Britain (1868), is now one of the better-known single-volume works of this kind, as is the American *The World Almanac* (1868).

Finally, mention needs to be made of *The Harmsworth Encyclopedia: Everybody's Book of Reference* that was published in London in 1905. This was edited by George Sandeman and met a genuine popular need. It rapidly sold a half-million copies.

An Italian encyclopedia founded by Giovanni Treccani of the Istituto della Encyclopedia Italiana is one of the finest examples ever produced of a national encyclopedia. This 36-volume set called the *Enciclopedia Italiana de Scienze, Lettere ed Arti* was published between 1929 and 1939 and was edited by the philosopher Giovanni Gentile. Although intended to provide "an inventory of Italian knowledge" for an exclusively Italian audience, it reflected a broader international approach, and its bibliographies cited books and periodical articles in many languages. Unfortunately, parts of this encyclopedia also contained some of the most blatant examples of a nationalistic bias in recent history. These parts were produced in accord with the views of Benito Mussolini's fascist regime. In fact, the article on Fascism itself was written by Mussolini. The encyclopedia's defense of Fascist ideology, however, did not impinge on the impartiality of much of the rest of the text.

Another example of such prejudice is found in the *Bol'shaia Sovetskaia Entsiklopediia*, or Great Soviet Encyclopedia, which the Soviet Union's Council of Ministers decreed, in 1949, "must show with exhaustive completeness the superiority of Socialist culture over the culture of the capitalist world." Reviewers in the West watched the publication of each volume of this encyclopedia with interest and amusement for its inclusion or exclusion of famous Russians according to the current state of their acceptance or condemnation by the government. When Secret Police Chief Lavrenti Pavlovitch Beria fell from power following the death of Stalin, the Great Soviet Encyclopedia removed the entry on Beria and provided all the encyclopedia owners with a special replacement section containing expanded entries on F. W. Bergholz (a forgotten eighteenth-century courtier), the Bering Sea, and the English philosopher Bishop Berkley.

The last edition of the Great Soviet Encyclopedia, begun in 1970, was generally considered to be a more objective reference work and one in which the political hues had been softened and sometimes even erased. In the earlier set Eugene O'Neill had been described as a "decadent" American playwright; in the newer one he is listed as a Nobel Prize winner. However, the Russian writer and Nobel laureate Alexander Solzhenitsyn, who had been expelled from Russia shortly before this edition was begun, is still omitted from the list of Nobel Prize winners.

Fortunately, several earlier Russian encyclopedias, although reflecting some nationalistic bias, were relatively good reference works. These include the eight-volume *Spravochnii Entsiklopedicheskii Slovar'*, completed in 1895 by the Russian journalist A. Starchevskii; and the 20-volume *Bol'shaia Entsiklopediia: Slovar' Obshchedostupnykh Svedenyii po vsem Otrasliam Znaniia*, published by S. N. Yushakov at St. Petersburg in 1905.

The *Espasa*, more correctly titled the Spanish *Enciclopedia Universal*

Ilustrada Europeo-Americana, not only is considered a great national ency-clopedia but also one of the largest encyclopedias currently in use in the world — 70 volumes. It was printed in Barcelona between 1905 and 1930. An entire volume is devoted to Spain alone, and this is separately revised and periodically issued. The *Espasa* is remarkable for its detail, lengthy bibli-ographies, international scope, and clear maps of even remote and obscure places. A miniature edition, the *Espasa-Calpe: Diccionario Enciclopédico Abre-viado,* has only seven volumes. This also has been printed in several editions.

Another Spanish production, the *Enciclopedia Labor,* published both in Spain and Argentina, began to appear in 1955 in nine volumes. It gives Span-ish and Latin American matters the most care and space, and tends to treat subjects such as Asia and Australia in much less detail. It is, however, lavishly illustrated with both color and halftone photographs as well as drawings. Each volume is complete with its own index.

Most countries have issued at least one good encyclopedia during this century. Among these should be mentioned the two-volume Austrian *Neues Welt-Lexicon,* the seven-volume Swiss *Schvizer-Lexikon,* the 11-volume Dutch *Oosthoek's Geïllustreerde Encyclopaedie,* the 20-volume Portuguese *Encyclope-dia e Diccionario Internacional,* the 24-volume Greek *Megale Hellenike Enkyk-lopaideia,* the four-volume Danish *Glydendals Nye Leksikon,* the 30-volume Swedish *Svensk Uppslagsbok,* and the nine-volume Norwegian *Aschehougs Kon-versations-Leksikon.*

In eastern Europe there are the six-volume Czechoslovakian *Ottuv Slovník Naucný,* the 21-volume Hungarian *Révai nagy Lexikona,* the 13-volume Pol-ish *Wielka Encyklopedia Powszechna,* the five-volume Bulgarian *Kratka Bal-garska Entsiklopedija,* the eight-volume Yugoslavian *Enciklopedija Jugoslavije,* the ten-volume Lithuanian *Lietuviskoji Enciklopedija,* the eight-volume Eston-ian *Eesti Entsüklopeedia,* and the three-volume Latvian *Latvju Enciklopedija.*

In Asia we find the modern 34-volume Turkish *Türk Ansiklopedisi,* the 19-volume Japanese *Japonica,* the 240-volume Chinese *Jiu Tong Tong,* and the three-volume Indonesian *Ensiklopedia Indonesia.*

In Latin America there is the eight-volume Mexican *Enciclopedia Yucater-nense* and the two-volume Venuzuelan *Enciclopedia Larense.*

Other English-language encyclopedias include the Canadian six-volume *Encyclopedia of Canada* and the ten-volume *Encyclopedia Canadiana.* There also are the ten-volume *The Australian Encyclopaedia* and the one-volume *The Oxford New Zealand Encyclopaedia.*

An attempt to chart a new direction for encyclopedias appeared in a series of speeches and essays written by novelist and historian H. G. Wells (1866–1946), which were subsequently collected in his book *World Brain,* as well in a famous article he wrote for the April 1937 issue of *Harper's* magazine.

Wells had begun life as a draper's assistant, achieved a university education by winning grants and scholarships, and eventually became a widely read professional writer. In his later years he gained fame as a proponent of many social reforms.

Long before thinking about how to compile a modern encyclopedia, Wells had surveyed the past with a broad sweep in his highly popular *The Outline of History* (1920). He had viewed the future in various science-fiction novels and in his fictional utopia *The Shape of Things to Come* (1933). He also had analyzed the present in some of his finest novels of lower-middle-class English life and in his writings on science. In the *Harper's* magazine article, he proposed a new type of encyclopedia that would encompass all the world's knowledge.

According to Wells, "This *World Encyclopedia* would be the mental background of every intelligent man in the world. It would be alive and growing and changing continually, under revision, extension, and replacement from the original thinkers in the world everywhere. Every university and research institution should be feeding it. Every fresh mind should be brought into contact with its standing editorial organization. And on the other hand, its contents would be the standard source of material for the instructional side of school and college work, for the verification of facts and the testing of statements — everywhere in the world. Even journalists would deign to use it; even newspaper proprietors might be made to respect it…. It would hold the world together."

Wells believed that the project should take little original writing, but be composed of selections from thousands of already-published works. "If a thing has been stated clearly and compactly once for all," he said, "why paraphrase it or ask some inferior hand to restate it?" He apparently never considered the problem of how utterly confusing such a conglomeration of styles might be should the publisher adhere to this kind of eclectic borrowing.

Despite the praise heaped on Wells' proposal, the *Harper's* article is a presumptuous example of British bias in Western scholarship. Wells begins it with a well-phrased attack on prevailing elitist attitudes among British and American scientists and other specialists. He then goes on to say that his proposed encyclopedia would bring together knowledge so as to act as "an organ of adjustment and adjudication, a clearinghouse of misunderstanding" not only for the average reader but for every specialist. In other words, it would be the source of absolute knowledge, a final authority. This is about as elitist an idea as anyone might ever suggest, and it is rather strange coming as it does after his earlier attack on other elitists.

He sees only two basic problems in producing this world encyclopedia. One is that of convincing individualistic and elitist scholars of the desirability of working on the project. He says they are so impatient and preoccupied with other work that this would be a problem. The other is the need to prevent advocates of various cults and propaganda groups from capturing or buying off the editors.

But the touch that most illustrates Wells' British prejudice is his discussion of why this encyclopedia for the whole world should be written in English. He says this is "because it [English] has a wider range than German, a greater abundance and greater subtlety of expression than French, and more precision than Russian." One can, of course, think of many German, French, and Russian people who would disagree with this depreciation of their languages. And what of the Chinese, who, even in 1937, constituted a larger number of persons speaking that language than those speaking English, and whose precise and subtle vocabulary ought to be considered seriously for any encyclopedia text designed to be read by all the world.

One advocate for Wells' proposal, Reginald A. Smith, has written a book titled *Towards a Living Encyclopedia: A Contribution to Mr. Wells' New Encyclopedia* that enthusiastically pushes Wells' theme further. Smith argues that what is needed is not the writings themselves, but a series of graded and annotated bibliographies of human knowledge to which the encyclopedia user might refer for extended study.

It is, of course, unlikely that any encyclopedia designed on Wells' model will be forthcoming in the near future, and I am not altogether sure such a project would do a commendable job in presenting knowledge in a legible and comprehensive manner. Wells' vision of the perfect encyclopedia already exists in a somewhat imperfect form in the great library collections in various countries throughout the world.

15. Modern American Encyclopedias

It might be said that Charles Anderson Dana (1819–1897), together with George Ripley (1802–1880), succeeded where Samuel Taylor Coleridge had failed. Coleridge only dreamed of setting up a utopian commune; Dana and Ripley lived in one for six years. Coleridge only designed plans for an encyclopedia; Dana and Ripley produced one — *The New American Cyclopaedia: a Popular Dictionary of General Knowledge.*

Dana was a journalist by trade. He also was a member from 1841 to 1847 of the Brook Farm Association at West Roxbury, Massachusetts, perhaps America's most famous intellectual commune. Its founder was the Unitarian minister George Ripley, and its more than 100 members included novelist Nathaniel Hawthorne, writer George William Curtis, consumer cooperative advocate John Orvis, a founder of the Roman Catholic Paulist Order Isaac Thomas Hecker, and a number of other leading New England intellectuals of that time. This commune also had the support, if not membership, of many other noted intellectual leaders, persons such as Ralph Waldo Emerson, Margaret Fuller, Henry David Thoreau, and Henry James. The Brook Farm experiment lasted six years, and Dana, while living there, wrote many articles for the two well-known magazines that were published at this commune, *The Harbinger* and *The Dial.*

After Brook Farm closed in 1847, Dana joined the staff of the New York *Tribune* and soon became its managing editor. Ripley also worked for this publication for a period of time as its literary critic. Dana resigned in 1862, however, because of his disagreement with the owner, Horace Greeley, over the paper's advocacy of compromise with the South during the Civil War. Dana then became part owner and publisher of the New York *Sun.* He was a friend of President Abraham Lincoln and served in Lincoln's administration as Assistant Secretary of War from 1863 to 1865.

While still working for the *Tribune*, Dana was commissioned by the

American publisher W. H. Appleton to design and edit *The New American Cyclopaedia*. Dana recommended that Ripley also be hired to work on the project. Both of them were already well-known as scholars and social reformers, and after their encyclopedia was completed it gained a wide reputation for its authoritative scholarship.

The 16-volume set was printed and sold volume by volume from 1858 to 1863. Most of its 364 contributors were Americans, representing almost every field of knowledge. Two were the German social scientists Karl Marx and Friedrich Engels, founders of the revolutionary communist movement. Marx at the time was one of the European correspondents for the *Tribune*. When Dana hired Marx to write some of the articles, mainly on military subjects, he wrote to Marx saying that the articles should give no evidence of partiality, not on political, religious, or philosophical questions.

Marx became somewhat handicapped in completing the assignment after Engels fell ill with glandular trouble, and he could offer no plausible explanation for his embarrassing delays in submitting the articles. Eventually Marx was reduced to pretending that they had been lost in the mail. Yet, in the end, 67 of the Marx-Engels articles were published in *The New American Cyclopaedia*, 51 of them written by Engels, though Marx had done much of the research for these at the British Museum.

The encyclopedia was sold house-to-house all over the United States and averaged sales of 20,000 sets a year. Dana and Ripley produced a second edition from 1873 to 1883 that also was highly successful. The second edition had 6,000 illustrations and cost an enormous sum to prepare. The publisher then issued supplements and cumulative indexes up to the year 1902. Though it is no longer in print, *The New American Cyclopaedia* is still consulted by historians, because of its valuable chronicle of the Civil War and Reconstruction periods and for the biographical material it contains relating to countless numbers of minor figures in American history.

The New American Cyclopaedia was not the first such work to be produced in America. Earlier, Francis Lieber (1800–1872), a German in exile living in America, designed the *Encyclopaedia Americana: a Popular Dictionary* that was published in 13 volumes by a Philadelphia printer between 1829 and 1833. Lieber based the work on the seventh edition of the German Brockhaus and named it the *Americana* in hopes of reaching the same market that was currently buying the British editions and pirated American editions of the *Encyclopaedia Britannica*.

Lieber was a distinguished scholar in the field of law and jurisprudence. He is credited with writing the first definitive proposal for the enactment of an international copyright law in a pamphlet published in 1840. After completing the encyclopedia, he accepted a post as professor of history and political science at South Carolina College, where he taught for many years. Then he became a professor of law at Columbia College in New York City. However, because his encyclopedia was selling well, he continued as its editor through several subsequent editions.

The set was an almost immediate success, and reprints and revisions appeared at various times between 1835 to 1858. At the end of the century, arrangements were made with *Scientific American* magazine to produce a new edition of the work. Frederick Converse Beach, then editor of the *Scientific American*, was appointed as editor. The new edition of 20 volumes appeared in 1911. Because of its connection with the magazine, this edition of the encyclopedia was particularly strong in science and technology. The next edition of 30 volumes was produced in 1920, though no longer in cooperation with the *Scientific American*, and the encyclopedia has been periodically revised and printed ever since.

Alvin J. Johnson's *New Universal Cyclopaedia* came out in four volumes in 1878 and was reissued almost 20 years later in eight volumes. This second edition was edited by Charles Kendall Adams, the former president of Cornell University. The set was then enlarged to 12 volumes before it was discontinued. A first edition of another encyclopedia, the *New International Encyclopedia* in 17 volumes, was issued in 1904. This was expanded to 20 volumes in 1916 and then to 24 volumes in 1922. The *New International* had one particularly unique feature. Its maps were mounted on inserts so that subscribers could replace them whenever new maps were issued to take account of any geographical changes.

By this time, the publishing of encyclopedias had become quite a lucrative enterprise, and many publishers and printers were making plans to enter the field. They began by either designing completely new works or by purchasing the rights to revise and reprint works that originally had been put out by another printer but which were not profitable because of their poor quality or because they came from another country and needed to be translated into English before they could be sold.

There are today, in fact, about 30 different encyclopedias printed and marketed in the United States, and perhaps just as many have been published and then discontinued since 1900, a few of which still can be found on the shelves of used bookstores. Some of the best ones and some of the worst ones are still being sold, because the life of any encyclopedia today is more dependent on clever sales techniques than on the quality of its content.

Sales of encyclopedia sets, which generally are made on a door-to-door basis rather than through bookstores, have expanded far beyond that of other types of books. Booksellers who at first feared that the purchase of an encyclopedia might discourage customers from buying other works soon found that they were as mistaken as newspaper proprietors were when they feared that the introduction of broadcast news might put them out of business. Yet most publishers who previously handled both standard books and encyclopedias now either dropped their standard book trade altogether or relegated it to a subsidiary role in relationship to the far more profitable encyclopedia business, which they dubbed the subscription books industry.

Nowhere in the world did salespersons so dominate the encyclopedia business as they did in the United States. Here they pioneered the innovations of time payment plans to overcome a householder's lack of ready cash, customer surveys to get the salesperson into a house, and bonus gifts to reward a buyer's prompt payment. They also succeeded in making their own profession respectable, talking of the art of selling as the capacity to get people to act, rather than as the capacity to get people to buy something they might not need or want.

In private, encyclopedia salespersons had to admit that the task of peddling encyclopedias was much the same as selling any other product. As a former sales manager for *Britannica* once put it, "The *Britannica* is sold with shoe leather. It doesn't matter in what section of the country you are selling. People in any part of the country buy a product for the same reasons, whether it is a vacuum cleaner or a *Britannica*. The technique of selling is basically the same everywhere. In the South we talk a little slower and we visit a little longer. But we say the same things."

The common sales appeal in the encyclopedia market was to the parents' aspirations for their children. Parents were warned that they would need a set of the *Britannica, Americana, Collier's,* or *World Book* in this highly competitive world if they were to hope to have their child get high enough grades to become eligible for college or a career. The implication was that any parent who failed to buy an encyclopedia for the youngster was depriving that child of the opportunity of doing well in school and, ultimately, in life.

American encyclopedia salespersons have pushed, pleaded, and aroused hopes, desires, and guilt feelings to place sets of these books in every home they entered. They have played upon the universal desire for greater knowledge. They have developed the skill of projecting sincerity and enthusiasm into every house call and of evoking awe on the part of the prospective buyer. With subtlety they have pointed to the potential buyer's ignorance. For example, the salesperson may sometimes ask, "Did you know there are catfish that climb trees?" and when the customer admits ignorance, turn to the page in the encyclopedia that pictures and describes such fish. The salesperson then will declare that the answer to every question the customer might ever ask can be found on other pages. By such methods salespersons eventually turned encyclopedias into household necessities on the order of the living-room piano, radio, or television set.

However, there is something singularly distasteful in this spectacle of using tricks of all sorts to sell parents the unwanted and perhaps unneedful. It is one thing to gull a car purchaser. It is another to hit below the belt with fake surveys and phony gifts, while playing on educational pride and parental responsibility.

Sometimes salespersons have instituted practices that courts have later ruled illegal. There is a long list of such actions by the Federal Trade Commission against various encyclopedia firms. A case against the *New Standard Encyclopedia* in 1940 revealed that this company's salespersons, in marketing their books, would state that the set was free, that customers need only pay for the annual supplement or for other services, that the offer was limited to a specific number of people in any community, and that the regular price of the books was greater than the one being stated in this offer by the salesperson. In 1960 *Collier's Encyclopedia* was charged by the FTC with similar deceptive methods and fictitiously reduced prices. The *Americana* also was fined severely in 1960 for violating FTC orders, and then again in 1965 and in 1970. The same was true for *Britannica*, which as recently as January 13, 1975, was convicted of deceiving its customers with numerous ruses, including misrepresentation by salespersons who said they were working for a large marketing firm rather than telling customers they were selling encyclopedias.

A certain awe surrounds any encyclopedia, because so many people assume that it contains, or initially was designed to contain, all the data anyone might need to know. Even in a home where the set has become covered with dust from nonuse, the owner will confess, when questioned, to feeling a certain security in possessing such books of human knowledge — volumes that might answer any question should they ever be opened. The owner may even tell you that the volumes are valued for nostalgic reasons. In this case, the person will describe a childhood before the days of television as a time when hours were spent leafing through each volume's pages to look at the pictures.

In many homes arguments are resolved by turning to the encyclopedia as the final authority, and when children go to their parents for help they will, as often as not, be directed to the encyclopedia shelf. Surveys show that most encyclopedia sales are made to families with school-age children. Parents clearly view the set of books as an aid to their child's academic development, and they probably are.

But encyclopedias also can cause frustration whenever they lack the specific information that the child or parent seeks. Of course, every encyclopedia fails to encompass all the material one might wish to know. People's interest and curiosity are far too diverse to ever be satisfied by a series of encyclopedia entries. At this point the frustrated user may assume either that the purchased set is inferior, since the information sought is not there, or that the fault lies in their inability to know where to look in the volumes for the needed material.

In one sense, the salespersons for encyclopedias performed a notable service. They brought into thousands of homes the only reading matter, other than daily newspapers and mail-order catalogs, that ever entered them. The sets demonstrated a sense of culture in homes where walls were bare and there was little furniture. They usually were placed where any visitor would immediately recognize that this was a home in which knowledge and education were taken seriously.

The books were even designed to be attractive to the average person with a limited education. With supplementary children's editions, a series of yearbooks, atlases, and dictionaries in complementary design, these encyclopedias conceivably could be said to bring knowledge to family members of all ages.

What the sales departments sometimes overlooked was the fact that an encyclopedia must be well written and informative if it is to have lasting appeal. It also must be thorough and neither too small nor too large. A small encyclopedia often indicates inadequacies in planning, while a large one is too costly to both publisher and reader. Too many of the rapidly appearing encyclopedias were written by hacks, who merely rewrote or abbreviated articles found in other sets. The salespeople didn't care. All they wanted to be assured of was that the set could be marketed.

Many writers and other intellectuals have despaired over what was happening to the book industry because of the domination of the sales mentality on the business. As early as 1910, publisher Henry Holt wrote several articles for *Putnam's Monthly* complaining of the "commercial enterprise that has come from Wall Street.... [It has] removed the publishing business from the control of the publishers into that of financiers." On his 70th birthday, he pointed out, "Probably the loss of very high literary quality is due to the fact that commercialism is draining off the talent into money-making pursuits."

Sales of encyclopedias in America kept steady pace with the growth of the population and rising standard of living. Of course, sales fluctuated with the economy, but encyclopedia publishers survived economic downturns, such as the Great Depression of the 1930s, in better shape than other divisions of the printing and publishing business. They experienced unprecedented prosperity during the Second World War, a time when automobiles, refrigerators, and durable items were in short supply. This was because encyclopedias were exempt from the government credit restrictions placed on most consumer goods. Their only limitations were paper supplies and printing and binding facilities. Millions of families with war-swollen incomes turned their cash into sets of these books at the ever-ready suggestion of door-to-door salespersons.

The encyclopedia with the best sales record — outselling the next three competitors combined — is the *World Book Encyclopedia*. Many owners of this 22-volume set probably would be surprised if they were to learn that the publishing company is now one of the leading vacuum cleaner companies and not an educational institution. But this transition should not come as a surprise. Selling books door-to-door is not much different from selling vacuum cleaners door-to-door.

The *World Book Encyclopedia* got its start just before the end of World War I when the Hanson-Bellows Co. of Chicago purchased the rights to a work for children called *The New Practical Reference Library* that had been designed by Michael V. O'Shea, professor of education at the University of Wisconsin. It was created in accord with the curriculum that children were then studying in school.

For the new eight-volume set named *World Book, Organized Knowledge in Story and Pictures*, O'Shea designed a questionnaire that reportedly was sent to 31,000 educators, parents, and businesspeople to learn what they considered would be the ideal encyclopedia for their needs. The encyclopedia, completed in 1917, was introduced at the National Education Association convention, where it received high praise from the assembled teachers. The favorable reaction was, of course, fully exploited by the *World Book* sales department, and the company recruited many of the teachers to be part-time salespersons for the set. The encyclopedia soon was selling well, with particularly good results in rural areas, where parents wanted to give their children educational advantages they themselves had lacked.

In 1919, W. F. Quarrie and Co. replaced the Hanson-Bellows Co. as publisher of *World Book*, and in 1954 that company was purchased by Marshall Field III, the millionaire grandson of the founder of a leading Chicago department store and owner of the *Chicago Sun* newspaper. After O'Shea died, J. Morris Jones, a native of Aberystwyth, Wales, was hired as the executive editor. Jones was already a distinguished editor and writer for children's magazines. He once had been a teacher and so had an understanding of the problems faced by educators. He further had a rare appreciation, among editors, for the needs of the sales force.

Under Jones, the encyclopedia was expanded first to 20 volumes and then to 22, and the contents were broadened so that it could be sold as both a school student's aid and an adult's encyclopedia. O'Shea earlier had made sure that a number of relatively small cities in the Unites States received description in the encyclopedia's pages to increase sales of sets in those cities.

Jones now tied the contents to a 34,000-word readability list developed by Edgar Dale of Ohio State University. This was used to guarantee that every article could be understood by the average reader. Jones also set up a number of review boards of distinguished scholars to annually review the contents of the encyclopedia. Such innovations are usually applauded by teachers, and, as Jones liked to say, teachers recommend encyclopedias to parents and this means more sales.

Perhaps the most important aspect of the *World Book*'s success lies in the fact that the publisher hired teachers as often as possible to act as salespeople. They sold the encyclopedia during their summer vacations, on weekends, and in the evenings. This helped poorly paid teachers earn more income, and it helped encyclopedia sales in school and out, for the sales department was fully aware that few parents can refuse a teacher who asks them to buy an encyclopedia, in this case *World Book*.

The genius of *World Book* sales was Bailey K. Howard, who had joined the company's sales staff following his failure to sell 300 sets of a rival encyclopedia to a midwestern school system. Howard decided *World Book*, which had picked up his lost order, must be a superior encyclopedia. He did so well with the new company that he soon advanced to the post of president. Howard promoted the encyclopedia's sales by widely advertising the company's sponsorship of Sir Edmund Hillary's climb of Mount Everest, cosponsoring the television broadcasts of both the 1960 Republican and Democratic political conventions, securing the exclusive rights to publish the stories of the lives of America's first astronauts, financing a scientific search for the Loch Ness monster in Scotland, and providing partial sponsorship of most television quiz programs. The profits of the company became so great that, in 1961, *World Book* was able to finance a Braille edition of the encyclopedia. It filled 145 volumes, comprising nearly 40,000 pages. The project was aimed at achieving goodwill, since the company could never hope to sell enough copies of this massive set to cover even a small part of the production costs. They finally donated all the sets of this Braille edition to various institutions for the blind. In 1964 the company also published a large-print edition for people with visual difficulties.

Other modern American encyclopedias of note include the 24-volume *Collier's Encyclopedia* published by the P. F. Collier Company. This was edited by Lewis Shores, an advisor to the American Library Association. The 18,864 pages of this work are matched by almost as many illustrations as well as many maps. Dr. Shores, in an address before the California Library Association in 1962, outlined his ideas in designing this encyclopedia and ended with these words: "Like librarianship itself, I consider the encyclopedia one of the few generalizing influences in a world of over-specialization. It serves to recall that knowledge has unity."

There also is the eight-volume *Compton's Pictured Encyclopedia*, which was started in 1922 by the educator Frank Compton and edited by Guy Stanton Ford. Today this has grown to 15 volumes. At the end of each volume is an index that relates both text and illustrations in that book to the material in the other books. And there was the *Nelson's Perpetual Loose-leaf Encyclopedia* edited by John H. Finley and published in 12 volumes in 1920. In theory, the new pages, issued twice a year, would keep this encyclopedia up-to-date and useful for many years to come, but the method eventually was abandoned because it could not attract enough sales.

Special mention should be made of *The Columbia Encyclopedia*, first issued in 1935 by the Columbia University Press. This one-volume work was a scholarly attempt to bridge the gap between the large encyclopedias and the cheap one-volume annuals. By omitting definitions and using many cross-references, the editors achieved an economy of space that has pleased many purchasers. The work concentrates on providing "first aid and essential facts" rather than technical details. It was issued in a second edition in 1950, a third in 1963, and a fourth in 1975.

Of course, no encyclopedia is complete in itself partly because it becomes out of date almost as soon as it is issued. Furthermore, even the lengthiest encyclopedia will provide only a introduction to the various subjects it contains. For this reason every good encyclopedia should provide comprehensive bibliographies along with its articles. In modern times, most encyclopedia editors have come to realize the value of even a short bibliography in providing other sources that may modify, correct, or amplify the information contained on the encyclopedia pages. Furthermore, an ideal bibliography should be international in scope if it is to fulfill its task of pointing the reader to the wider horizons beyond the confines of the article just read.

The twentieth century and the end of the nineteenth century saw the development of many specialist encyclopedias devoted to limited branches of knowledge. Some of these works, although primarily focused toward only a particular audience, took on the characteristics of a general encyclopedia. The *Catholic Encyclopedia* (1907–1918), for example, was neither limited to ecclesiastical matters nor to the activities of church persons. It is especially useful for medieval history and philosophy. The *Encyclopedia of Religion and Ethics* (1908–1926), *New Schaff-Herzog Encyclopedia of Religious Knowledge* (1882–1884), and the *Jewish Encyclopedia* (1901–1906) also are broad in coverage and useful to the general reader.

The *Encyclopedia of the Social Sciences* (1930–1935) is particularly noted for its articles on political science, economics, law, anthropology, ethics, education, and philosophy. Examples of other excellent encyclopedias that give detailed information only in specific fields are *Grove's Dictionary of Music and*

Musicians (1897–1889), *Dictionary of American Biography* (1928–date), *Cyclopedia of American Government* (1914), *Thorpe's Dictionary of Applied Chemistry* (1890–1893), *Dictionary of Applied Physics* (1922–1923), and the *McGraw-Hill Encyclopedia of Science and Technology* (1960).

16. The Growth of Libraries

The world's earliest surviving book on the craft of librarianship comes from China. Here Cheng Ju (1078–1144) wrote the *Lin-tai Gu-shi* ("Tale of the National Library") to encourage the emperor to reestablish an imperial library. The earlier one had been destroyed by a tribal army from Manchuria that pillaged the capital and nearly conquered the empire. The author claimed that such a library was essential to good government.

Interestingly enough, Cheng argued that the library would be a resource for scholars, historians, and encyclopedists. It would allow the experiences of earlier rulers and the wisdom of sages to be consulted in considering present problems, and it would provide resources for students preparing for the imperial examinations. Added to this proposal was a listing of technical matters relating to library management — acquisitions, cataloging, classification, circulation, staffing, and even the kind of building that should be erected to house such a collection of books and documents.

Cheng's petition was accepted, and the government constructed the library according to his instructions. They rewarded those who donated books or loaned works that could be copied and then returned with gifts of silk and money. Those who provided the best collections of books were even permitted to name candidates for the imperial examinations.

A few years later, a celebrated scholar named Zheng Qiao (1103–1162) wrote a book called *Jiao Zhou Luo* ("Theory of Library Science and Bibliography") to set forth "eight methods for collecting and purchasing books." His primary concern was not one of finding sources for such library collections but of the need for subject determination based on a careful review of each volume before it was added to the library shelves so that the book could be classified according to the nature of its contents.

Similar classification problems faced the custodians of libraries all over the world. Most of the libraries that had been established in Europe by that time were connected to monasteries; those in the Islamic world were associated with mosques. The Grand Mosque of Damascus reportedly had a collection of works that totaled more than 5,000 volumes housed in 20 huge glass cases. The Muslims also began, as early as the tenth century, to set up public libraries with charitable endowments, called *waqfs*. This occurred at much the same time that the various Islamic sects were developing and growing — the orthodox Sunni, the messianic Shi'a and Ismal'ili, the rationalist Mutazilites, and the mystic Sufi— and each sect gathered its own literature and set up its own libraries to be used by members of that sect.

Although books in the medieval libraries of Europe often were chained and scholars could not remove unchained books from the specified reading room, many Islamic libraries freely loaned out their works believing it was their religious duty to facilitate the study of scientific knowledge and the copying of religious texts. One Arab historian of the thirteenth century, Ibn Hayyan, praised the generosity of these Islamic libraries, saying, "Whatever book I want to have I can get on loan from any library, while if I want to borrow money to buy these same books I can find no one who will lend it to me."

Many of the best libraries in the Muslim world, however, were destroyed by the European Crusaders as they swept through Syria and Palestine, and some of the libraries they spared were later destroyed by zealots of the Islamic sects intent on suppressing what they thought might be heretical works. Later, when the Mongols arrived during their conquest of the great cities of central Asia, these followers of Genghis Khan destroyed almost all of the remaining Islamic book repositories. In one week, in 1258, the Mongols burned all 36 public libraries in the city of Baghdad alone.

In Europe, where some of the early monastic libraries had served as models for the universities, much the same kind of destruction occurred on a somewhat lesser scale during the period of the Reformation. Followers of Martin Luther in Germany burned and pillaged these book repositories as they eradicated elements of Catholicism in their various states. But Luther himself was an advocate for the establishment of libraries. In a pamphlet he wrote in 1524, Luther said, "No effort or expense should be spared to provide good libraries or book repositories, especially in the larger cities which can well afford it." He even blamed the poor condition of education in Germany on the fact that the city fathers were not founding libraries and were letting good books deteriorate while holding onto the poorer ones.

In England it was the Civil War, which broke out in 1642, that resulted in the devastation of the monastic library system. Many books, Catholic religious ornaments, and other popish elements were removed from the monasteries, cathedrals, and universities and subsequently destroyed. Some of the paper from the books was used, according to one witness, "to serve their jakes [latrines], some to scour their candlesticks, and some to rub their boots." Yet in many places the destruction of the monastic libraries resulted only in the relocation of the volumes, which were taken away to augment the collections of rich private landowners.

It took a long time and a great deal of energy to rebuild the destroyed libraries in Protestant Europe, just as it did in the Islamic world. In France, where the Reformation never took hold, the great Mazarine Library of Paris, founded in 1643 by Jules Cardinal Mazarin, became public property following the French Revolution, as did the king's private library that is now the Bibliothèque Nationale, one of the largest and most important libraries in the world.

The more famous Vatican Library in Italy was established by Nicholas V, pope from 1447 to 1455, as a repository for handwritten manuscripts. Prior to this, although many of the popes had collected books, no permanent papal library had been established. The Vatican Library now has more than 50,000 manuscripts in its collection, most of which are valuable old Latin works, as well as almost 4,000 Greek and Oriental manuscripts. The library also contains about 350,000 printed books.

The British Museum, the oldest of the great national museums of the world, has a fine library that was initially gathered by the Italian political exile Antonio Panizzi (1797–1879), who was appointed Keeper of Printed Books for the museum in 1837. Panizzi set out to collect "every book that was printed either by Englishmen or in English or relating to England," and he even found an American who would regularly supply the library with books from the New World. The influence of this library eventually spread far beyond London. Here scholars from around the world found information about the economy and history of their own lands that they could not locate at home. Karl Marx based much of his work on his research into the British Museum's collections, and Lenin here found not only revolutionary literature from Russia that he could not locate in his native land but also a great deal of information about the French and English revolutions.

The largest library in Russia, the Lenin State Library in Moscow, dates from 1862 and contains a collection of 25 million books and two-and-a-half million manuscripts. Other national libraries around the world that have particularly large collections include the Bibliothèque Royale Albert I in Brussels, Belgium; the Dutch Royal Library in the Hague, The Netherlands; the Biblioteca Nazionale Centrale Vittorio Emanuele II in Rome, Italy; the National Library of Australia in Canberra; the National Library of Beijing, China; the National Library of India in Calcutta; the National Library of Argentina in Buenos Aires; and the National Library of Mexico in Mexico City.

The Library of Congress in Washington, D.C., is believed to have one of the largest collections and to be one of the most valuable research libraries in the world. Its collection is comprised of more than 70 million items, including 17 million books and pamphlets, and millions of engravings, maps, motion pictures, musical compositions, recordings, and photographs. It owns the largest collection of incunabula (books printed before 1501) in the Western Hemisphere as well as one of the few perfect copies of the Gutenberg Bible. Its collections of Chinese, Japanese, and Russian books is the most extensive outside of the Far East and Russia.

Since 1870, the Library of Congress has automatically received by statute two copies of every book copyrighted in the United States. In 1900 it was the only library in America that had more than one million items. But the accumulation of books being what it is, more than 90 United States libraries reported collections that large by the early 1970s.

The Library of Congress has taken the lead in searching for ways to preserve books and other library materials from decay. They have microfilmed newspapers, laminated precious documents, and experimented with chemical compounds designed to remove or neutralize the destructive acids found in pulp paper, acids that eventually may destroy all the pages of old, untreated books.

Keeping track of all the material contained in this library and the other large collections throughout the world is a major endeavor that employs many people for long hours each day. That was not the case during the Middle Ages, when library catalogs were simple shelf-lists compiled not to identify the contents of books but to inventory them as valuable pieces of property. In most instances these lists gave no indication of the subject matter of such books, and because many of the works were volumes of composite writings, it was next to impossible for any researcher to find a desired volume by consulting these lists. The only one who truly knew the intellectual value of a library's collection or of any of the individual books would have been its librarian.

The first attempt to catalog books by subject took place at the library of the abbey of St. Gall in Switzerland in the ninth century. Books about the lives of the saints were arranged in calendar order so that they could be easily located for reading on the saints' feast days. As other medieval monasteries later adopted various arrangement processes, the librarians often grouped the books in their collections as follows: the Bible, writings of the Church Fathers, theological works, homilies, saints' lives, and finally secular literature. In Islamic libraries the order was much the same, with books arranged from the most sacred (i.e., the word of God) down to the profane. At the Christian monastery of Altenzelle in Saxony the monks attached colored labels to their books to distinguish them by subject: red for theology, green for medicine, and black for law.

Union catalogs (lists that included the holdings of several libraries) began to emerge in France, England, and Germany as early as the thirteenth century. The abbey of Savigny in France compiled a list of its holdings that included books from four neighboring Benedictine abbeys, and a similar listing at the Regensburg abbey in Germany included the book titles from three other monasteries.

At that time books were so expensive that no library could hope to own more than a few of them, and so these union catalogs offered a way for the scholar-monks to discover to what location they might need to travel to consult specific texts. Today, however, many national libraries have proclaimed their intention to collect and store all the available works printed in their own national languages.

Yet as more and more knowledge accumulates in printed form and in an increasing number of non-print forms, it is becoming impossible for any library to collect everything, or even all of the most recently printed books. It is said that the main library building at Indiana University sinks more than one inch every year, because the engineers who constructed it failed to take into account the weight of all the books that eventually would be stored there. It is also estimated that the world's great libraries are doubling in size every 14 years.

Cooperative acquisition agreements have been instituted by most of the university libraries in the United States to assure that scholars will have access to the materials that cannot be housed by their home institutions. The first such agreement was the Farmington Plan in which several dozen academic libraries decided among themselves to act together in collecting all the new books and pamphlets from foreign countries that might reasonably be of interest to any research worker at one of their schools. Each institution took responsibility to stock particular types of documents and then made these available on loan to the other schools. Standards for interlibrary loans between nonacademic libraries were adopted at about the same time.

The National Union Catalog, maintained by the Library of Congress, has for some time distributed its list of books in card form to more than one hundred leading American libraries and major libraries abroad, and the *Union List of Serials*, published in five massive volumes, can be found in all of the larger libraries of North America. Furthermore, catalogs are available that relate to special collections such as Columbia University's Avery Architectural Library and the American Geographical Society's research library.

Prior to World War II, the leaders of Nazi Germany viewed the public library as a vehicle for spreading their racist doctrines. They greatly increased the number of public libraries in Germany and stocked them with their "approved books." They also set up libraries in border areas to counteract

Danish, French, and Polish cultural influences. Books by Jewish and communist writers were removed from all existing libraries, as were other titles deplored by the Nazis. Even the German catalogs and classification systems were revised to reflect Nazi views on questions of nationalism and race. Fortunately, after the war ended the German library system was returned to the standards of librarianship practiced elsewhere in the world.

Most librarians historically have viewed themselves as the upholders of the moral values and ethical standards of society. Thus during the eighteenth and first half of the nineteenth centuries librarians deplored popular fiction and kept such books off their library shelves. But by the 1850s a general hope arose among them that in stocking some fiction they might attract readers whose tastes would be improved as they came into contact with the "better types" of literature.

Even as late as 1928, the American Library Association warned its members through its publications that "many of the staid old conservative magazines of the past now are distributors of social and political theories of at least doubtful desirability and of fiction of whose desirability there is, unfortunately, little or no doubt." Few libraries in America at that time contained any books with minority viewpoints, and books advocating political radicalism were always banned.

Yet the climate was changing and opposition to censorship became, and today still is, a part of any librarian's professional ethics. In 1939, when the United States celebrated the 150th anniversary of the Bill of Rights, the American Library Association composed and issued the following *Library Bill of Rights*:

1. As a responsibility of library service, books and other reading matter selected should be chosen for values of interest, information, and enlightenment of all the people of the community. In no case should any book be excluded because of the race or nationality, or the political or religious views of the writer.

2. There should be the fullest practicable provision of materials presenting all points of view concerning the problems and issues of our times, international, national, and local, and books or other reading matter of sound factual authority should not be proscribed or removed from library shelves because of partisan or doctrinal disapproval.

3. Censorship of books, urged or practiced by volunteer arbiters of morals or political opinion or by organizations that would establish a coercive concept of Americanism, must be challenged by libraries in maintenance of their responsibility to provide public information and enlightenment through the printed word.

4. Libraries should enlist the cooperation of allied groups in the fields

of science, of education, and of book publishing in resisting all abridgment of the free access to ideas and full freedom of expression that are the tradition and heritage of Americans.

5. The rights of an individual to use of a library should not be denied or abridged because of his race, religion, national origin, or political views.

6. As an institution of education for democratic living, the library should welcome the use of its meeting rooms for socially useful and cultural activities and discussion of current public questions. Such meeting places should be available on equal terms to all groups in the community regardless of the beliefs and affiliations of their members.

Unfortunately, this *Library Bill of Rights* is not always honored when significant public pressure is applied. Pressure groups of all sorts, both conservative and radical, have demanded that their views be represented in any library collection, and they have called for the banning of books that were in opposition to their views. During the McCarthy period of the 1950s, when Senator Joseph McCarthy of Wisconsin conducted Congressional hearings to rout out alleged Communists in the government, a great many books were removed from library shelves at the insistence of self-proclaimed patriots. Even now, some librarians still succumb to such pressures. A list of the 50 most frequently banned books taken off the shelves of school libraries during the 1990s includes *Of Mice and Men* by John Steinbeck, *The Catcher in the Rye* by J. D. Salinger, *The Adventures of Huckleberry Finn* by Mark Twain, *I Know Why the Caged Bird Sings* by Maya Angelou, *Lord of the Flies* by William Golding, and even *Little Red Riding Hood.* The entire list can be found by accessing one of the Internet Web sites relating to banned books.

National, university, and public libraries form the backbone of any country's general library system. Yet one should not forget that these are supplemented by libraries that have been established to meet the highly specialized requirements of business and professional groups.

The National Library of Medicine, America's and perhaps the world's greatest medical library, began as a collection of books in the office of the United States Army's surgeon general. Its catalog in 1840 listed only 134 titles. Today its collection is truly enormous and its catalog, recorded in a computerized database, is available on request to doctors everywhere.

There is no equivalent of this National Library of Medicine for lawyers because the practice of law varies from state to state, but every large law firm in the United States has its specialized law library, and in England lawyers rely on the libraries of the Inns of Court and the Incorporated Law Societies. Other countries have comparable law libraries that jurists can consult.

The Hamburg Commercial Library in Germany was the first special library established to serve people in the fields of commerce and trade. It was started by the Hamburg Chamber of Commerce in 1735. As the size of this library's collection grew, it became a symbol of the city's importance to commerce. The library collected as many books as possible relating to trade and navigation from England, France, Holland, Italy, Russia, and Sweden. Later, similar libraries were established in England and in the United States. Many industrial companies today maintain large libraries of their own that relate specifically to their business specialties.

As early as 1876, the United States Patent Office Library had 23,000 volumes in its collection and was considered at the time to be "the best technological library in the country." The number of volumes has, of course, increased enormously, and searching through the library's records to find a single item takes a great deal of time. In fact, the Patent Office now receives more than 100,000 applications for new patents each year and every one must be thoroughly examined to make sure that another patent has not already been issued for that same invention. In England, the British Patent Office Library eventually evolved into the National Reference Library of Science and Invention and became a constituent part of the British Museum. And a whopping 30 million patents, covering 63 countries including Japan and the United States, can be reviewed on a free Internet Web database (ep.dips.org) run by the European Patent Office.

On the whole, special research libraries have been among the pioneers in adapting to new library technology, whether it be microfilm, microfiche (four-by-six-inch microfilm cards), or computerization. They also have been the first to catalog their collections in greater depth, develop their own indexing vocabularies and classification schemes, and enter document and book data on magnetic tape so that information could be found quickly by using pattern-matching techniques invented by computer scientists. Furthermore, as computers and optical storage devices such as CD-ROMs became available, special research libraries were among the first to begin to take advantage of the rapid search capabilities and multimedia content of these devices. The aim of the special libraries always has been to place the right piece of information in the right hands at the right time.

The role of public libraries has changed just as much in recent years. Such libraries now sponsor a wide variety of activities from story hours for children to afternoon musicales, international events workshops, and public poetry readings for adults. Through such means as radio, television, and newspaper announcements, librarians publicize the benefits to be derived from using library materials. They operate bookmobile services to carry library collections throughout cities, towns, and rural areas. Some of the most modern libraries even send out information by way of cable television.

With the storage capacity that computers and microfilm make possible, library archivists face an increasingly difficult problem in deciding what information is worth storing for present reference and for the edification of future generations and what is not. Everyone agrees that books, magazines, and newspapers are not the only receptacles for knowledge. But there is no consensus on what information should be saved by a library beyond such printed data. One library, for example, keeps a large collection of posters and billboard displays that were designed for advertising beer, cigarettes, and underwear. Another maintains a collection of political cartoons.

Workers in the modern library also are having to learn a whole new vocabulary derived from electronics, communications, information theory, and systems engineering. Terms such as malfunctioning, programming, noise, mathematical model, online, lattice, and PERT (Program Evaluation and Review Technique) have become a part of the library researchers' daily language. And the ranks of librarians are being invaded by engineers, data processors, and systems designers who have brought their technological concepts with them.

Subject headings now have become descriptions. The librarian is now an information specialist, and the library is now an information center. Even collections of library materials have been redesignated as the store of information. There have been some discussions in library circles about creating "information supermarkets," complete with membership fees and parking-meter rates for time spent in the reading room. Yet through providing public access to the World Wide Web and giving instructions to library users on how to find information from the countless sources available in cyberspace, librarians are continuing to provide the services that they traditionally have supplied over the centuries.

The ability to search for material under a wide range of categories — author, date, key word, title, report number, and others — and to use various search techniques to specify with increasing precision the subject matter being sought has made the computerized catalog a necessity in both specialized and large general libraries. University students now consult the bibliographies of many specialized libraries on their campus as well as general libraries at other institutions by computer, and in a matter of minutes determine whether the book they are seeking is currently available or out on loan. If it is on loan, a "save" in the caller's name is automatically recorded by the computer. As yet, the researcher, though able to browse through the various library catalogs and other library resources, cannot read the books online. In fact, there remains quite a gap between knowing that a particular book is available in a particular library and being able to see its contents on the computer display.

Quite a number of books, however, can be downloaded from the Internet for a small price. It is indeed easy and cheap to publish works on the Internet. Unfortunately, no mechanism exists to make sure that the information appearing there is accurate.

17. The Complexity of Learning

We learn from our parents, from our teachers, and from the general store of knowledge that circulates within our environment, some of which is merely mythology. Any conflict in information on the same subject from two different sources sets up cognitive dissonance in our minds, which we can resolve only by making a decision to accept one source over the other. In a surprising number of cases, human beings tend to opt for the most tenuous data.

Opinion polls, for example, show that at least one-fourth of all Americans believe in astrology, even though scientists have shown that it is just superstition and they have produced many scientific studies to support that fact. Indeed, there are about ten times as many astrologers in the United States as there are astronomers, while in France there are more astrologers than there are Roman Catholic clergy.

Only nine percent of Americans, again according to opinion polls, accept the central finding of modern biology that all species, including human beings, evolved naturally over the millennia from primitive one-celled organisms. When people are asked if they accept the idea of evolution, 45 percent will say yes, but when asked the same question in terms of Darwin's theory of evolution, this number declines precipitously. Yet all professional biologists would affirm the statement by one of their leading members, Theodosius Dobzhansky, that nothing in biology makes sense except in the light of Darwin's theory of evolution.

One-quarter of all Americans believe in reincarnation, the mystical concept that comes from India and for which there never has been any empirical or logical proof, while one-third of these same adults believe they have made contact with the dead on some level or other.

The results of these surveys demonstrate that much of what we learn in school, where scientific facts are commonly presented in an undistorted fashion, is all too often discounted in favor of popular and unsupported beliefs. The fault lies not with our schooling; it apparently comes from the way our minds process data.

Today scientists know a great deal about how the mind works (short-term and long-term memory, left and right brain activity, and so forth) yet no one has formulated an adequate and comprehensive explanation as to exactly how the learning process takes place. This is because hundreds of subtle influences affect the ingestion of knowledge. We learn through our eyes, our ears, our taste and smell, and through touch. We learn by sensing movements, temperatures, and distances from other people and objects. We learn from television, from conversations, from reading newspapers and books. And we learn from our feelings — through the often irrational links between feelings and sense experience, and through the perception of conflict between one feeling and another.

The subtlety of this influence of sensations on our ability to learn has been demonstrated by several simple experiments proving that room design, lights, and noise clearly affect our comprehension and speed in reading a newspaper. Architects report that redesigning a meeting room can change the character of the deliberations conducted within it. Arguments occur less frequently when there is more space so that the participants feel less crowded. Even the arrangement of seats apparently can determine the liveliness and tone of discussion.

The limited theory of learning put forward by behaviorist psychologists, such as B. F. Skinner, fails to include the multitude of subtleties that go into acquiring knowledge. Perhaps the theory is popular because of its simplicity and measurability in laboratory experiments. However, it is woefully inadequate as an explanation of the many ways in which we actually learn.

The theory holds that a person acquires the ability to perform an action as a result of the response to that action. For example, a child learns to beg for candy because such behavior often results in the child receiving candy. Every time the child receives such a reward, the tendency to beg becomes greater because it is reinforced by the receipt of the sweets.

Behaviorists insist that this is the way all learning takes place, and a multitude of experimental results back their claim. Rats have been trained by food rewards to press levers to get more food. Cats have been trained to follow a series of intricate movements to avoid electrical shocks. Chickens have been trained to dance on piano keys and to pull pinball machine levers.

There is no doubt, of course, that behavior can be conditioned by reward and punishment. The threat of retaliatory violence has long kept people from doing harm to others. And it is certainly true that many of our habits are developed as a result of unconscious rewards. But it is absurd to conclude from this that all our past learning — or present learning — is purely the result of such conditioning. Most of what we learn never becomes habit. Activities that result in great rewards may never again be repeated. And people act over and over in ways that they know will result in punishment rather than reward, because they are responding to some moral or ideological principle.

In real-world situations, as distinguished from those in a laboratory, the possibility of foretelling human response to particular rewards and punishments is so slight that it has no predictive value at all. Free choice always is there as a human attribute. It remains so even in situations where behavior is most predictable — as in a prison or concentration camp. Here, often enough, a prisoner risks death by refusing to follow what he is "conditioned" to do.

Behaviorists claim that persuasion is a relatively ineffective method for controlling behavior. They say that learning takes place only through the reward-punishment process. When punishment works, they argue, it is related to some reward, even when the individual is not conscious of that fact. They point out that persuasive arguments regarding the hazards of not wearing seat belts while driving a car, the danger of lung cancer to smokers, and the threat of air pollution to every city dweller's health have little perceptible effect on increasing seat-belt usage and decreasing smoking and air pollution.

Whether persuasion is effective or not depends on the content of the argument, not on hidden rewards and punishments. Again, there are too many examples of human free will in opposition to expected rewards and punishments to argue otherwise. The behaviorist theory may be true to a limited extent, but that's the problem. It holds only for the type of learning that leads to habits and not for the much broader and more general types of learning that all people experience.

When we want to explain more complex aspects of learning — the attraction of certain philosophical concepts, the beauty of mathematics for particular individuals, the joy of language to others — the behaviorist explanation quickly collapses. It is too limited to account for much more than that which has long been obvious.

One area of learning generally ignored by behaviorists is that which grows from the arts — painting, literature, music. Art presents us with tools that can probe to depths of understanding we would not otherwise reach. This is because the artist's creative vision reveals previously hidden internal dimensions of life, enabling us to see a totally new world. The inspiration of a poet invites us to recognize our own buried emotions and desires. The music generated by a composer allows us to recognize new sounds and rhythms in life.

Art is expressive of human existence. It is the extra vision by which an artist perceives the truth and conveys it to us through suggestion. It is expressed in language by writers, in stone or clay by sculptors, in paint or chalk by graphic artists, and in sound and rhythm by composers. Each artistic work achieves power through its design or structure. And each work can add something to our learning.

Susanne Langer, who has written perhaps the most perceptive books on the philosophy of art, describes the arts as symbols of reality — symbols that enable us to increase our understanding of our own emotions and of the world in which we live. As she puts it, the artist's eye and ear turns ordinary sights (or sounds, motions, and events) into inward visions that, in turn, are captured in a finalized artistic form. To create a work of art is to create an illusion that magnifies and spotlights aspects of the real world, and thus brings it to everyone's consciousness. To experience and learn from a work of art is to grow in self-knowledge.

Langer has demonstrated that every art image is a purified and simplified aspect of reality created by the subtle laws of human experience that express the nature of this reality. The art of dance, for example, creates the illusion of power made visible by the unbroken fabric of gesture. The elements in a painting combine to create the illusion of space. The elements of music create the illusion of time. Poetry, in turn, creates the illusion of reality through its imagery, grammatical form, and word rhythm.

Each of the arts teaches us in a somewhat different way, and these variations are due to more than just how the particular art form impacts our senses. Take, for example, the differences in the way the same story is conveyed to us through television or through a novel. The television image is a captive of time and space in a way that no book needs to be. Television cannot really show a thought or reflect on ideas as can the printed words in a book. Despite slow-motion and fast-cutting techniques, television is limited to showing people in action at a normal human pace. Each television event takes place at a single time and in a single place.

Television resembles day-to-day happenings, resembles them in that if you miss something on the screen, it's gone forever — unless you can catch it on the reruns. Television is thus experiential. Printed words, on the other hand, are reflective. No matter how concretely an author writes, the words transcend time and space. They can be looked at now or later. They can be read, put aside, and reread at any time you might wish. They can be skimmed over rapidly or they can be ponderously followed syllable by syllable.

Television, stage plays, and music are all art forms that require audience control if they are to succeed as art. The playwright achieves success with a play to the extent that the audience has been made to laugh or cry at the moment the playwright wanted them to do so. The audience relates to the play at the particular speed and according to the dynamics set by the author. If the playwright's desired effect is lost on the audience, the play fails. The author cannot ask the audience to go back and review the scene until their reaction fits the desired purpose.

The pictorial arts and literature are not so restricted. The audience can look at a picture again and again. Each time, an individual may experience a different emotion or see something new in the deep structure of the artwork.

The dire predictions about the impending demise of books under the impact of television that were published by Marshall McLuhan and others in the 1960s just haven't proven true. More people are buying and reading books now than ever before — when television is at the height of its influence. The form and type of knowledge provided by books just cannot be replaced by a television screen.

In a sense, a book is the most compact and convenient leisure product and knowledge preserver in existence. You can take it anywhere except underwater and read it anytime you have enough light. Ever since writing was first developed, it has given human beings a broader dimension to their learning process. Through literature people have experienced situations and environments without ever having to meet them in the real world.

But we need to remember that reading is more than just seeing and interpreting a series of words. It is a joint creative process involving a dialogue between the author and the reader. It involves as much skill on the part of one as it does on the part of the other. Indeed, with practice, the reader grows in the ability to deal with written material, just as an author grows in the skill of using words to accurately convey meanings.

Learning a common grammar and alphabet may be the first step to reading, but it no more qualifies one to be a reader than knowing how to hold a violin and interpret a staff of music makes one a musician. Reading is an art and skill acquired through careful exercise and kept in working order through use.

Frequently the most rewarding reading — that which is most satisfying and information producing — is the writing that is the most difficult to read. Chaucer's *Canterbury Tales*, for example, are today no longer easy to understand. They have idioms that are not always clear to us. The sentences are long and somewhat convoluted by present standards. Their content reflects ways of life that are now quite alien. Yet anyone who is willing to struggle through this work will agree that it is far more productive in terms of knowledge and the sparking of new ideas than are 90 percent of contemporary short stories and articles.

The acquisition of knowledge requires mental discipline. This, much like physical discipline, is gained through practice. Untrained muscles when first put to work are always clumsy and soon begin to ache. With training, the athlete learns to control them. Mental muscles behave in much the same way. We improve our knowledge, sensitivity, and capacity to learn through exercising our minds. Indeed, words take on power as readers exercise them through their minds.

Fortunately, mental exercise can take advantage of the fruits of others in a way that physical exercise cannot. We can twist and turn the thoughts we find in centuries of encyclopedic lore and thousands of handwritten and printed books to look at them in different ways, much as we might twist and turn a piece of colored glass to see what happens to the light shining through it. We can apply another author's concepts to situations in the text we are currently looking at and discard the elements in those ideas that prove useless to our deliberations.

Rapid reading is in vogue today because so much printed material deserves no more than a rapid reading. The gems of knowledge within it are few and far between. It is as if our society, now that it has developed the technical capacity to produce large quantities of paper and highly sophisticated methods for printing, finds it necessary to fill that paper with a mass of redundant and trivial words. Many of these, no matter how well packaged in succinct paragraphs and chapters, are useless drivel that will not stand the test of time.

Yet rapid reading sometimes can be quite useful. It allows you to cover a wide range of printed materials in a short span of time. But you simply can't read in depth rapidly. Nor can you grow much in knowledge by speeding up the assembly line of data intake.

Studies have shown that people place more value on the information they themselves seek out than they do on the information they are given by others. In fact, we learn best and remember longest those things in which we are most interested. We also tend to learn most readily about things that are related to those we already understand. Psychologists refer to this as the process of apperception, or the assimilation of new perceptions by means of the mass of ideas already in the mind.

John Locke described this kind of learning in his article *An Essay Concerning Human Understanding*, written in 1690. Locke says that ideas, "always keep in company, and the one no sooner at any time comes into the understanding, but its associate appears with it.... This wrong connexion in our minds of ideas, in themselves loose and independent of one another, has such an influence, and is of so great a force as to set us awry in our actions, as well moral as natural, passions, reasonings, and notions themselves, that perhaps there is not any one thing that deserves more to be looked after."

The astronomer Carl Sagan, while working with his students, developed what to my mind is one of the most useful lists one can use to separate truth from fiction. He published this "baloney detection kit" in the last book he wrote before he died, *The Demon-Haunted World*. It can be of great help to anyone in recognizing some of the most common traps in our own and others' logic. As Sagan put it, "many good examples of the common fallacies of logic can be found in religion and politics, because their practitioners are so often obliged to justify two contradictory propositions."

Below, I have rearranged his list somewhat and have substituted my own examples for his. Perhaps you have even better ones, but you probably will find the list of categories useful:

1. *ad hominem* (Latin for "to the man") — attacking the person rather than the position taken, or in other words, saying that the argument put forward by Mr. Smith is obviously wrong because Smith is such an immoral person. The same kind of fallacy often is applied to groups when someone says that "Chinese scientists can't produce anything of value because China is a largely agricultural country."

2. straw man — setting up an imaginary argument so that it can be easily attacked, as, for example, saying that labor unions exist only to give jobs to high-paid union officials. Another example is the argument used by those against women in the military because they might distract the men in time of war.

3. argument from authority — relying for evidence on the statements of an accepted leader or group of leaders without seeking further confirmation. As everyone knows, this human tendency to believe what any "authority" might have to say is frequently used in advertising to promote one or another drug through pictures of "doctors" (really actors dressed in laboratory gowns) praising the product.

4. appeal to ignorance — arguing for something because it has never been proved untrue, or vice versa. Sagan uses the example of many people's belief in UFOs because no one has yet been able to prove that beings from other worlds have never visited the Earth. Another example might be the widespread belief in extra sensory perception, which has never been proven not to exist even though the proof of its existence rests on rather flimsy grounds. Remember that absence of evidence can hardly prove the evidence of absence.

5. special pleading — any argument that ignores or sets aside points or features that are unfavorable to one's own position. Thus some Christian fundamentalists argue against evolution and for the belief that God created the world in just seven days by saying that dinosaur fossils were placed by God on the Earth at the time of creation as an enticement to human curiosity and never have been remnants of extinct species.

6. begging the question — some call this fallacy "assuming the answer"

and it is seen in the often stated argument that we should censure children's television programs in order to discourage violence among youth. Yet it is an open question as to whether or not youth violence can be linked to television viewing.

7. observational selection — listing only those facts favorable to one's argument and ignoring negative ones. For example, the success of American medicine in performing complex (and expensive) organ transplants is cited as proof of our advanced medical system, while the high rate of our infant mortality statistics in comparison with those of other industrialized nations is ignored. Francis Bacon spoke of this as counting the hits and forgetting the misses.

8. argument from adverse consequences — assuming that some action or situation will automatically lead to a negative result. For example, saying that if the death penalty were to be abolished capital crimes would increase, even though there is no evidence to prove this.

9. misunderstanding the nature of statistics — The classic example here is that of the man who drowned in a river that averaged only six inches in depth. But Sagan points out an even better example of this fallacy, that of President Eisenhower who was shocked when he learned that half of all American citizens are below average in intelligence.

10. statistics of small numbers — basing one's conclusions on a limited number of facts. Thus one assumes that the stock market will go up tomorrow because it did over the last three days, or (the gambler's folly) deciding that luck is going your way because the slot machine paid off twice already.

11. *non sequitur* (Latin for "it doesn't follow") — The classic example here, the one that Sagan uses, is the belief that God is on our side in war and peace, even though the people of almost every nation firmly believe that God is on their particular side. A less often cited *non sequitur* is the statement that homosexuality is unnatural even though most doctors tell us and psychological studies show that at least one out of every ten persons is homosexual or bisexual and this has been true throughout recorded history.

12. inconsistency — reaching a conclusion in which one or several of the arguments conflict with one another. For example, a person argues that everyone should have the right to carry a gun for hunting pleasure and protection, while ignoring the increase in the number of school shootings and the number of police officers who are murdered by people carrying guns.

13. *post hoc, ergo propter hoc* (Latin for "it happened afterward and so it was caused by") — For example, many people are of the opinion that because the Russian scientists were able to build a hydrogen bomb after the Americans did, they must have stolen the secret from us, despite the fact that nuclear physicists in many countries already were working in this area. It should be

noted that many of the best physicists who developed our nuclear capability were immigrants rather than native-born Americans.

14. excluded middle — holding onto the two extremes among a series of intermediate possibilities, as in the statement "better to be dead than red" or "my country right or wrong."

15. slippery slope — somewhat like the excluded middle in that one statement quickly slides without justification into a widely variant conclusion, such as if we permit free distribution of clean needles, the problem of drug abuse will escalate beyond control.

16. short-term vs. long-term — promoting immediate goals at the expense of the future, such as calling for a massive reduction in the tax rate when the national debt remains at an all-time high.

17. meaningless question — raising an issue that is basically irrelevant, such as what do we need to do in preparation for the next ice age. There is the story of the little girl who broke out in tears when she found out that Niagara Falls was retreating toward the city of Buffalo at the rate of three inches per year; she was worried because her favorite aunt lived in Buffalo.

18. confusion of correlation and causation — prevalence of something does not necessarily point to its cause. For example, some say that the use of birth control pills has lead to promiscuity among women, or that AIDS is a "gay disease."

19. suppressed evidence, or half-truths — An example of this is the statement that education is not important among the African-American population because most of them drop out of school anyway, while neglecting to take into consideration the social and economic causes of such high-school dropouts or neglecting to take into account those African-American scholars who have made contributions to our society.

20. weasel words — using euphemisms to hide reality, such as "pacification" in place of military invasion, or speaking of "collateral damage" when a bomb kills people who are not the intended targets. Euphemisms are most often used when speaking of the economy, such as referring to the "working poor" instead of acknowledging that there is widespread poverty among many groups of working people.

The above list includes the most important principles of logic developed by the Greeks as well as some modern ones. But there is one caveat to keep in mind. It is always easier to find fault with the logic of others than it is to find it in yourself.

In conclusion, it is the very complexity of the learning process that results in our often holding onto faulty and contradictory ideas. We learn in so many different ways that our minds sometimes have difficulty in determining reality from illusion. This is why the Greeks developed tools of logic in an attempt to protect themselves from irrational thinking. Such rules have proved helpful throughout the ages for finding the fallacy in the thinking of others. They are not too helpful in analyzing our own thinking, however — probably because we are too protective of our cherished ideas and prejudices to see our own logical fallacies.

18. Entering the Computer Age

There is one thing of which we can be certain — the workings of a computer are nothing like those of the human brain. A computer, in fact, is almost exactly what the brain is not. A computer is capable of paying undivided attention to unlimited detail. It is precise and reliable. It is immune to distraction. It can carry out the most intricate and lengthy calculations with ease, and in much less than a millionth of the time it would take its human counterpart. It suffers neither boredom nor fatigue, and it has to be told to do something only once to do it perfectly thereafter.

But computers cannot be made to think for themselves, i.e., without the installation of a computer program created by human design. Computers cannot do their job unless they have the whole program laid out in advance, which is something people don't usually need. When the program is faulty, the computer will turn out rubbish, or GIGO (Garbage In, Garbage Out) as computer technologists call it.

The human brain has many more processing units than does a computer, roughly as many as there are stars in our galaxy. Millions of them are destroyed during one's lifetime without any noticeable loss in efficiency. Most of the brain consists of connections, each unit having thousands of which lead to other units and back to themselves. In a computer chip there are usually fewer than six.

Both the brain and the computer have speed and power. The brain seems able to perform as many as 200 trillion operations a second, far more than any computer can. It does many things easily that a computer cannot — recognize people's faces, understand language, direct intricate muscle movements throughout the body. But when the normal brain is called upon to multiply large numbers without the aid of paper and pencil, it fails miserably in comparison to even the simplest of computers.

Computers are woefully inadequate as posers of new ideas and concepts. They cannot make up questions on their own, talk back independently, imagine, dream, aspire, or create. They can find no new problems, and quite often they can be found running a human user off in the wrong direction. Frequently new ideas come to a person while searching the mind for a bit of information among the mass of remembered facts and images. The unrelated idea takes hold, and the searched-for data is then no longer important. In a computer the data will be found much more quickly, and no unrelated idea will ever evolve. The computer can go over the same ground innumerable times and never produce a single new idea.

When people and computers work together in a symbiotic relationship, the shortcomings of each are compensated for by the other. Then the individual and the computer can perform the kind of activity for which each is best suited. The person can be creative and the computer can be fast and exact.

Ever since the development of the first computers, progress in science no longer has been determined by the number of people who are able to solve intricate problems, because the supreme problem solvers have been the machines. A mathematical computation that took the astronomer Johannes Kepler nearly two years to solve, for example, was answered by a computer in eight seconds. Another computer program enabled the solving of as many as 350 theorems taken from the first 13 chapters of Whitehead and Russell's *Principia Mathematica* in just under eight and a half minutes. In the past, the deciphering of just one of these theorems might have been the subject for an entire Ph.D. thesis. In a surprisingly short time science, with the aid of computers, has extended our knowledge all the way from the behavior of galaxies to the behavior of particles in the subatomic world.

The chief consequence of the computer revolution, however, is that human beings now are relieved of much of the dull and stultifying labor to which they were subjected for all of history. Yet when computers first were used for some white-collar as well as blue-collar tasks in the 1950s it shocked the humanitarians, who feared that the machines might make human beings obsolete. Norbert Weiner, the noted mathematician who played an important part in developing these machines, did nothing to alleviate such anxieties when he spoke of "machines doing complex intellectual tasks."

Since then, however, we all have come to accept without fear the usefulness of these electronic brains in assembling, classifying, calculating, and summarizing a whole variety of data. Computer technology now inundates us at every turn, whether we are withdrawing cash from an ATM machine, buying airline tickets, using a telephone, playing Nintendo, or surfing the Internet. In fact, we refer to our times as the computer age, and we talk of the "information sciences" that have been spawned by computers, of the "information superhighway," and of performing "information work."

Computers are highly versatile. They have been programmed to draw pictures; to play chess; to respond to sounds, smells, and touch; and to reproduce some of their own parts. All kinds of data, even music, can be reduced to 1s and 0s (the basic binary computer code) that is inserted into the computer's memory system. Later the same data can be retrieved as a series of printed numbers, as lines on a graph, as words, as music coming through a loudspeaker, or as pictures on a monitor.

Supercomputers, manipulating billions of commands a second, forecast the weather and analyze complex medical images. Sensory computers recognize parts on assembly lines, and robotic computers build those parts into complete products. Millions of personal computers, along with a wide variety of software packages, assist people at work and at home with thousands of different tasks.

As they relate to knowledge acquisition, computers provide storage for vast amounts of data in huge databases that make even the most complete libraries of books seem small by comparison. A portion of this data has been recorded on CD-ROM disks for desktop computer use, and much of the rest of it can be accessed through the Internet.

The computer evolved over the past 60 some years from a roomful of vacuum tubes and wires capable of executing perhaps 500,000 instructions per second into a chip one square centimeter or less in size that works 20 times faster. The number of components that can be contained on a single chip has been doubling every 18 months as estimated by the Aspen Institute for Humanistic Studies.

Relatively intuitive instructions, icons, and desktop metaphors have replaced the strings of alphanumeric instructions long dreaded by early programmers. Optical fibers with a carrying capacity of millions and perhaps eventually billions of bits of information per second are replacing copper wires carrying 64,000 to one million bits per second. The compression technology now in use is multiplying such numbers by a factor of two or three. New computer words such as keyboard, mouse, modem, interface, online, hardware, software, and information access now have become entrenched in our vocabulary.

The person credited with developing the idea for a digital computer was Charles ("Sir Alphabet Function") Babbage (1792–1871). He spent all his large fortune in meticulously constructing such a machine, which he called his Analytical Engine. Babbage explained that, "One evening I was sitting in the rooms of the Analytical Society at Cambridge ... with a table of logarithms lying open before me. Another member coming into the room, and seeing me half asleep called out, 'Well, Babbage, what are you dreaming about?' to which I replied, 'I am thinking that all these tables might be calculated by machinery.'"

The device that Babbage constructed consisted of two parts: "1st. the store in which all the variables to be operated upon, as well as those quantities which have arisen from the result of other operations, are placed. 2nd. the mill into which the quantities about to be operated upon are always brought." Today, we talk of what he named "the store" as memory; his "internal information" is our numerical data; and his "mill" is our central processing unit, or CPU.

Although the Babbage machine was much more advanced than anything of this sort that had been designed before, it was more of a calculator than a computer. And it was capable of calculating only two orders of difference in a mathematical series of numbers. It took another British genius, Alan Turing, to come up with the radical and exciting concept of constructing a single machine that had no fixed purpose, one that could tackle any or all of the tasks an owner might wish to perform.

Computer development flourished during World War II when such machines were needed to make calculations that could be used for aiming antiaircraft guns, breaking the enemy's secret codes, and computing airplane wing flutter. The Mark I, built in 1944, was controlled by many mechanical and electrical devices. Next came the ENIAC (Electronic Numerical Integrator and Computer) in 1946. It was a huge machine controlled by 18,000 vacuum tubes. It occupied 3,000 cubic feet of space, weighed 30 tons, and consumed 140 kilowatts of electricity.

During these years perhaps the most important of computer advances came from the work of John von Neumann (1903–57), a Hungarian mathematician who had immigrated to the United States. Von Neumann developed the technique for storing a computer program in the machine's memory. Of course, earlier computers also had used programs, but these were fed into the machine as needed and not stored within them.

Like Turing, von Neumann stressed the fact that a computer's power would derive from its ability to connect logical operations to electronic circuitry. Logic could set the rules for moving symbols about in a completely determined manner, according to Turing. Electronic circuitry corresponding to these logical rules, according to von Neumann, could manipulate the symbolized information in a series of electronic impulses that passed through a sequence of controlled or branching points.

By the 1950s, computers were able to perform thousands of calculations per second. Those of the early 1960s could perform ten times as many per second, and by 1965 there were machines that could do one million calculations a second — one thousand times as many as could be done in the 1950s.

A few basic concepts about computers should be helpful to anyone in understanding how they work. First, although the rapid strides in digital electronics have taken the computer industry on a wild gallop through three generations in as many decades — from large vacuum tubes to small transistors to micro-processors — it is the chip's complex structure and not its diminutive size that has made it so important. Single chips have become complete systems or major portions of systems, and thus they have achieved a flexibility previously unknown. At a relatively early stage, for example, an experimental device built in California demonstrated that with one chip a computer could become a digital clock; with another it could be turned into a radio-like unit that played a set tune; and with still another it could be converted into a rudimentary piano that the operator could play by depressing a few keys.

The second thing to note is that the basic architecture of a computer is the same whether the machine is mammoth or miniscule. It consists of three systems that recently have been separated and inscribed on different silicon chips. One of these three systems is an arithmetic, or logic, unit that performs the mathematical operations. Another is the memory unit where information is stored. The third is a control unit that guides the computer in sending electric signals through the mathematical and memory units.

Finally, one needs to recognize that the way data is recorded in the computer's memory system and the way it is retrieved depends on the program that is written for the particular task it is meant to do. And this brings us to the language of computers. In the earliest computers, instructions had to be painstakingly written out by hand as an endless string of 1s and 0s. But by the early and mid–1960s, computer programmers could manipulate the machines' operations with high-level computer languages such as FORTRAN (Formula Translation), COBOL (Common Business Oriented Language), and PL-1 (Programming Language 1). They could write the programs in a kind of computerized Pidgin English, and other special programs called compilers would translate their instructions into the machine code of 1s and 0s.

The first attempts in using the machine code to create programs that would translate noncomputer languages, such as Russian or Chinese, into English proved somewhat faulty. The phrase "the spirit is willing but the flesh is weak" when translated into Russian came out as "the vodka is agreeable, but the meat has spoiled." An attempt to turn the advertising slogan "Coke adds life" into Chinese produced "Coke brings your ancestors back from the grave."

Despite such difficulties, it has been in the area of word processing that the computer has proved most useful for the average layperson. Few authors use a typewriter anymore. Aunt Grace sends out her Christmas letters after inputting them on a computer keyboard and printing them directly from the console. Uncle Jim sends his college-based daughter daily e-mail messages through his computer's connection to the Internet.

Although typing a few words seems simple enough, the computer operations that take place are much more complex than they ever were on a typewriter. Each letter of the Roman alphabet, upper and lowercase, as well as the standard punctuation marks, numbers, tabs, and carriage returns are read by the computer as a single unit, or byte, of eight digits (separate combinations of 1s and 0s). There are altogether 128 such combinations that stand for the numbers, letters, and punctuation marks used in the English language. When an operator's finger depresses a key on the keyboard, the action results in producing the electrical impulse that sends one of the eight-digit units through the logic and memory chips so that it will appear on the computer screen as a recognizable letter of the alphabet.

When one wishes to reproduce French, German, or other languages that require accents and umlauts in their written form, the number of characters (eight-digit units) must be doubled to 256. Virtually every desktop computer in use has these additional characters at its disposal, which was never true with the ordinary typewriter. However, these special symbols are embedded in the memory chip and cannot be easily located on the keyboard. The numbers for each character must be entered as a particular series of 1s and 0s before they will appear on the computer screen. Fortunately, simple programs have been added to most operating systems that allow the user to produce the necessary numbers for this ASCII (American Standard Code for Information Interchange) alphabet code by pressing various key combinations on the keyboard to insert the desired special characters.

Yet even the 256 combinations of the ASCII set will not account for some of the unique characters used by other European languages, such as Swedish and Greek. At present a new universal alphabet of about 35,000 units is in the making. This eventually will replace the ASCII character set. Once it is completed, a computer will be able to reproduce every distinct symbol in every writing system known to humankind. The universal alphabet is being dubbed the Unicode, and it should allow for a far more flexible representation of all the writing systems in the world.

Computer manuscript production and editing has proved particularly useful in the field of encyclopedia publishing, since as much as 80 percent of the editorial work on such publications involves the revision of existing materials. The computer can hold an almost unlimited number of such pages in its memory bank and display them on the computer screen at the demand of an editor.

Using a sonic sketch pad and a special stylus, the editor and layout artist can designate what corrections are needed on any page by drawing them on the layout pad. The lines of the stylus are electronically sensed by the pad and converted into digital signals (the 1s and 0s of the binary system) for electronic reproduction as lines on the display screen. The editor or layout artist thus is able to erase and adjust the layout at will. When the work is finished, the push of a button sends the revised layout into the computer's permanent memory bank.

Word and paragraph additions to any page can be typed on the computer keyboard, viewed on the screen, and then stored in the memory bank to be recalled and edited at will. Page proofs from the computer then can be produced in printout form for circulation and approval by others in the editorial department. After all the page changes have been approved, the computer can produce a magnetic tape that drives a phototypesetter in reproducing the pages as offset printing plates.

Because of computers, typesetting has moved from the printing plant to the desktop. While human typesetters in the early part of this century spent as much as one-half of their time inserting metal typefaces in sequence and the rest of their time arranging the white space on a page surrounding the characters, there are now many computerized ways for rapidly formatting information into text pages. The results are quite attractive on either the computer screen or on printed pages. And the number of distinct typefaces (from Old English to Circus Modern) available to any computer user are far greater in variety than were those available to the average printing house in the days of metal type.

The editing process itself also has changed dramatically in recent years due to the computer software now available. These software programs can read through documents and find all the split infinitives, occurrences of the passive voice, archaic and foreign words, improper punctuation, doubled words, hackneyed words, clichés, and so on. Such programs can even rate the written material as to its reading level and potential interest.

The very ease and flexibility of the electronic media has raised serious issues relating to copyright protection. Even when photocopiers first came into use, copyright protection was in danger, because it was so easy to make almost exact copies of printed material and whole books without the author's or publisher's knowledge. But making photocopies still required time as well as quantities of photocopying paper. Now, when information exists as a pattern of 0s and 1s on a hard disk, it takes less than one second to make an identical copy that can be read on one's monitor or printed out in multiple copies for distribution. The computer technology to make such copies is cheaper and more lightweight than are most photocopying machines. Furthermore, the fact that such an electronic copy has been produced is easily concealed and almost impossible to trace.

The computer age, of course, is resulting in an ever greater amount of knowledge being created and stored. Some estimates have it that every year this amount doubles. The value of most of this data may be a matter of conjecture, but consider the fact that a weekday edition of the *New York Times* contains more information than the average person in seventeenth-century England was likely to encounter in a whole lifetime. That much and probably more is added to the accessible Internet archives every single day.

Never has the cost of collecting, processing, and transmitting information been so low. The linking of computers with telecommunications has made not only the large-scale processing of tremendous amounts of information but their almost instantaneous collection and analysis a matter of relative ease. The complex system for getting approval in Paris to make a purchase using an American-based credit card, which involves a 46,000-mile journey over phones, relay stations, and computers, now is usually completed in fewer than five seconds.

Much of the information stored in computers exists in large mainframes and central data banks that can be accessed through the Internet from desktop machines. However, as noted above, some of this also can be accessed from CD-ROM disks, each of which can store up to 600 megabytes of data. That is equal to 250,000 pages of printed material, or nearly 1,700 of the 360K floppy disks that used to be used to distribute software and data for the personal computer. Unlike the disks, however, these CDs are read-only so that the data on them is permanently encoded and cannot be erased or modified. (The term "CD-ROM" stands for compact disk, read-only memory.)

CD-ROM disks are five-inch slices of plastic that look exactly like any of the plain old audio compact disks that have mostly replaced phonograph records as the media of choice for music enthusiasts. In fact, most computer CD drives also can play music disks, provided they are connected to a pair of speakers or a home stereo sound system.

Because they hold so much data and because they also can hold software, CD-ROMs are excellent knowledge containers. A single disk can replace a wall of books, hold an entire encyclopedia, a set of huge reference manuals, or an auto company's entire parts list. A CD-ROM disk is lightweight, rugged, and easy to store. Every telephone number in the United States, for example, can be stored on perhaps five disks and kept in a desk drawer.

One of the major attractions of CD-ROMs is their portability. Internet connections are not universally available throughout the world, and phone service in some countries is chancy at best. Even within the United States, a librarian may not be able to access a particular database through the Internet, because all the access ports are at that moment in use or the computer system itself is down. A copy of the needed database on a CD-ROM disk takes care of such problems.

Despite the density of data, the error rate for a CD-ROM disk is lower than for magnetic tape, and random access makes CD-ROMs ideal as reference book replacements, because they provide quick and easy access to specific information. Accessing data on such disks may be slower than getting the same information from the Internet, but the ease of use clearly makes up for this slight difficulty.

CD-ROMs are orders of magnitude cheaper to produce than books in terms of per unit of data, and they are virtually indestructible. The data on them is easily updated, because only new data needs to be added at the premastering step. Duplicates can be stamped out mechanically at a much faster rate than magnetic tape can be reproduced. The largest single expense associated with CD-ROM disk production lies in the conversion of text, pictures, or music into the digital 0 and 1 binary form. And much of this can be done by an electronic scanner rather than by the labor-intensive typing of a human worker.

CD-ROMs may last as long as a few decades or even for centuries. But the software programs that run them don't last, because these are constantly being upgraded. The series of 0s and 1s that were recorded on magnetic tape for use in the 1960s cannot be read today, because the hardware and software that originally created them is now obsolete and probably has been destroyed. This, like the infamous Y2K problem, is something the computer programmers didn't anticipate when they stored the original data two or three decades ago.

Thanks to CD-ROMs, along with a new generation of hardware and software, computers are no longer limited to just words and numbers. They are becoming multimedia tools. A single home computer can now inform and entertain you with pictures, animation, sound, graphics, and video, as well as more pages of printed words than you will probably ever desire.

19. The New World of Hypertext

The best known encyclopedia designers — Francis Bacon, Denis Diderot, and Samuel Coleridge — probably would have thought hypertext to be some kind of magic. H. G. Wells, who wrote about plans for a "world brain" that would contain all relevant knowledge, never even dreamed of any such process. It took the invention of the computer and the vision of Vannevar Bush and Ted Nelson to bring this miracle into being.

Vannevar Bush was the science advisor to President Franklin D. Roosevelt in the 1940s. In those days, when the first room-sized computers were being constructed, he published an article in the July 1945 issue of the *Atlantic Monthly* titled "How We May Think." His contention was that human beings follow thought processes in terms of associations and patterns that are rarely alphabetic in nature, as are indexes in books and topic guides in libraries. Thus all text storage systems, he said, should be organized by association rather than by the letters of the alphabet or numbering systems. This essay laid the groundwork for hypertext.

Bush envisioned a text storage system that he called Memex, a system in which all the documents and their contents were indexed by association. Each time a new document was placed into the system, logical links would be entered leading to the contents of other documents already in storage. The links then could be used by any researcher to point to any or all the related documents.

Twenty years later Ted Nelson, another computer visionary, refined the Bush idea and named it hypertext — meaning a nonsequential assembly of ideas. According to Nelson, "The ultimate hypertext goal is the global accumulation of knowledge.... It would be a universal publishing system where every interested person has direct access to humanity's accumulated knowledge — in effect, the ultimate publishing system where each person is both contributor and user."

Documents in hypertext now can be found on the Internet and on some CD-ROM disks. The hypertext system allows a reader to jump at will to related ideas instead of reading a text from beginning to end. Of course, it is always possible to read any hypertext article sequentially, but with this system readers can link to other items and ideas as they move through the document, and go back and forth to follow other leads. Reading hypertext is open-ended, the path being determined by the needs and interests of the reader. The process might be compared to that of using a dictionary or thesaurus where, each time you consult the work, you enter it at a different location based on the word with which you began your search.

Consider reading a book about civil rights — a multifaceted topic. As you are reading, you come to a sentence about Dr. Martin Luther King, Jr., in a portion describing the historic 1963 march on Washington. At this point you might like to skip elsewhere in the book to learn more about Dr. King. You could keep plodding along through the text in the hope of eventually coming to a section on Dr. King, or you could flip to the index to find references to the man. In either case, it would take time before you located what you wished. As you progress through the text and find other names or topics that interest you — Rev. Shuttlesworth, Stokely Carmichael, the Montgomery bus boycott — flipping back and forth from the index to the text becomes quite cumbersome.

Now let us say you are viewing the same book on the Internet or with a CD-ROM program that has been designed to use hypertext. Again you are reading about the march on Washington and you come to the mention of Dr. King. Here you just click your mouse on his name and his biography appears on the monitor, overlapping the main article. When you finish reading the biography, you can return to the main article to continue reading, perhaps later clicking on another subject that catches your interest, and so on.

Hypertext is designed to work in a fashion similar to the way people actually think — not processing information in a linear way from A to B to C — but by free association, starting with A but taking you to G or M or F before you continue on sequentially to B. Hypertext thus is a totally different method for accessing information. It is nonsequential, allowing for the nonlinear organization of text. Unlike other storage schemes, hypertext has no dead ends.

Hypertext allows people to create, annotate, link together, and share information from a variety of media such as text, animation, audio, graphics, video, and computer programs. It provides flexible access to information by incorporating the notions of navigation, annotation, and tailored presentation. When multimedia elements have been added to hypertext — linking pictures, video sequences, or music to the text — the system is usually called hypermedia, another word coined by Ted Nelson.

Some of the first attempts to create hypertext documents were contained in programs such as Apple's HyperCard, Owl's Guide, and MaxThink's Houdini. But as interest in the Internet increased, a hypertext markup language called HTML was developed, and various tools, such as Java, were created to write programs using the hypertext system. These placed markers throughout any text that pointed to other documents or sections of documents that related to the marked words.

When you look at a document that includes hypertext, you will see words in almost every paragraph that are marked in some way (usually by underlining). If you click your computer mouse on one of these words, a different document appears that will give you more information about the item selected. The new information might come from another section of the document you are reading, from a different document in that data file, or even from a totally different location on the Internet's World Wide Web. It all depends on what the author chooses as that particular link at that point in the text.

Some links are even set up to automatically retrieve the supporting or opposing arguments related to the content of the text. The linked ideas can be shown as words, as an image, as viewed from the back or front, and even inside out. Furthermore, one link can point to another that points to still another so that by the time the reader has learned all they might want to know about a selected topic many overlays will have filled the monitor.

The computer and hypertext have given those with desktop machines the potential to access much more information than existed in the Great Library of Alexandria. In fact, computer technology is drawing together all of today's reference books, scholarly journals, research reports, specialized encyclopedias, atlases, lexicons, and so forth into one huge comprehensive electronic encyclopedia. Some of this data on the World Wide Web is updated daily. There also are small-scale examples of how such knowledge can be organized so that duplication will be avoided. For example, the Yale Human Relations Area Files have electronically organized and systematized all the verifiable knowledge about anthropology for certain geographical areas, sorting out new facts, correcting existing facts, and removing all duplications in the process.

It was always possible for the compilers of printed encyclopedias to justify their omissions on the grounds of space limitations. But with the data warehousing capabilities of computers almost all the information one might ever want can be readily available, and with hypertext one can access this through the computer monitor in written text form, four-color illustrations, film clips, and sound recordings as an interactive talking reference work. A student can listen to a symphony by Brahms while reading about the composer's life and looking at segments of the musical composition.

Most of us were taught in school that we "knew" something when we had memorized a series of facts. We passed an examination when we could recall the information we had thus learned. Now, however, "to know" can no longer refer to the facts we have stored in our memories. Instead, it should be used to refer to the skills we have developed for accessing a system that will lead us to the facts, i.e., knowing how to use a search engine on the Internet to find desired information and how to follow the hypertext links to unearth gems of knowledge.

A college student looking at a World Wide Web page placed on the Internet by the instructor of a course may find everything there from the course syllabus to an extended reading list and even the handouts that were available after the professor's lecture. There also will likely be links to databases elsewhere that contain much more information about the subject than any professor could ever hope to provide in the series of assigned lectures.

Hypertext proves particularly useful, because information is intermeshed like a network of fine wires so that to deal with one fact is to touch a thousand others. Ask why the price of a loaf of bread went up last week and you are soon dealing with crop failures, fertilizer production, weather conditions, labor costs, machinery replacement, merchandising markups, energy supplies, advertising rates, printing needs, shelf life, pollution problems, minority rights, and many other topics related to a single loaf of bread. Or, if you want to find out some specific data about the workings of a plant cell, do you turn to a botanist, a biologist, a biochemist, a biophysicist, or a cytologist? They each would have information you might need, yet their subject areas are distinct, even though interlocked.

Databases now exist on the Internet and on some CD-ROM disks that keep track of thousands of medical journals published annually throughout the world. Others catalog the minute details of archaeological investigations at many sites. Still others include hundreds of maps, charts, and satellite and aerial photographs collected by the National Oceanographic Service. There is the *Isocrates* database of all the Greek texts up to A.D. 600 developed by the University of California, and the *Database of Macromolecular Movements* that classifies hundreds of proteins and other biomolecules by how they move in living cells (such as sliding or swiveling like a hinge) that can generate movies of the action on the fly from any data presented to it by researchers.

On the Internet one can consult the *MLA Bibliography*, a huge resource of literary scholarship, or the *New York Times Biographical File*. One also can consult the many-volumed *Oxford English Dictionary*, the *Reader's Guide to Periodical Literature*, and the ever-growing list of *Books in Print*. A business consultation database includes a wide variety of publications from government agencies such as the Department of Commerce, Veterans Administration,

Defense Department, and General Services Administration, as well as publications from accounting firms and other business enterprises.

Furthermore, a complex genome database for any scientist to consult is presently being compiled by researchers throughout the world. When completed, it will stockpile massive amounts of data on cells, chemicals, microbes, proteins, and DNA sequences that can be used for future research into biological development.

The daily updating of knowledge in areas such as medicine or law may help save a life or win an important case. This kind of updating and coordination of information is clearly something quite different from just a more efficient library. It eventually may shape human thought itself.

We need computers and hypertext today if for no other reason than to digest the mass of records that proliferate throughout our society. The amount of published information is increasing at an explosive rate. One research institute has estimated that one trillion pieces of paper were on file in the United States in 1964, and that at least 175 million pieces more have been added each year since that date. This means that in the few seconds it takes to read this paragraph, there were more than 22,000 additional pages of writing generated in this country.

Book publishers issue 30,000 titles in America each year. There also are 35,000 journals in more than 60 languages published every year, and the rate of publication is doubling every 15 years according to one estimate. The current collection of electronic journals listed on the Internet alone numbers nearly 8,000. A group of educators meeting in July 1967 calculated that human knowledge doubled from A.D. 1 to A.D. 1750, and doubled again from 1750 to 1950. It now is estimated that the total of all printed information doubles every eight years.

We are, in fact, inundated with new data. Some scientists even claim that it takes more time to research whether an experiment already has been conducted than it does to perform the experiment itself. Hypertext is designed to meet this problem of information overload.

The figures may overwhelm us, but the problem is not new. It is said that the great naturalist Johannes Müller died by his own hand in 1858 out of frustration, because he could not keep up with developments in biology. As early as 1613 Barnabe Rich, a popular author and soldier, wrote, "One of the diseases of this age is the multiplicity of books; they doth so overcharge the world that it is not able to digest the abundance of idle matter that is every day hatched and brought forth into the world."

At this point we should perhaps deliver a word of caution regarding the new technology. Every new invention or discovery results in its virtues being oversold. Don't forget the "friendly atom," the totally mobile society of the automobile, and the era of universal education that would result from television. There now are similar claims for the Internet, where the expansion of knowledge already is explosive and getting faster. However, though hypertext makes access to data much easier than it was in the past, the physical limitations of a computer screen, amount of installed memory, and speed of electronic transmission puts restrictions on many of these utopian claims. As Pulitzer Prize winner E. Annie Proulx puts it, "No one is likely to sit down and read a novel on a twitchy little screen."

Yet Kofi Annan, the current Secretary-General of the United Nations, said in a recent speech, "The Internet holds the greatest promise humanity has known for long-distance learning and universal access to quality education.... It offers the best chance yet for developing countries to take their rightful place in the global economy. You have only to look at the production of software in India.... And so our mission must be to ensure access as widely as possible. If we do not, the gulf between the haves and the have-nots will be the gulf between the technology-rich and technology-poor."

Even with the computer and hypertext one can't conveniently retrieve all pertinent records in response to all possible questions. Any record we might choose to examine has an infinite number of possible attributes that could serve by their presence or absence to answer a potential question. Links to even most of these might stretch the capabilities of any computer beyond its limits.

Consider, for example, what links might be required to locate an ordinary color slide among many other such slides. In different contexts we might want to find and retrieve this slide by the names of the individuals in the picture. Or, we might want to retrieve it by the date of the photograph or by the location at which it was made. Other possible categories for retrieval would include the name of the photographer, the type of camera, the type of film, the type of lens, the exposure time, the date of developing, the developing procedures used, the developing solutions used, the light and weather conditions when the photograph was taken, and the predominant colors in the picture. The possibilities go on and on. We could retrieve the slide on the basis of the relationship of the people photographed to one another or, for that matter, to the photographer. We also could consider the presence or absence of specific plants and animals, known or conjectured geological formations, types of clouds, types of building or other man-made structures, and so on ad infinitum.

Almost any computer could be programmed to search through our hypothetical group of slides and pick out this one on the basis of any of these categories. But it would be impossible to create any information storage and retrieval system that might fully respond to all such questions, no matter how complex and speedy the computer. It also would be prohibitively expensive to try to approach such a condition.

Electronic search technology is a vast improvement in most respects over conventional indexing. Digital methods can make use of any of the traditional techniques and move beyond them. Boolean logic and intelligent searches based on various encoded dictionaries offer reference capabilities not available elsewhere, although these may at first confuse the inexperienced information searcher.

All the electronic retrieval systems are based on the matching of terms or images. In the example above, if we were to want to use a computer to quickly locate all slides with pictures of Uncle Willie in them we would first have to list the term "Uncle Willie" (as well as all other desired terms) in the computer memory bank. This is simple enough. Yet because normal English offers so many variations of the same term and so many ways to phrase the same question, a dictionary or thesaurus of synonyms and antonyms probably should be consulted to make sure that our list was comprehensive enough to adequately employ the computerized retrieval system.

Several years ago, before the creation of hypertext, a study by scientists working for International Business Machines Corporation showed that one particular collection of documents could be accessed by four sets of possible index terms, each with between two and nine thesaurus synonyms — a total of nearly 1,500 possible word combinations. The use of *methods* instead of *principles*, for example, or *methods* instead of *procedures*, greatly affected the results of the search and the documents retrieved.

Thus, as the number of documents and the word index grows, the search time needed and the capacity of the computer increases. Such coordinate systems perhaps will eventually reach a natural and inescapable limit on their size and utility because of the limitations in the logic methods of the retrieval systems.

We now can turn to the practical steps involved in searching for information on the Internet. For this it is helpful to know something about the rules of symbolic logic, or what is generally called Boolean logic. These rules were created by the English mathematician George Boole (1815–1864), and his "algebra of logic" is used not only in searching for knowledge with a computer but are the basis for the operation of all of the electrical switching circuits that take place within the memory and program chips of the computer itself. For the purpose of computer searching, however, only three rules of Boolean logic need to be known — those that deal with AND, OR, and NOT.

To begin a computer search, it is usually best to start with one of the general search tools that have been developed for this purpose, such as those offered by AltaVista, Dogpile, Excite, HotBot, InfoSeek, Lycos, or Yahoo (see chapter 20 for information on each). These search tools, or search engines as they are usually called, do not look through all the available databases. That would take much too long. But they do locate articles in many different databases, and even though their choices sometimes overlap, one search engine will likely cover some areas that the others do not. Therefore, you may need to use several of them to find the specific data you desire. Each will probably locate dozens to thousands of sites that contain the information — and misinformation — that you may be seeking. But you don't need to be daunted by the number of sites that a single search produces. You can always find ways to refine your search so that the number of sites becomes manageable.

Choose words wisely to identify the item you are seeking. A generic search phrase, such as "American history" or "computer memory," will yield too many results to be useful. You will get better results if you enter a few related words rather than a single word. Thus "Archimedes law of the pulley" will be more effective than just the word "pulley." Most of the search engines will automatically ignore words like "the" and "of." You also can enter questions such as "Who discovered the law of the pulley?" to get good results.

If you don't get what you want on the first try, don't give up. Try again with a different set of synonyms or related words. If you find you are getting far too much information from one query, make your request more precise and try again.

Most of the search engines respond well when you use the Boolean logic terms AND, OR, and NOT in your searching. Plus and minus signs also work well. Use the logic term AND to link all the words that need to be found in each search result. For example, "art and schools" will retrieve all the records that contain both the keywords "art" and "schools." Using a plus sign before each term in the query produces much the same result: "+art+schools."

The use of the Boolean OR results in the retrieval of all records that contain one term or the other. Thus the query "ceramics or pottery" will retrieve all records containing the words "ceramics" or "pottery," as well as all those containing both words. You don't need to worry about excessive duplication. The search engine will omit duplicate entries. Inserting the word NOT or the minus sign before a word can be used to exclude words that must not appear in the search result. Thus "film not photography" will retrieve all records containing the keyword "film" but not the keyword "photography." In using the minus sign, you would write the query in this way: "film -photography."

Parentheses can be used to create more advanced searches. For example, "art and (school or college)" will result in finding all records containing information about general art schools and about the colleges that give degrees in art. Put quotation marks around specific, verbatim phrases that you want to find exactly as written: "All the world's a stage."

In most cases you can click with your mouse on the title of any desired document that is listed among those that appear on your screen when the search engine has completed its work, and the entire document will pop up on your screen ready for reading.

All the Internet search engines base their searching capabilities on the index they have previously generated. They comb through that index in a matter of milliseconds and sort out the results to display them on your screen. But each site handles these tasks differently and thus can yield different results. Often it is the knowledge in a single, obscure database that will provide the vital piece of information you might be seeking.

Most of the search engines use "spider" software that crawls across the Internet's World Wide Web to create their indexes. The software targets various sites and follows every link on all the pages there, indexing each page. Because spider indexing may include invisible descriptions put there by the creators of the various Web pages, the results provided by one search engine will perhaps differ from those results provided by another, even though they have both indexed the same material.

Some of the best search engines invest in human site-indexing, but most do it mechanically. Whatever the case, you will get the most thorough results if you use several search engines when looking for a single topic. None of these will take as long to find the necessary documents as you probably would by searching manually at the local library.

Besides search engines, the Internet has various programs that will monitor other sites and collect and store information you might desire so that you can tap into it at a later time. The various regional sites for *Business News* and the *Area Business Databank* are such databases that cover hundreds of local newspapers and business journals.

In conclusion, it is computers and the technology involved in the Internet that are bringing about the free flow of information throughout the world. Instantaneous transmission of knowledge by way of modems, satellites, fiber optics, and such is causing a blurring of national boundaries. No government can any longer control the flow of data, and the pooling and exchanging of information is tending to homogenize the different cultures. Eventually, as all people in the world gain access to the same information, the cyberspace built by the Internet will indeed be a new land of knowledge.

20. Using the Great Electronic Encyclopedia

It is conceivable to view printed encyclopedias as early attempts to produce hypertext on paper. They were not designed for linear, sequential reading, and much of their usefulness depends on indexing, cross-referencing, and the various bibliographies that were inserted within the content of the individual articles themselves. But printed encyclopedias can in no way compete with the multimedia components of their CD-ROM hypertext counterparts. With the addition of photographs and drawings, audio recording, MIDI music synthesis, digital maps, animation, motion video, and still-image-plus-audio sequences, these CD-ROM encyclopedias have turned electronic research into something vastly different from traditional encyclopedias.

Multimedia adds life to the text much as colorful illustrations do to the printed page. Images and sounds provide entertainment value that may keep students motivated as they make use of such electronic encyclopedias. And CD-ROMs enrich the information content by illustrating complex processes and by placing users in other times and situations. Electronic search technology is indeed a great improvement over conventional indexing.

All CD-ROM encyclopedias permit the printing of text and graphics, as well as the copying of sections or whole articles to a disk file. In preparing a school term paper, this is easier than making photocopies and certainly better than taking notes by hand.

CD-ROM encyclopedias have several other advantages over the printed editions. They are extremely compact, compressing several feet of shelf space onto only one or two small CDs. They provide rapid and flexible retrieval of information through their various electronic search techniques. And new editions of CD-ROM disks offer the addition of more and higher quality multimedia content. As multimedia technology improves, purchasers can expect to have longer audio clips, better motion video, and better sound.

Compton's Encyclopedia Deluxe

Based on the 26-volume printed *Compton's Encyclopedia*, this two-disk CD-ROM is focused toward middle school and high school students, so it is one of the easiest to use. It comes with a dictionary, a thesaurus, and perhaps the best set of term-paper tools: a topic finder, note organizer, integration with one's word processor, presentation manager to create a multimedia report, and Compton's own online library staff that the user can reach through Compton's Web site. Questions posted to this Web site are answered by e-mail within two business days. This feature, called "Ask a Librarian," also lists neighborhood resources, such as the libraries and museums located within driving distance of the user's ZIP code and even directions to particular locations.

This CD-ROM package also is one of only two electronic encyclopedias that has a built-in planetarium. The other is Webster's. The user can specify longitude and latitude, as well as the date and time, and this program will indicate which stars and planets should be visible that night in the sky. Finally, in preparing reports, the Compton's program lets a user bookmark articles and media items so that they can be assembled into a slide show — with or without voice-over narration.

Encyclopedia Britannica

This two-disk version of the printed original — including its Micropaedia, Macropaedia, and *Britannica Book of the Year*— contains 44 million words. But its multimedia content is slimmer than that of most of the other CD-ROM encyclopedias. Users can pose a question in plain English and immediately get a list of the articles that will most likely provide an answer. If the user wishes to browse further by accessing the "Knowledge in Depth" feature, more information about the subject in question than is desired may appear.

One particularly useful feature, the "Analyst," brings up comparisons of the statistics for any two countries or regions in the world. This can be printed out in custom tables, graphs, or charts. The Britannica CD also offers time lines that cover nine subject areas and provides some 15,000 Internet links. The Merriam-Webster dictionary is included on one of the disks.

Eyewitness World Atlas

The statistics on this one-disk CD-ROM come to life through the multimedia effects of this interface — either a 3-D rotating globe or flat maps.

The user can zoom in on any section of each map or let each one fly by in a determined order. It also is easy to print out whatever one might wish to use for a business presentation or term paper. Even the animated opening logo may prove fascinating when the user first examines this electronic atlas.

Grolier Multimedia Encyclopedia

The text nucleus for this two-disk CD-ROM encyclopedia is the 20-volume *Academic American Encyclopedia,* published in its printed edition by the New York-based Grolier Publishing Company. It is designed for the middle school and above range, but it also offers access to two Internet-based resources: The *New Book of Knowledge* (for younger children) and the *Encyclopedia Americana* (for college-age researchers). In keeping with its school orientation, the encyclopedia includes an Activities and Study Guide and curriculum-oriented Guided Tours.

The Grolier Multimedia Encyclopedia was the first electronic encyclopedia to be issued on a CD-ROM disk, and each new edition has added more multimedia elements. The user also can purchase three additional CDs that will provide *Bartlett's Familiar Quotations,* the *Hammond Atlas of the World,* and *The Wall Street Journal Almanac* to enhance the information provided by this electronic encyclopedia.

Microsoft Encarta Encyclopedia Deluxe

This CD-ROM, which many consider to be the best of all the electronic encyclopedias, includes 41,000 articles that cover a wide range of material. There are also Internet connections to keep all the facts up to date. The text originally was based on Funk & Wagnalls' *New Encyclopedia,* a respectable if not deep or inspired general-purpose work. But in 1998, in the hope of appealing to college students, Microsoft acquired the rights to Collier's multimedia encyclopedia (no longer available), which is targeted toward a slightly older audience.

In the case of this electronic encyclopedia, the user can obtain answers to questions asked in plain English or, if one's computer is equipped with voice recognition, through voice commands. The user also can purchase, for a small additional fee, five extra CDs that include an atlas, an information manager, and a revision of much of the information that was previously included in Microsoft's first CD-ROM, the *Microsoft Bookshelf.* These extra disks also contain a dictionary, a thesaurus, an almanac, time lines, quotations, a writing guide, and another (briefer) encyclopedia.

Finally, the *Encarta* encyclopedia can be purchased on DVD (Digital Virtual Disk—a new type of CD-ROM that holds 28 times as much data and needs a DVD disk reader to access) that shows high-resolution, full-screen video.

Simon and Schuster New Millennium Encyclopedia

This two-disk CD-ROM includes dictionaries, a thesaurus, an almanac, and an atlas. It is based on the Funk and Wagnalls' *Encyclopedia* and is the least expensive of the various CD-ROM types, but it is also the leanest, omitting some of the extra features found elsewhere.

Webster's International Encyclopedia

The core of this one-disk DVD encyclopedia is the printed *Cambridge Encyclopedia* originally produced by the Cambridge University Press. It is marketed by an Australian company and includes a large number of books, such as a dictionary, a natural history dictionary, foreign phrase guide to 20 languages, and various histories of medicine, astronomy, warfare, archaeology, Australia, Ireland, and Great Britain. There also is a "Star-Gazer" module that resembles the planetarium feature in Compton's multimedia encyclopedia.

This electronic encyclopedia even has one or two games as well as a great deal of information about the United Nations and other items that bear no particular relation to one another, and it is heavily weighted in regard to British and religious matters. Although its multimedia features are many, a topic search will likely frustrate most users because of its somewhat clumsy navigation tools and lack of outlines with which to navigate. For example, when users click on a link in the text to find out more about a particular subject, they may be taken to an entirely different book on the disk without ever getting any kind of overview of their surroundings.

Webster's New World Dictionary and Thesaurus

This one-disk CD-ROM may prove useful only to a person who doesn't already use a word processor with a built-in dictionary. It includes perhaps a half-million words listing the entries and definitions for each, but all of these can be found in the various printed dictionaries, which are probably easier to access than a computer's CD-ROM drive. They certainly can be found on the Internet, where the range of dictionary resources is far more comprehensive.

World Book Family Reference Suite

This two-disk set comes with a microphone headset for use with IBM's "ViaVoice Technology." It contains the full text of the printed *World Book Encyclopedia* that is designed for elementary and secondary school use, and in which the reading level varies according to the article content so as to appeal to the full-grade span of pre-college students.

All the major articles come with bibliographies (organized by reading level) as well as suggested study questions. Where appropriate, links take the user to Internet Web sites that offer further research and curriculum support. A set of "Homework Wizards" helps students assemble text segments and media into published reports, while a "Quiz Wizard" feature allows the creation of flash cards and quizzes for exam preparation.

A third CD related to this electronic encyclopedia can be purchased that will provide the user with the *Merriam-Webster Reference Library* and the *Information Please Almanac*.

Web Encyclopedias

While no discussion of information gathering and storage would be complete without mention of the numerous web sites that serve that specific purpose, the very nature of the burgeoning World Wide Web precludes their examination here. The breakneck pace of technological advancement has resulted in a "here today, gone tomorrow" situation on the Internet. Web addresses are tenuous at best.

Suffice to say that many excellent encyclopedias reside on the Web, among them Britannica, Encyclopedia Smithsonian, Encarta, and Grolier. Venerable dictionaries are likewise available, as are *Roget's Thesaurus* and Bartlett's *Familiar Quotations*. Some are available by subscription; others may be accessed free of charge. To navigate your way to these and other sites, several search engines are available to ease you along the information superhighway.

Web Search Engines

Almost anything can be found on the Internet, but with so many available search engines, each working somewhat differently from the others and possibly accessing different Web sites, it still can be something of a challenge to find exactly what you are looking for. In terms of sheer size, AltaVista and HotBot index the largest number of pages. But if you are looking for something obscure, you probably will need to try a number of sites to find it. Below is a listing of the best search engines currently available.

It is wise to become conversant with the use of the Boolean terms AND, OR, and NOT discussed in the previous chapter. While most search engines aren't yet capable of recognizing natural-language inquiries, most of them can do a few simple substitutions. For example, searching for the word "Einstein" will also bring up "Einstein's." And wild cards work too: theor* matches theory, theorem, and theoretical.

AltaVista (www.altavista.com)

This powerful general-purpose search engine has been available on the Web longer than most of the others. When you type a simple question into its query box, along with giving you the search results, it will guess at several related questions you might wish answered. Its basic search form lets the user specify which language they want to use — 25 in all, including Icelandic and Lithuanian, but not Old English.

Dogpile (www.dogpile.com)

This site performs metasearches of many types of sites. In other words, it obtains results from the available listings of other specialist search engines. The user can choose specific types such as newswire services, Usenet, FTP sites, and other sources such as maps, weather reports, and stock quotes. The results are not collated, but instead are posted in groups as arranged by the search engine that found them.

Excite (www.excite.com)

Considered one of the best all-around content sites, this search engine makes a broad search of the Web (not just Web page links) and returns a categorized list of its results. For a quick overview of a subject, the answers given by this program are hard to beat.

HotBot (www.hotbot.com)

This is a time-related search engine, great for finding Web pages posted during a specific period of time. The user can search for phrases, page titles, people, and links to particular sites, linking the results to any of nine languages. The user also is permitted to restrict the search to particular domain names (such as pcworld.com) or to domains (such as .com, .gov, or .edu). If the user doesn't need a directory, this is a good place to start any search.

InfoSeek (infoseek.go.com)

This is a particularly good search engine for business topics, although it also has an array of Web content sites affiliated with Disney and ABC. InfoSeek has a handy filter called GoGuardian that allows the user to screen out content from those locations where the pictures or text may be unsuitable for children. This filter can be turned on with a single click.

Lycos (www.lycos.com)

This is a convenient search engine that lets the user easily refine searches by letting the user enter a second query related to the first after the initial search is completed. Its ProSearch page helps the user find specific content, such as images, music clips, books, or news groups.

Microsoft Network (www.msn.com)

This site, originally designed for the Microsoft browser, provides searches using several different search engines (AltaVista, Infoseek, Lycos, and Snap). It is capable of handling a variety of mixed phrase as well as single operator searches.

NetCenter (www.netcenter.com)

Set up by Netscape, the foremost browser in competition with Microsoft, this search engine collects information from a half-dozen different Web search sites, including Excite, InfoSeek, Lycos, Snap, and LookSmart. But if you know which particular sites you prefer to use, go directly to one of them rather than becoming mired down in NetCenter's interface.

Yahoo (www.yahoo.com)

This is by far the most popular search engine on the Web. In fact, it is one of the best places to start any search, because it maintains and regularly updates a carefully constructed subject catalog. Rather than focusing on specific pages within a site, Yahoo lets the user locate entire sites and their index pages. Because this search engine allows the user to search by categories or by sites, its results tend to be more manageable than those from most other sites.

More Search Engines

Several search engines specialize in perusing other search engines and then providing the user with listings from each one. These metasearch engines are different from the search sites such as Dogpile, because they can be freely downloaded to one's computer where, when activated, they will open the Internet and do their searching before they close it. My favorite is WebFerret, which is available from (www.ferretsoft.com/). It provides the search results it obtains through AltaVista, AOL Netfind, EuroSeek, Excite, Infoseek, LookSmart, Lycos, Search.com, and Yahoo. But the user will probably want to do any searching with WebFerret somewhat sparingly, as the results can be overwhelming. I entered the search word "abacus" recently and received a listing of 267 sites. The word "Einstein" brought up 500 sites.

Another free metasearch utility of this sort is Copernic 99, available from Copernic Technologies (www.copernic.com). Enter a query and it will produce hits from more than 30 search engines simultaneously, returning results as fast as the modem connection allows. For a small fee Copernic 99 can be upgraded to access more than 130 different search engines at one time.

Libraries on the Web

The world's libraries have begun to use the Internet to present their research guides and holdings on the Web, which allows people to visit the facilities of these libraries without ever leaving home. Primary among these is the Library of Congress that lists most of the books in its collection and provides several other useful tools for research. To access this site, go to (www.loc.gov/) and follow the instructions.

Another library site of note is the University of California's Berkeley library, which has links to a number of academic libraries throughout the world. It can be accessed at (sunsite.Berkeley.edu/Libweb/). And then there is the Public Libraries on WWW Servers list, which provides links to all the libraries listed on the Internet. This can be accessed with the rather cumbersome command (sjcpl.lib.in.us/homepage/PublicLibraries/PubLibSrvsGpherWWW.html#wwwsrv).

Books to Aid One's Search

Until a person has developed a great deal of skill in searching for information among the more than 3,000 Internet online databases available to the general public, it may be wise to read what the experts have to say on the matter. Here is a list of some of the books that can be found at many bookstores.

CyberHound's Web Guide
by D. Farrell
Published by Visible Ink Press

Great American Websites: An Online Discovery of Hidden America
by Edward J. Renehan, Jr.
Published by Osborne

Harley Hahn's Internet & Web Yellow Pages
by Harley Hahn
Published by Osborne McGraw-Hill

How to Look It Up Online
by Alfred Glossbrenner
Published by St. Martin's Press

The Internet Kids and Family Yellow Pages
by Jean Armour Polly
Published by Osborne

Official AT&T WorldNet Web Discovery Guide
by Adam Engst
Published by Osborne

Appendix:
General Encyclopedias
Published in English

Title	Date (first published)	Place of publication	Vols.
Aiton's Encyclopedia	1910	Minneapolis	5
American Educator	1919	Lake Bluff, IL	10
American Educator Encyclopedia	1931	Lake Bluff, IL	14
American Home Library	1962	Steubenville, OH	1
American Oxford Encyclopedia	1965	New York	14
American Peoples Encyclopedia	1948	New York	20
Anglo-American Cyclopedia	1911	New York	50
Appleton's Annual Cyclopaedia	1902	New York	14
Austin's New Encyclopedia	1948	Chicago	3
renamed Everyday Reference Library			
Australian Junior Encyclopaedia	1956	Sydney	3
Basic Everyday Encyclopedia	1954	New York	1
Black's Children's Encyclopaedia	1964	London	1
Book of Knowledge	1912	New York	24
Britannica Junior	1934	Chicago	15
British Cyclopaedia of Arts and Sciences	1835	London	2
British Encyclopaedia	1809	London	6
Cabinet Cyclopaedia	1849	London	133
Cassell's Concise Cyclopaedia	1883	London	1
Cassell's Storehouse of General Information	1894	London	4
Caxton Encyclopaedia	1960	London	6
Century Dictionary and Cyclopedia	1901	New York	10
Chamber's Cyclopedia	1728	London	2
Chamber's Encyclopaedia	1868	London	10
now published in 15 volumes			
Chamber's Encyclopedia, New Edition	1950	London	15
Children's Encyclopaedia	1910	London	20
Children's Encyclopedia	1959	New York	1
Children's Guide to Knowledge	1958	New York	1

Children's Illustrated Encyclopedia of General Knowledge	1957	New York	1
Child's First Encyclopaedia in Colour	1964	London	6
Collier's Encyclopedia now published in 24 volumes	1951	New York	20
Columbia Encyclopedia in One Volume	1935	New York	1
Columbia-Viking Desk Encyclopedia	1960	New York	1
Compact Encyclopaedia	1929	London	6
Complete Reference Handbook	1964	New York	1
Compton's Pictured Encyclopedia	1922	Chicago	15
Concise Encyclopedia	1937	New York	8
Dictionarium Polygraphicum	1758	London	2
Dictionary of Arts and Sciences	1807	London	2
Doubleday's Encyclopedia	1931	New York	10
Edinburgh Encyclopaedia	1830	Edinburgh	18
Encyclopaedia Britannica	1768	Edinburgh	24
Moved to America	1911	Chicago	29
Encyclopaedia Edinensis	1827	Edinburgh	6
Encyclopaedia Grolier	1947	Montreal	10
Encyclopaedia Metropolitana	1845	London	28
Encyclopaedia Perthensis	1806	Perth, Scotland	23
Encyclopedia Americana edition published today totals 30 volumes	1833	New York	13
Encyclopedia International	1963	New York	20
Encyclopedic Dictionary of American Reference	1901	Boston	2
English Encyclopaedia	1862	London	22
Enquire Within Upon Everything	1856	London	1
Everybody's Cyclopedia	1911	New York	5
Everybody's Encyclopedia also issued as Webster's Universal Encyclopedia and La Salle Extension University Encyclopedia	1909	Chicago	1
Everyman Encyclopaedia	1913	London	12
Facts: the New Concise Pictorial Encyclopedia later named New Concise Illustrated Encyclopedia and Comprehensive Pictorial Encyclopedia and World Home Reference Encyclopedia	1934	New York	4
Funk & Wagnalls Standard Reference Encyclopedia also known as Universal Standard Encyclopedia	1931	New York	25
General Dictionary, Historical and Critical	1741	London	10
Globe Encyclopaedia of Universal Information later named Student's Encyclopaedia of Universal Knowledge	1881	Edinburgh	6
Golden Book Encyclopedia	1959	New York	16
Golden Home and High School Encyclopedia	1961	New York	20
Golden Treasury of Knowledge	1961	New York	16
Great Encyclopaedic Dictionary	1964	London	3
Grolier Encyclopedia	1944	New York	20

Grolier Universal Encyclopedia	1965	New York	10
Harmsworth's Universal Encyclopedia	1905	London	10
Home University Encyclopedia	1941	New York	15
Human Interest Library	1914	Chicago	4
renamed New Human Interest Library			
and now issued in 20 volumes			
Hutchinson's New 20th Century Encyclopaedia	1964	London	1
Illustrated Encyclopedia	1959	New York	1
Illustrated Encyclopedia of Knowledge	1955	New York	21
renamed Illustrated World Encyclopedia			
Illustrated Globe Encyclopedia	1881	Edinburgh	6
Illustrated Home Library Encyclopedia	1954	New York	12
renamed Illustrated Encyclopedia	1956		
of Knowledge			
Imperial Encyclopedia	1814	London	4
International Reference Work	1927	Chicago	10
International World Reference Encyclopedia	1942	Chicago	16
Knowledge	1963	London	20
Library of Universal Knowledge	1942	Chicago	1
Lincoln Library of Essential Information	1924	Buffalo, NY	1
Little and Ives Illustrated Ready	1962	New York	20
Reference Encyclopedia			
Lloyd's Encyclopaedic Dictionary	1895	London	7
London Encyclopaedia	1829	London	22
Macmillan Everyman's Encyclopedia	1913	New York	12
Modern Encyclopaedia	1820	London	11
Modern Encyclopaedia, Illustrated	1963	London	1
Modern Encyclopaedia of Universal Information	1907	London	8
Modern Encyclopedia	1933	New York	1
renamed New Modern Encyclopedia	1943		
National Cyclopedia of Useful Knowledge	1851	London	12
National Encyclopaedia	1868	Glasgow	14
National Encyclopedia	1932	New York	11
edition published today equals 20 volumes			
Nelson's Perpetual Loose-Leaf Encyclopedia	1920	London	12
New Age Encyclopaedia	1921	London	10
New Age Encyclopaedia	1957	London	1
New American Comprehensive Encyclopedia	1906	New York	5
New American Cyclopaedia	1863	New York	16
New American Encyclopedia	1938	New York	8
renamed American Family Encyclopedia	1963		
New Century Book of Facts	1965	New York	1
New Champlin Encyclopedia for Young People	1926	Chicago	12
renamed Champlin Encyclopedia			
New Concise Pictorial Encyclopedia	1938	New York	1
New Cyclopaedia	1820	London	44
New Funk and Wagnalls Encyclopedia	1932	New York	36
renamed Funk and Wagnalls Standard			
Reference Encyclopedia			
New Golden Encyclopedia	1963	New York	1
New Gresham Encyclopedia	1921	London	6

New International Encyclopaedia	1904	New York	17
New Masters Pictorial Encyclopedia	1955	Washington	8
New Practical Reference Library	1907	Lake Bluff, IL	10
New Standard Encyclopedia	1906	New York	12
New Teachers' and Pupils' Cyclopedia	1927	Chicago	8
New Universal Encyclopaedia	1878	New York	4
New Wonder Book Encyclopedia of World Knowledge	1954	Philadelphia	12
New World Encyclopedia	1919	New York	6
New York Post World Wide Illustrated Encyclopedia	1935	New York	15
New Zealand Junior Encyclopaedia	1962	Wellington	3
Newnes Popular Encyclopaedia	1962	London	8
Our Wonder World	1914	Chicago	10
renamed New Wonder World, then New Wonder World Encyclopedia, and now New Wonder World Cultural Library	1932		
Our Wonderful World	1955	Chicago	18
Oxford Illustrated Dictionary	1962	London	3
Oxford Junior Encyclopedia	1956	London	13
Oxford New Zealand Encyclopaedia	1964	London	1
Pantologia	1813	London	12
Pears' Cyclopaedia	1897	London	1
Penny Cyclopaedia	1843	London	27
People's Cyclopedia	1914	New York	5
Pictured Knowledge	1956	New York	14
Popular Encyclopaedia	1841	Glascow	7
later called New Popular Encyclopaedia and then Modern Cyclopaedia of Universal Information			
Progressive Reference Library	1928	Chicago	10
Purnell's New English Encyclopaedia	1967	London	12
Richard's Cyclopedia	1933	New York	24
renamed Richard's Topical Encyclopedia			
Royal Cyclopedia, and Encyclopedia	1788	London	3
Standard American Encyclopedia	1916	Chicago	16
Standard International Encyclopedia	1953	New York	20
also issued as New World Family Encyclopedia			
Twentieth-century Encyclopaedia	1955	London	1
Twentieth Century Encyclopedia	1901	Philadelphia	6
Twentieth-century Encyclopedia	1930	Cleveland	10
also called American International Encyclopedia and Encyclopedia Library			
Unified Encyclopedia	1962	New York	30
Universal Cyclopaedia	1900	New York	12
Universal World Reference Encyclopedia	1916	Chicago	15
University Illustrated Encyclopedia	1938	New York	15
Volume Library	1911	Chicago	1
renamed Cowles Comprehensive Encyclopedia			
Webster's Unified Dictionary and Encyclopedia	1953	New York	1

Weedon's Modern Encyclopedia	1932	Cleveland	8
Wonderland of Knowledge	1937	Chicago	14
Wonder-world of Knowledge in Colour	1961	London	1
World Book Encyclopedia	1918	Chicago	8
edition published today equals 22 volumes			
World Educator Encyclopedia	1963	Miami	16
World Home Reference Encyclopedia	1951	Chicago	1
World Scope Encyclopedia	1945	Chicago	20
renamed New American Encyclopedia			
World University Encyclopedia	1964	New York	12
World-wide Cyclopedia	1919	New York	6
World-wide Encyclopedia and Gazetteer	1908	New York	12
World Wide Illustrated Encyclopedia	1937	New York	15

Bibliography

In addition to the publications listed below, I have consulted many general encyclopedias, the *Dictionary of American Biography*, *Oxford English Dictionary*, and *International Encyclopedia of the Social Sciences*.

ALA World Encyclopedia of Library and Information Services, American Library Association, Chicago, 1986.

Allen, Leslie H., ed., *Bryan and Darrow and Dayton*, Russell and Russell, New York, 1967.

Andrade, E. N. da C., *Sir Isaac Newton: His Life and Work*, Doubleday Anchor Book, New York, 1958.

Artz, Frederick B., *The Mind of the Middle Ages*, Knopf, New York, 1953.

Benton, William, "The Great Soviet Encyclopedia," *Yale Review*, New Series 47: 552–568.

Bonino, José Miguez, *Christians and Marxists*, William B. Eerdmans, Grand Rapids, Mich., 1976.

Boulding, Kenneth E., "The Dodo Didn't Make It," *Bulletin of Atomic Scientists*, May 1971.

Bush, Vannever, "How We May Think," *Atlantic Monthly*, July 1945.

Campbell, Jeremy, *The Improbable Machine*, Simon and Schuster, New York, 1989.

Childe, V. Gordon, *Man Makes Himself*, New American Library, New York, 1983.

Chomsky, Noam, "The Case Against B. F. Skinner," *The New York Review*, December 30, 1971.

Collison, Robert, *Encyclopedias: Their History Throughout the Ages*, Hafner, London, 1966.

Darnton, Robert, *The Business of Enlightenment*, Harvard University Press, Cambridge, MA, 1980.

Dobzhansky, Theodosius, "Nothing in Biology Makes Sense Except in the Light of Evolution," *The American Biology Teacher*, March 1973.

Einbinder, Harvey, *The Myth of the Britannica*, MacGibbon & Kee, London, 1964.

Eiseley, Loren, *The Man Who Saw Through Time*, Charles Scribner's Sons, New York, 1961.

Eliade, Mircea, *Shamanism: Archaic Techniques of Ecstasy*, Princeton University Press, Princeton, 1972.

_____, *The Sacred and the Profane*, Harcourt, Brace & World, Inc., New York, 1957.

Evans, Christopher, *The Making of the Micro: A History of Computers*, Victor Gollancz, London, 1981.

Farb, Peter, *Man's Rise to Civilization as shown by the Indians of North America from Primeval Times to the Coming of the Industrial State*, E. P. Dutton, New York, 1968.

Farrington, Benjamin, *Francis Bacon, Philosopher of Science*, Lawrence and Wishart, London, 1951.

Gay, Martin K., *The New Information Revolution*, ABC-CLIO, Santa Barbara, CA, 1996.

Gerbi, Anotello, *The Dispute of the New World: The History of a Polemic, 1750–1900*, University of Pittsburgh Press, Pittsburgh, 1973.

Gillespie, Charles, *Reproduction of Some Plates from the Encyclopedie* (2 volumes), Dover, Mineola, NY, 1959.

Gomes, Peter J., *The Good Book: Reading the Bible with Mind and Heart*, William Morrow and Company, New York, 1996.

Hanson, N. R., *Patterns of Discovery*, Cambridge, England, 1958.

Harding, D. W., "How's Your Gestalt," *The New York Review*, December 18, 1969.

Hayes, H. R., *In the Beginnings*, G. P. Putnam's Sons, New York, 1963.

Hazard, Paul, *The European Mind, 1680–1715*, Yale University Press, New Haven, CT, 1953.

Hobart, Michael E., and Zachary S. Schiffman, *Information Ages: Literacy, Numerancy, and the Computer Revolution*, Johns Hopkins University Press, Baltimore, 1998.

Jackson, Sidney L., *Libraries and Librarianship in the West: A Brief History*, McGraw-Hill, 1974.

Johnson, Paul, *A History of Christianity*, Atheneum, New York, 1977.

Kogan, Herman, *The Great EB*, University of Chicago Press, Chicago, 1958.

Kuhn, Thomas S., *The Structure of Scientific Revolutions*, University of Chicago Press, Chicago, 1962.

Langer, Susanne K., *Feeling and Form*, Scribner's, New York, 1953.

_____, *Philosophy in a New Key*, Mentor, New York, 1951.

_____, *Problems of Art*, Scribner's, New York, 1957.

Lerner, Fred, *The Story of Libraries*, Continuum, New York, 1998.

MacDonald, Dwight, "Book-of-the-Millennium Club," *New Yorker*, November 29, 1952.

Madison, Charles A., *Book Publishing in America*, McGraw-Hill, New York, 1966.

Marc, David, "Understanding Television," *The Atlantic Monthly*, August 1984.

McLellan, David, *Karl Marx: His Life and Thought*, Harper & Row, New York, 1973.

Mollenkott, Virginia Ramey, "Feminine Images of God in the Bible," *Circuit Rider*, June 1982.

Muller, Herbert J., *The Children of Frankenstein*, Indiana University Press, Bloomington, IN, 1970.

Needham, Joseph, *Science and Civilization in China* (Vol. 1 and 2), Cambridge University Press, England, 1954 and 1956.

_____, *Within the Four Seas*, George Allen & Unwin, Ltd., London, 1969.

Nelson, Ted, *Computer Lib/Dream Machines*, Microsoft Press, Redmond, WA, 1987.

O'Donnell, James J., *Avatars of the Word*, Harvard University Press, Cambridge, MA, 1998.

Rubinstein, Annette T., *The Great Tradition in English Literature from Shakespeare to Shaw*, Citadel Press, New York, 1953.

Sagan, Carl, *The Demon-Haunted World*, Ballantine Books, New York, 1996.

Schurman, Franz, and Orville Schell, *China Reader #1, Imperial China, The Decline of the Last Dynasty and the Origins of Modern China*, Vintage, 1967.

Smith, Reginald A., *Towards a Living Encyclopedia: A Contribution to Mr. Wells' New Encyclopedia*, Andrew Dakers of London, 1948.

Spong, John Shelby, *Living in Sin*, Harper & Row, San Francisco, 1988.

_____, *Rescuing the Bible from Fundamentalism*, Harper, San Francisco, 1991.

Steinberg, S. H., *Five Hundred Years of Printing*, Faber and Faber, London, 1959.

Swift, Jonathan, *Gulliver's Travels*, Oxford University Press, New York, 1998.

Swift, Lindsay, *Brook Farm, Its Members, Scholars and Visitors*, Corinth Books, New York, 1961.

Toffler, Alvin, *Future Shock*, Random House, New York, 1970.

Trevelyan, G. M., *English Social History*, Longmans, Green, London, 1942.

Tsien, T. H., *Written on Bamboo and Silk*, University of Chicago Press, Chicago, 1962.

Van der Post, Laurens, *The Lost World of the Kalahari*, Penguin Books, New York, 1958.

Walsh, James P., *General Encyclopedias in Print*, Newark, DE, 1964.

Wells, H. G., "The Idea of a World Encyclopedia," *Harper's*, April 1937.

Wilson, A. M., *Diderot: The Testing Years, 1713–1759*, Oxford University Press, Oxford, England, 1957.

Wurrman, Richard Saul, *Information Anxiety*, Doubleday, New York, 1989.

Wright, Willard Huntington, *Misinforming a Nation*, B. W. Huebsch, New York, 1917.

Yates, Frances A., *The Art of Memory*, Penguin Books, New York, 1966.

Index